Bo Belinsky

ALSO OF INTEREST
AND FROM MCFARLAND

The New York Mets in Popular Culture: Critical Essays (edited by David Krell, 2020)

The New York Yankees in Popular Culture: Critical Essays (edited by David Krell, 2019)

"Our Bums": The Brooklyn Dodgers in History, Memory and Popular Culture (David Krell, 2015)

Bo Belinsky

*The Rise, Fall and Rebound
of a Playboy Pitcher*

DAVID KRELL

McFarland & Company, Inc., Publishers
Jefferson, North Carolina

ISBN (print) 978-1-4766-8888-6
ISBN (ebook) 978-1-4766-5515-4

Library of Congress cataloging data are available

Library of Congress Control Number 2025026201

© 2025 David Krell. All rights reserved

No part of this book may be reproduced or transmitted in any form or by any means, electronic or mechanical, including photocopying or recording, or by any information storage and retrieval system, without permission in writing from the publisher.

Front cover image: Angels pitcher Robert "Bo" Belinsky
(Los Angeles Public Library)

Printed in the United States of America

McFarland & Company, Inc., Publishers
Box 611, Jefferson, North Carolina 28640
www.mcfarlandpub.com

Addicts can leave trails of heartbreak behind them.

This book is dedicated to their loved ones who get injured emotionally, physically, or both.

Table of Contents

Acknowledgments   ix
Preface   1
Prologue   3

1. From Trenton to Los Angeles   5
2. "The most pleasant surprise of the 1962 Los Angeles Angels"   23
3. Bo and Dean   43
4. Belinsky's Beauties   58
5. Aloha!   77
6. Basebrawl   91
7. Philadelphia   103
8. Play Me or Trade Me   119
9. Aloha, Again!   133
10. The End of a Long and Winding Road   147
11. Say It Ain't So, Bo   162
12. Las Vegas   177

Epilogue   187
Chapter Notes   189
Bibliography   209
Index   211

Acknowledgments

Writing a book may seem to be a solitary endeavor, but it's not. I'm grateful for several people who assisted me on the journey of chronicling Bo Belinsky's life.

The staff at the New York Public Library was invaluable in locating copies of the *New York Mirror* on microfilm, allowing me to read Walter Winchell's columns mentioning Belinsky. The Inter-Library Loan program at the NYPL procured microfilm of the *San Diego Union* and *Los Angeles Herald Examiner*, great complements to newspapers that I could access through ProQuest and newspapers.com.

Cassidy Lent in the Giamatti Research Center of the National Baseball Hall of Fame and Museum did a yeoman's job in fulfilling my research requests. Laura Poll, archivist of the Trentonian Department at the Trenton Free Public Library, played a vital role in helping me gather information about Bo Belinsky's formative years in Trenton. Longtime friends Art Carine and Lisa Bloomfield provided substantive feedback. Belinsky's friends and colleagues shared memories: Tyler Corder, Al Ferrara, Bob Case, Ray Dinardi, Cliff Findlay, Scott Keene, and Bruce Trampler.

Eileen King was my liaison at the Los Angeles Public Library for a mystery solved by her colleague, Robert Anderson. During my research of Mamie Van Doren's career, I came across a review of the 1957 film *Untamed Youth* with no byline but the initials GMW at the end. Robert's sleuthing revealed that the critic's name was Geoffrey M. Warren.

Geraldine Engel at Davis Memorial Park in Las Vegas generously took time from her schedule to locate Bo Belinsky's gravesite and accompany me there during a visit.

The Los Angeles Public Library Photo Collection staff, Matthew Lutts at the Associated Press, and Frank P. Hardy facilitated the licensing of photographs and made it a smooth process.

Gary Mitchem and his team at McFarland gave the green light to this project.

My thanks to everyone.

Preface

All that glitters is not gold.
It's a statement rooted in truth and a throughline for Bo Belinsky's life. On the surface, Belinsky had the world in his hands. A professional baseball player, he threw a no-hitter as a rookie with the Los Angeles Angels in 1962, launching him into a stratosphere of fame, sex, and idolatry that would satiate most men, if not exhaust them. His social calendar listed the most famous actresses of the 1960s, a benefit accorded the pitcher from playing in southern California, where he had proximity to show business.
But relationships proved elusive. Three marriages led to three divorces. Estrangement from children hovered over him in his later years like a dark cloud. Alcohol and drugs became prominent in his life, leading to violent behavior. Belinsky went into recovery in the 1990s. He died in 2001.
When I found out that Maury Allen's biography of Bo Belinsky—written with the ex-ballplayer's full cooperation—had been published 50 years ago, I realized that the time was right for an objective, comprehensive biography. I had a major benefit not available to previous generations of journalists—the website newspapers.com, containing hundreds of newspapers going back decades. It proved to be an invaluable resource for finding information about Belinsky, particularly his years with the Hawaii Islanders in the Pacific Coast League.
Newspaper titles are listed in the bibliography. There aren't any recorded interviews of Belinsky on YouTube, so I used information and quotes from articles, then cited the sources in the Chapter Notes. Additionally, Belinsky's colleagues and friends were extraordinarily helpful in giving me information about his state of mind in the 1990s, when he embraced sobriety. Regarding photographs, there are fewer than in my other books due to the rising cost of licensing fees.
I aimed to chronicle Bo Belinsky's life without judgment. No condemning. No condoning. From what I've learned through those who knew him best, he would approve. It's all here. The good. The bad. The ugly.

Prologue

Cashman Field, Las Vegas, 2000.

Bo Belinsky looked like he could still fit into his baseball uniform and throw a few pitches in the strike zone.

When the 63-year-old former baseball player entered Cashman Field for Bo Belinsky Night at a Las Vegas 51s home game, he absorbed the energy, attention, and applause from the crowd. With so much hype surrounding him, a montage of memories must have raced through his mind.

Decades ago, he had it all. Fame. Money. Women. Pitching a no-hitter as a rookie for the Los Angeles Angels made him a celebrity and gave him a gateway to glamour in southern California. If you had a favorite actress of the 1960s, there's a good chance that Belinsky dated her. Carefree and cocksure, Belinsky provided great fodder for newspapermen, led by Bud Furillo of the *Los Angeles Herald Examiner* and Walter Winchell of the *New York Mirror*.

There was a tremendous downfall. Liquor, drugs, and self-destructive behavior made for a terrifying combination that not only impacted him severely but also imploded relationships with those who tried to love him.

Things got better since he moved to Las Vegas. Recovery. Work. But the path had been far from smooth. Only a few people knew the true story. If he told the crowd at Cashman Field the truth about his journey from growing up in Trenton to overindulging in LA's nightlife to hitting rock bottom to finding a balance in a city notorious for sin, they probably wouldn't believe him. His story was hard to believe.

But it happened.

1

From Trenton to Los Angeles

Beginning a Pro Career

Robert Belinsky had been restless ever since anyone could remember.

"When I was a kid of 13 or 14, I knew something was wrong," said the major leaguer in 1965. "I read about Florida and California. I couldn't wait to get on the Greyhound Bus."[1]

Born on December 7, 1936, to Edward and Anna Belinsky—a Polish American Catholic and a Russian Jew—he viewed unstructured leisure time as a destination, not merely an oasis. This approach stayed with him into adulthood. Even his nickname had a certain aura of fun. Bo. Baseball attracted him early. But his interest passed reasonableness. "He never would come home for supper," revealed Anna. "I didn't want to let him stay out until it got dark. He didn't care about eating. He would just play ball all day and night."[2]

As a teenager, Belinsky played on sandlot and semi-pro teams but refused the opportunity to display his God-given athletic ability for the Trenton Central High School baseball team. His free spirit fueled the decision. "It was too regimented," explained Anna. "He didn't like practices and all that. He played in the sandlots. He could come and go as he pleased. I don't think he was that interested in ball to tell you the truth. I think what he really wanted then was a car."[3]

Indeed. Belinsky figured to be more like an eagle soaring alone than a bird belonging to a flock. "I kept myself loose," he explained. "No gangs, no cliques, just me, ready to move wherever I wanted. I could fly the way the crow flies. Looking back, I didn't want it any other way. What the hell for, for a lot of rah-rah, gee-whiz bullshit? That's why I never played on the high school baseball team."[4]

Belinsky spent a chunk of his formative years absorbing lessons about the nuances of pool from colorfully named players like Goose and Cincinnati Phil, identifying, assessing, and hustling marks. His billiards skills became well known during his baseball career. A 1969 profile of *Mannix* actress Gail Fisher in the *Hollywood Citizen-News* mentioned her playing pool and asking the writer, Allen Rich, if he knew how to play. He wrote that he learned the game at a Manhattan pool parlor and "studied under Bo Belinsky." After Belinsky retired, colleagues and friends marveled at the ex-ballplayer's ability to dominate with a cue stick at any bar, nightclub, or home.[5]

Belinsky graduated from Trenton Central in 1954, a year when America birthed cultural touchstones defining innovation, creativity, and commercial growth. NBC premiered *Tonight*, later titled *The Tonight Show*; Eddie Mathews graced the cover of the first issue of *Sports Illustrated*; Swanson accelerated annual sales of its TV dinners from five thousand to ten million; Hyatt entered the competitive arena of hotels and hospitality; President Eisenhower signed a bill into law establishing the U.S. Air Force Academy; the USS *Nautilus* became the navy's first nuclear submarine in service; Dr. Joseph Murray led his surgical team in the first kidney transplant; and Decca Records helped boost the popularity of rock and roll in its infancy with the iconic song "Rock Around the Clock."

The teenager who enjoyed playing baseball would soon get the opportunity to satiate his craving for the game and get paid for it after attracting the attention of Pittsburgh Pirates scout Rex Bowen, who visited the family at 244 Hewitt Street and offered the young Trentonian a job in the minor leagues. He suffered financially, according to Anna. "They didn't give him any money," said Anna. "Nothing. Just a bus ticket. They don't ever tell you things like that. They just tell you about all the big bonus money they give out and how well they treat the boys. Let me tell you, it's a lie." Further, she said, "I don't know why he signed. He just didn't have anything else to do and he wanted that car."[6]

A couple of years after graduation, Belinsky began his journey in professional baseball when he headed southward to join the Brunswick Pirates in the Georgia-Florida League for the 1956 season. He pitched in 11 games, compiling a 2–3 record with 29 strikeouts, 24 walks, and a 7.36 ERA.[7]

In the first game of a twin bill on June 2, Brunswick got blanked, 3–0, in a perfect game tossed by Fitzgerald Athletics hurler Henry Szostak. But it had another significance for Belinsky as an early signal of the control problems that bothered him during his career. Szostak struck out nine in the seven-inning game; Belinsky got shelved in the third inning after Fitzgerald tallied its trio of runs on three hits, a hit-by-pitch, and a walk.[8]

Skipping his obligations two months into his stint with the Brunswick club, Belinsky headed to Jacksonville, where he employed his skills with a pool cue by "hustling the sailors" and committed a sexual act with voyeurism for one opponent. "He made me shack up with his old lady while he watched before he would shoot pool with me," claimed Belinsky.

"I didn't care much for his wife, but he was an easy hustle so I did it. A few days of that and I went back to the ball club."[9]

When the season ended, Belinsky returned to Trenton and worked in a pottery factory, which prompted a declaration never to work in that kind of environment and instead focus on baseball. "I'm going to make it big in baseball, I'm going to make it real big."[10]

But he got sidetracked by criminals on Manhattan's West Side, where he helped them sell stolen goods and then associated with the same types back home in Trenton. "He got in with the neighborhood thugs, never in the mainstream of the action, but always close enough," explained Belinsky's biographer, Maury Allen. When cops began arresting guys in his circle, Belinsky jumped at an opportunity to play baseball far from his environs.[11]

Pitching in Pensacola

The following March, Belinsky signed with the Pensacola Dons in the Class D Alabama-Florida League. "Throws hard and has a nice curve" was the description that manager Lou Fitzgerald gave the pitcher as he assessed the team.[12] For leisure, Pensacolans saw the Dons play at Admiral Mason Park, abutting Pensacola Bay on Ninth Avenue, when they weren't going to movie theaters featuring Andy Griffith giving a bravura performance as lusty, charming, folksy TV personality Lonesome Rhodes in *A Face in the Crowd*; Dean Martin starring in his first movie without Jerry Lewis, *Ten Thousand Bedrooms*; Donald O'Connor channeling a comedy icon in *The Buster Keaton Story*; Jack Webb representing military authority in *The D.I.*; and Jimmy Stewart depicting Charles Lindbergh's aviation achievements in *The Spirit of St. Louis*.

Pensacola's baseball community had bigger stories to enjoy in 1957 with Belinsky on the mound, beginning with the honor of starting for the Dons—Pensacola's first baseball team since the 1949 Southeastern League champion Fliers—against the Whiting Field Blue Jays from Naval Air Station in the home exhibition opening game on April 20. Described by the local press as a "smooth-working" southpaw, Belinsky allowed two singles, five walks, and three runs but recorded five strikeouts in the 5–4 loss.[13]

He lasted six and one-third innings against the Montgomery Rebels on May 5, striking out five and walking six. Montgomery's batters achieved four hits in the second inning, though they couldn't manage a hit off Belinsky at any other time. The Rebels won, 7–5. Pensacola's defense contributed to the loss with four errors while Belinsky toiled on the mound.[14]

In his next start on May 8, Belinsky proved his worth against the Fort

Walton Beach Jets with a complete-game, 10-strikeout, 3–1 victory that looked like it could be a one-hitter until the opposing batsmen got on base several times in the later innings. A shutout remained a possibility into the ninth inning, but the Jets got two baserunners when Belinsky hit a batter and walked another. A fielder's choice ground ball forced out the runner going to second and advanced the other runner to third; he scored on a single. Belinsky scattered seven hits.[15]

The Graceville Oilers put up a bigger fight in their 9–4 victory against the Dons on May 13. After suffering through the first three innings with a lack of hits, they pounded Belinsky for eight runs across the fourth and fifth innings. The next day, he saw action against the Panama City Fliers when he relieved Dick Fletcher, who had "bruised his shoulder" in a collision with a runner at home plate. Belinsky started the bottom of the fourth inning and got credit for the 6–4 victory.[16]

A 16–9 victory against Panama City on May 22 gave Pensacola's baseball fans a reason to cheer as Belinsky struck out seven in four and one-third innings on the mound; his time in the batter's box yielded two hits and a run scored.[17] On May 31, he engaged in a compelling battle with Jets righty Bill Felker. Both teams suffered in an offensive quagmire, scoreless until an RBI single off Belinsky in the ninth inning gave Fort Walton Beach a 1–0 victory. Though he kept the opposition in goose eggs and scattered seven singles, his outing could not be described as smooth. "Belinsky, the calm, poised lefty suffering from a mild case of wildness, faced 37 batters and thrice the Jets stranded two runners," wrote *Pensacola News-Journal* sports editor Earle Bowden.[18]

His next two performances delighted baseball-minded Pensacolans, who could get paper cuts thumbing through *Roget's Thesaurus* to find adequate descriptors. Stellar. Bravura. Superior. On June 4, Belinsky allowed five hits and tallied 17 strikeouts in a 6–2 victory on the road against the Jets. He had great control until the ninth inning, when he walked two batters.

On June 8, the Dons' wunderkind threw a one-hitter and counted 16 whiffs in a 9–1 victory at home over the Graceville Oilers—who occupied first place in the Alabama-Florida League—thanks to a fastball that "hopped" and a curveball that "snapped effectively" as he dispatched batter after batter. Graceville scored its sole run in unearned fashion. It happened in the second inning, when Belinsky hit a batter and walked another, followed by Dons shortstop Jim Strickland's throwing error. "But his mastery over the offensive-minded Oilers made the estimated 235 fans braving threatening weather forget everything but a new strikeout record," wrote Bowden.[19]

More dominance manifested against the Montgomery Rebels on June 12. As he had in the previous two contests, he threw a complete game—eight strikeouts, four hits, three walks—and the Dons' offense gave him a huge cushion as he kept the opposition scoreless for a 7–0 shutout.[20]

Dons fans who expected a continuation of authority found disappointment on June 20, when the Jets slashed at the left-hander's pitches for 12 hits and seven runs; three runners scored in the first inning. Belinsky, suffering from acute tonsilitis, went the full nine. Fortunately, Pensacola's batsmen answered the call with 13 runs to secure the fourth straight victory for their star pitcher.[21]

At the beginning of July, Belinsky got a tonsillectomy. He rebounded with an appearance for the league's All-Star team in a 13–9 victory against Graceville and showcased his productivity again with 13 strikeouts against the Selma Cloverleafs on July 10. The Dons supported Belinsky with seven runs. Selma had scored once against the southpaw, whose 7–1 lead began to collapse like a house of cards in a wind gust during the top of the ninth. A walk, two singles, and a double caused two runs; an error by Pensacola's left fielder with the bases loaded accounted for an additional three runs. Relief pitcher Rex Ford preserved a 7–6 win.[22]

The next time that Belinsky faced Selma, he underlined his effectiveness with 11 strikeouts in a two-hit complete game for his 10th victory of the season. The Dons won, 7–3 as defensive errors caused Selma's runs. Belinsky had an admirer besides the fans, though. Chattanooga Lookouts general manager Zinn Beck saw the July 18 game and eyed the ballplayer—described by Bowden as "rapidly becoming a desirable commodity on the baseball market"—for a potential graduation to the Double-A Southern Association. Chattanooga's club belonged to the Washington Senators organization.[23]

Belinsky raised his record to 11–5 on August 10. A six-hitter highlighted by 11 strikeouts against Graceville culminated in a 6–1 entry for the Dons' win column, but an item in the *News-Journal* dampened hopes of Belinsky's ascent beyond Class D baseball despite his fantastic groove. At least for the moment. "Washington scouts, who once were seriously considering buying Pensacola southpaw Bob Belinsky, are no longer interested," stated Bowden.[24]

On August 16, Panama City did as well against Pensacola's ace as outlaws trying to evade the Lone Ranger and Tonto in the Old West as the left-hander utilized "a hopping fastball with a baffling curve" in a three-hit shutout helped by four runs for the Dons.[25]

Ending his season with a 13–6 record, Belinsky captured the #2 slot in the Alabama-Florida League for strikeouts with 202. He pitched 195 innings, allowed 90 walks, and finished the season with a 3.00 ERA.[26] But baseball didn't provide the only drama for Belinsky, who tried to make

Bo Belinsky went 13-6 for the Pensacola Dons in 1957. It was his best record in the minor leagues before breaking into the majors with the Los Angeles Angels in 1962. Belinsky is the last player on the right in the back row (courtesy Frank P. Hardy).

some headway with a sailor's girlfriend. "The sailor broke a beer bottle over Belinsky's head," wrote Maury Allen, who authored his 1973 biography of Belinsky with the pitcher's approval and participation. "When Bo recovered, he smashed the guy's face down hard on the bar and broke his nose. The Shore Patrol arrested Belinsky." Dons owner Fred Davis bailed out his pitcher and told him to take a breather for a week in Mobile. The charges were dropped.[27] Another incident involved the police, though it was benign compared to that clash. Belinsky got arrested after ignoring 17 parking tickets. Davis got him out of jail by paying them.[28]

His performance for Pensacola earned him a price tag of $1,000 and a jump from Class D ball to the Knoxville Smokies in the Class A South Atlantic League. Moreover, Belinsky now belonged to a major league organization; Knoxville played under the auspices of the Baltimore Orioles, which had brought the Pensacola Dons into their nest because Davis, an independent operator, succumbed to the financial benefits of being associated with the Orioles.[29]

Knoxville, Aberdeen, Amarillo, Stockton, and Vancouver

Smokies fans didn't have enough time to get used to Belinsky in 1958—he played in seven games and compiled an 0–2 record before getting sent to the Aberdeen (South Dakota) Pheasants of the Northern League in mid–May. The "Sally" League limited its rosters to 18, so Knoxville removed Belinsky and two other players to meet that number. Belinsky's inconsistency manifested in two mid–July games. In the first game of a doubleheader on July 10, he didn't even last through the first inning against the Duluth-Superior White Sox though he had a three-run lead. His tenure got truncated with two outs and the Pheasants down, 4–3. Duluth-Superior scored twice more for a 6–3 win; Aberdeen won the second game, 2–0.[30]

Against the St. Cloud Rox four days later, he threw a 2–0 shutout with 11 strikeouts.[31] Then he dominated the Fargo-Moorhead Twins with a two-hitter, racking up 11 strikeouts and limiting walks to two.[32]

Belinsky's exploits earned him the starting slot for the All-Star Game pitting the Winnipeg Goldeyes against the rest of the Northern League's greatest players. Managers, umpires, and sportswriters voted on the selections.[33] Fargo-Moorhead Twins manager Ken Silvestri piloted the All-Star team; his paradigm conceived Belinsky on the mound for three innings. "Everybody's going to get a chance to play," declared Silvestri.[34]

Alas, the star southpaw threw just one inning, allowing one walk and no hits. His pitching compadres in the 1–0 victory for the All-Stars in front of a crowd nearly 4,500 strong were Dick Stewart (Fargo-Moorhead Twins), Bob Quinn (St. Cloud Rox), Rex Rupert (Grand Forks Chiefs), and Ernie Christoff (Eau Claire Braves).[35]

Belinsky led the Northern League with 184 strikeouts and a 2.24 ERA as he went 10–14 against Northern League opponents in Class C ball for Aberdeen. He placed second in Northern League MVP Award voting, getting 24 votes to 27 for Goldeyes catcher Jim Schaffer. The voters consisted of sportswriters, four league umpires, and the league's eight managers, who were forbidden from voting for players on their respective squads.[36]

His achievements on the field didn't suffice for excitement, a template that continued throughout his career. Belinsky sought women. But female companionship led to physical injury in the winter of 1958–1959, when he roomed with a prostitute in New Orleans. According to Maury Allen, "Every time she did a trick Belinsky had to go out and get some coffee. He did it because he liked the girl and needed the money." One time he returned and got attacked by three guys, who had also done a number on the woman. A former acquaintance came by, but Belinsky offered her a selfless caveat to keep her distance. "I told her she better stop coming after me. I was a loser and would only cause her grief. Never stopped her. She gave me some dough, cut out again, and showed up the next season in Aberdeen."[37]

Before the 1959 season, the Orioles labeled Belinsky—who had clearly matured on the mound with Aberdeen—as a prospect for promotion. Amarillo Gold Sox manager George Staller noted his "fine curve ball" in an uncredited article for the *Amarillo Globe-Times*, which also framed him as a "happy-go-lucky fellow off the field but he's all business when he is pitching."

Belinsky's "Bo" moniker had not yet caught on, demonstrated by Aberdeen manager Billy Demars observing his commitment and calling him Bob. "He hates to lose," said the skipper. "Once he made a date before a game he was to pitch. Bob lost the game. When he walked off the field his date was standing there waiting, but he walked by without a word and didn't go out that night. He takes his losses hard."[38]

Amarillo's baseball fans learned to read beyond the numbers of their new acquisition when his 10–14 record with Aberdeen in 1958 received a description of "deceiving" because of an inferior squad. Plus, Belinsky had notched four shutouts and allowed 79 walks in 181 innings. His first start delighted Gold Sox fans: a two-hit shutout.[39]

Belinsky lived in a suitcase for the Orioles organization in 1959, bouncing from farm team to farm team like a pinball. In addition to pitching in four games for the Aberdeen Pheasants and compiling a 2–0 record, Belinsky pitched for the Gold Sox (Double A, Texas League, nine games, 1–3); Stockton Ports (Class C, California League, eight games, 1–0); and Pensacola Dons again (Alabama-Florida League, nine games, 4–4).[40]

His voyage to the Golden State caused him to reunite with his Aberdeen manager, now piloting the Stockton club. "Ports skipper Billy DeMars' daily prayers for a certain fastballer to join the club were answered when New Yorker Bob Belinsky arrived from Amarillo," reported the *Stockton Evening and Sunday Record*, which also labeled his fastball as "blazing."[41] Belinsky got his sole victory for Stockton on June 2, striking out 10 and pitching a complete game for a 6–2 "W" against the Bakersfield Bears; he allowed eight walks.[42]

Stockton enjoyed another formidable but not dominant performance from Belinsky during his brief residency in northern California. On June 15, the Modesto Reds notched nine hits and seven runs off Belinsky, whose solid control during his seven and one-third innings yielded 11 strikeouts and two walks. He also hit a batter in Stockton's 12–8 victory but did not get credit for the victory.[43]

The Stockton tenure lasted about a month, consisting of six starts and two relief appearances before he was released on June 23.[44] Next stop: Pensacola. Although Dons fans may have been thrilled to see Belinsky back in the Florida panhandle, his brief stay on the mound in his debut likely gave them pause. With the Dons trailing the Dothan Cardinals, 4–1, on July 5, Belinsky got the call for relief in the ninth inning and produced a nightmarish sequence—a single, a walk, and three balks leading to a fifth run for Dothan.[45]

He returned on July 8 with a masterful display in a complete game against the Cardinals, throwing a five-hitter punctuated by 10 strikeouts. Pensacola won, 7–3. It was Belinsky's first start in his second Pensacola spell. Lack of control led to two Dothan runs; one transpired in the first inning. With two outs and the bases clear, the Cardinals worked Belinsky for three walks but didn't capitalize further. His reputation preceded him. Noting his stay with the Gold Sox, the *Dothan Eagle* reported, "This season, he pitched in the Texas League but saw only limited duty as the wildness which has plagued him throughout his career returned. He was returned to Pensacola to 'recover.'"[46]

Another outstanding game followed. Belinsky struck out 12 and limited the opposition to five hits in Pensacola's 3–0 victory over Panama City on July 12; he added to the offense with a solo home run. A ninth-inning Fliers rally had not only threatened the shutout but also the game. Belinsky loaded the bases with a walk after a single and a ground ball bobbled by Pensacola's second baseman, then went to full counts on two batters before striking them out. When the next batter hit a "spinner in front of the plate," Belinsky fielded it and threw to first to secure the out and the victory. Panama City's skipper Al Ronning, also the team's catcher, protested to no avail.[47]

Belinsky's desire for companionship and lack of judgment led to another boondoggle. A woman who had sex with Belinsky in Pensacola claimed to be 18 years old. Later, she said that she was 17 and threatened to have him arrested for statutory rape unless he married her. Davis presented Belinsky with more information that exacerbated the problem—the mother of the accuser had a relationship with Pensacola's chief of detectives. It wouldn't take much for him to investigate the matter, with the result being prosecution and prison. Another female acquaintance smuggled the ballplayer under a blanket in her car's back seat and deposited him in New Orleans, which partially solved the problem. Davis picked the farthest spot from Pensacola in the Orioles' farm system, Aberdeen. He had an 0–2 record playing again for the Pheasants, now piloted by Earl Weaver.

At the end of the season, Belinsky quit. It wouldn't be the only time. He felt stagnant, plus the beating by the trio of goons didn't help matters. Orioles farm director Harry Dalton received the phone call from his unhappy player, digested the situation, and called Weaver back with a solution—Belinsky should come to Baltimore and pitch batting practice for the Orioles.[48]

He traveled with a Pheasants teammate who had a rural upbringing and a thirst for the sexual opportunities in an urban environment. Belinsky's compadre reached his breaking point in Chicago. After parking "on some dirty street," Belinsky made a deal with a pimp; when the pair returned to the street after their dalliance, they found the car vandalized and their belongings gone.[49]

But when they arrived in Baltimore, only to get assigned one room with one bed for the two of them at Baltimore's Southern Hotel, the left-hander quit baseball. Again.[50]

Dalton called on the Belinsky matriarch for reinforcements when he presented an opportunity to play in Florida for the Orioles' Instructional League team during the offseason. He also had a meteorological asset. Clearwater, Florida, provided a nice antidote to New Jersey winters. But temptations abounded when a groupie hung around outside the Orioles' field and asked Belinsky for his autograph. Whether it was a line or his policy, Belinsky said that he didn't sign "in front of ball parks" but asked if they could get coffee and then "I'll sign anything you want." They agreed to go on a date, beginning with the woman coming to his apartment.

Belinsky wasn't there yet, but two other ballplayers hosted two women. One took them to a back room, and the other attacked Belinsky's date. "When I finally get to the apartment the girl is hysterical," remembered Belinsky. "She had been raped and her dress was torn and she is screaming. This nut was laughing. I had a hell of a time soothing that broad that night."[51]

He seemed to be a magnet for controversy where women were concerned. In 1960, he served in Army reserve duty in Fort Knox, Kentucky. A woman named Penny, whom he had been dating, arrived at Fort Knox, gave herself the moniker of Mrs. Belinsky, and claimed that that their baby was sick. It gave Belinsky the rationale for a leave of 48 hours. Penny had cash. Lots of it. She told the ballplayer that her late husband left her a lot of money, plus she had robust income from working as an interior decorator.

The kid from Trenton rode on cloud nine until the Army's Criminal Investigation Division targeted him and his "spouse" for prosecution. Reason: bad checks totaling $4,000 in Columbia, South Carolina. Belinsky came clean about his marital status; the FBI okayed his story. The woman got prosecuted and later went to the Belinsky house in Trenton. Belinsky said, "My mother is a compassionate woman."[52]

In the middle of the 1960 season, Baltimore promoted Belinsky to the Triple-A Vancouver Mounties after a brief period in the army. Now managing Vancouver, George Staller used Belinsky to start three games and tapped him to relieve in seven others; he had a 1–3 record and 4.50 ERA against Pacific Coast League opponents. But the friction between the manager and the pitcher hadn't lessened. Staller stated his position quite clearly: "Well, I don't want you here."[53]

Drama off the field affected Belinsky physically. When he found that a guy stole his coat from a bar and camped out in the coffee shop across the street, he went with another player to get the coat back. They had words. Belinsky got his coat back but punctuated his triumph with a left hook, which hurt his pitching hand. An excuse that he fell on his hand when he ran and "slipped in the outfield" did not suffice for Staller, who put the lefty on suspension without pay.

If Belinsky had a shot at pitching in the major leagues in 1961, another incident interfered when a previous winner of the Miss Universe contest stayed at the same hotel that the Orioles used in spring training and resided in the room next to Belinsky's. An imposing mother served as bodyguard to the striking Colombian woman, preventing any chance that the lothario could spend time with her. So he let it go. When Steve Dalkowski and Steve Barber came up to his room before dinner, Dalkowski "almost passed out with excitement" when he saw her in the hall and schemed to get an up close and personal look.

A quick jaunt to the hotel's maintenance room allowed him to procure a drill, which he used to make 20 holes for him to invade her privacy. Word spread. Maury Allen describes a dozen players coming up to the room to look at her the following night, but one had a flashlight. It doomed them. When she turned off the lights, she noticed the beam. A call to hotel security led to a call to Orioles general manager Paul Richards, which led to Belinsky et al. being summoned. Belinsky and Dalkowski got their walking papers with the destination of Little Rock, where they'd join the Travelers—Baltimore's Double-A team in the Southern Association. Richards kept Barber with the Orioles.[54]

Big Times in Little Rock

When the southpaw played for the Little Rock Travelers, he began talking to a guy at a bar. An everyday occurrence. Two guys enjoying a drink and shooting the breeze. But Belinsky's conversation partner was not just an ordinary Joe looking to dull the sharp edges of life with a couple of belts. Through the conversation, Belinsky realized that the man was Penny's husband, who had two kids. The four grand had come from their marital assets. Penny left them and shacked up with some ballplayer.

When Belinsky revealed his identity, there were no outbursts. Rather, they continued drinking "to Penny" for a couple of hours. Belinsky offered a consolation of sorts. "If this is any satisfaction to you, sir, we had a hell of a time on your four thousand dollars."[55]

In his first pitching opportunity, Belinsky threw one and one-third innings in relief against the Shreveport Sports on April 10 and kept them scoreless with one strikeout but reinforced the "wild" quality that seemed to be attached to him. Little Rock won, 9–6.[56]

He got three innings of relief work in the middle of a game on April 14 against the Macon Peaches, who won, 3–2, on a bases-loaded single in the 10th inning. The box score shows that Belinsky's output amounted to three strikeouts, two walks, a base hit, and a hit-by-pitch, but the article in the *Arkansas Gazette* mentions five strikeouts. After the Shreveport and Macon contests, Travelers manager Fred Hatfield revealed a promising opinion of Belinsky's future with the ball club. "That Belinsky (Bob) looks good enough to be a starter, too. He's done real well in relief and he looks like he'll be strong enough to go the distance."[57]

On April 20, Hatfield backed up his words by naming Belinsky the starting pitcher against the Birmingham Barons. Belinsky confirmed Hatfield's instinct. During a prevailing stretch of 20 at-bats for the Barons, he ended 17 with an out. Additionally, Belinsky struck out six and allowed six hits in six-and-one-third innings. The Travelers had built a 3–1 lead when he left the game, but the Barons came back in the later innings with four runs; Little Rock scored in the bottom of the ninth, resulting in a 5–4 loss.[58]

In his second start, Belinsky shone like Shabbat candles on Friday night as he notched 11 strikeouts in his first Southern Association victory—a 5–4 victory against the Barons in Birmingham on April 24. Hatfield used two relievers in the 10th inning to preserve the win for Belinsky, who had allowed six hits and three walks in his nine-inning occupation of Rickwood Field's pitching mound.[59]

Belinsky's personality attracted attention in Little Rock as well as his pitching exploits. Like the fictional slugger in *Casey at the Bat*, the southpaw had an ease about him. *Arkansas Gazette* columnist Orville Henry wrote, "This swarthy New Yorker is the sort who'd look and probably feel right at home if you suddenly dropped him into the starting slot of a World Series game." Additionally, Henry observed that Belinsky's demeanor matched his physicality: "As far as he's concerned, pitching like he talks, which is smooth and sure, it is a left handed league."[60]

Another victory followed on April 29. Going into the ninth inning, the Mobile Bears trailed the Travelers, 5–2, and they scored a run on an infielder's error, a walk, and an RBI single. Belinsky responded with his eighth strikeout, but Hatfield pulled him for "showing signs of wear," plus Mobile's right-handed batters were about to get another chance at the southpaw. Relief pitcher Jimmy Lehew replaced him and retired the next two batters to end the game with a 5–3 victory.[61]

Belinsky raised his record to 3–0 on May 4 with a 12-strikeout performance against the Atlanta Crackers, managed by former Cub and Dodger Rube Walker. Atlanta showed a strong offense. Little Rock, more so. The Travelers won, 10–6. Acknowledging the power of his teammates, Belinsky said, "This club of ours is going to make some runs. My job is to get out there and bear down and throw as hard as I can for six, seven innings. The rest of it has to take care of itself. If we've got a good lead, I can get by the rest of the way without my best fast ball. If we haven't then we've got somebody who can come in and take over for me."[62]

Owning a 6–1 lead, Belinsky got nicked for three runs in the top of the eighth and a pair in the top of the ninth to tie the game, but Atlanta's batsmen and baserunners did not accomplish this solely by their skill. Belinsky walked three batters and the Travelers made three errors. Result: four unearned runs.

The Travelers crossed the plate four times in the bottom of the eighth inning. Their victory didn't overshadow Belinsky's challenge, which he admitted after the game to battery mate Chuck Staniland. Because his recent employment in the minor leagues offered neither stability nor opportunity in significant doses, Belinsky needed to adjust his approach if he wanted to be a starting pitcher in the major leagues. "What I've really got to do now is to learn how to pace myself to go nine. I've got to learn how to be a starter all over again. I haven't been one in two years."

Staniland believed that Belinsky's "breaking stuff is good enough for the majors," but another pitch threatened stamina. "You've got take something off your fast ball when you're not in trouble so you'll have something left when you need it."[63]

His first loss came in his next opportunity, a one-inning relief job in the first game of a twin bill at Shreveport on May 9. Beginning the bottom of the sixth inning with two men on base courtesy of walks by starting pitcher Charlie Ready, Hatfield summoned Belinsky and witnessed a see-saw presentation: another walk, two strikeouts, and a grand slam. The Travelers lost, 5–4, and got trounced in the second game, 7–1. The Nashville Volunteers were responsible for his second loss, a 3–0 shutout on May 12 in which they struck out seven times against the lefty and managed seven hits in his six and one-third innings.[64]

The Nashvillians had an edge, according to Belinsky. They knew what he was going to pitch because of his body language. So he adapted with "a very limited windup," shielding his repertoire, a strategy sourced from playing with Vancouver and facing keen-eyed batsmen in the Pacific Coast League who could decipher pitch selections. "If you just put your fingers a quarter of an inch differently on the ball, they'd know what to look for," explained the southpaw.

Restricting one's body movements on the mound before releasing the ball gave pitchers a double advantage in strategy and stamina. "You're able to keep the ball hidden better, and the hitters don't have nearly as long to look at it before you throw," offered Belinsky. "And, too it saves a lot of energy. If you use the full windup, it's like throwing 15 more hard pitches a game. Sure, I can throw a little harder with a full windup, but I can't throw as many hard ones during a game if I use it."[65]

Belinsky registered 10 strikeouts in a 10–8 victory over the Vols in the first game of a doubleheader on May 21. He threw nine innings, but it took the Travelers two more to win; Pat Gillick got credit for the "W." Nashville won the second game, 6–1. The Chattanooga Lookouts handed Belinsky a loss on May 26, bringing his record to 3–3. In his seven innings, Chattanooga scored a quartet of runs; three were unearned. An additional three tallies established a decisive 7–1 victory, but Belinsky, the Southern Association strikeout leader, presented a cause for celebration with nine whiffs.[66]

Topping the league gave as much consolation as Burgess Meredith having time to read his favorite books after his glasses break on an iconic episode of *The Twilight Zone,* when Belinsky and his cohorts began June with a 15–2 loss to the Crackers. He struck out six in a punishing five and two-third innings at Ponce de Leon Park as the Atlanta lineup confronted him with 10 hits and eight walks, boosted by Little Rock's five defensive errors. "The Travelers, after a long bus trip from Little Rock, were never more sluggish or inept," declared the *Arkansas Gazette.*[67]

Atlanta's press corps showed more bite. In addition to using the word "inept," the *Atlanta Constitution* called Little Rock's performance in the field—which included allowing five walks and seven runs in the bottom of the sixth inning—a "comic opera defense," while the *Atlanta Journal* emphasized an "assortment of frustratingly fast and slow curves" from Crackers hurler Ed Dick being the real reason for the win.[68]

At 3–4, Belinsky's record obscured a fantastic start. Orville Henry sourced the problem to the team's defense, stating that Belinsky "falls off" when he followed through, putting him at a disadvantage to field ground balls hit back to the pitching mound or cover first base on grounders hit to the second baseman. Further, the strikeouts that he tallied with the regularity of sales at a Macy's cash register on Black Friday caused an unintentional nonchalance. "Behind this sort of pitching, with the counts mounting, fielders get used to the whiffs and anticipate them and when they don't come off, they're back on their heels, not ready for the peculiar things that a hitter is apt to produce against unusual stuff," opined the *Arkansas Gazette* scribe.[69]

Hatfield used Belinsky for an inning in relief during the 7–4 loss to Macon on June 5 after Little Rock squandered a 4–0 lead; he got his fifth loss a couple of days later courtesy of the Peaches, who split a doubleheader with the Travelers.[70] Another relief opportunity happened on June 11, when the Barons tapped John Papa for five runs in the second and third innings. They tacked on another score during Belinsky's occupancy, which ended after the eighth inning; Birmingham won, 6–3.[71]

In a home game for the Travelers on June 13, Macon handed Belinsky his sixth loss. Hatfield had already used three pitchers in this pulse-raising battle at Travelers Field when he called on the lanky left-hander later in the game. Little Rock trailed, 3–0, in the second inning, but rebounded with a pair of runners crossing the plate in the eighth inning and tied the game in the bottom of the ninth. The Peaches scored two runs off Belinsky in the top of the 10th and kept the home team scoreless in the bottom half to win, 5–3.[72]

On June 17, Birmingham swept a doubleheader, 3–2 and 7–3; Belinsky lost the first game, his seventh loss.[73] His drought ended with a 3–2 victory against the Atlanta Crackers on June 23. It seemed that Belinsky had paid attention to Staniland's caveat about creating an even tempo throughout the game. "Belinsky paced himself better than usual and though he worked in the constant shadow of trouble, he went out with a four-hitter," wrote Jim Bailey in the *Arkansas Gazette*. Indeed, Belinsky walked eight in his eight innings.[74]

In his next chance, Belinsky dominated. His complete-game, 2–0 shutout against the Mobile Bears on June 28 encompassed 11 strikeouts, two hits, and the last 11 batters retired in order. Little Rock's offense lacked the authority of their pitcher, managing their runs on four hits.[75]

Inconsistency

Things were looking up for the 24-year-old. His recent exemplary displays elevated his record to 5–7, proving that baseball is a game of patience, discipline, and skill. But his next opportunity, a relief effort on July 2, resulted in a downward slide when he lasted one-third of an inning in an away game against the Shreveport Sports ending in a 19–4 defeat for the Travelers. Trailing 10–2, Hatfield brought in his ace. Walks plus a sacrifice loaded the bases, which Belinsky followed by giving up a triple; Don Bradey replaced him. Shreveport amplified the score with four more runs and scored twice in the bottom of the eighth.[76]

The Volunteers swept an Independence Day doubleheader hosted by the Travelers, 6–2, 6–4. Belinsky started the first game, threw three wild pitches, and left after three and two-thirds innings with the home team trailing, 3–2. His defense faltered as well. Orville Henry reminded readers that Belinsky erred "in fielding a grounder and allowing a base runner caught in the middle to reach the base ahead of him."[77]

A rainout plus the Southern Association's upcoming All-Star break provided an opportunity for the fourth-place Travelers to regroup. Owning a 43–48 record, they had a bright spot with Belinsky even if his 5–8 record didn't reflect it. SA managers voted him among the eight fastest pitchers in the league. He maintained his strikeout leadership with 118, far outpacing the pitcher in second place; Barons right-hander Howie Koplitz, who had torn through the league so far with an 11–1 record, had 90.[78]

An item in the July 12 edition of the *Gazette* stated that Hatfield would shift Belinsky from a starting pitcher to a long reliever along with Chuck Daniel. That maneuver didn't last long; Belinsky started the July 16 game against the Lookouts and threw five innings of shutout ball, complemented by relief pitcher Jim Lehew, who also kept the opposition in zeroes. An explosive Travelers offense racked up nine runs, four in the first inning. His loss in the first game of a July 21 doubleheader against the Crackers in Atlanta pushed his record to 6–9. The defeats were less than decisive: 1–0 and 5–4.[79]

Belinsky's season to date had a roster of signifiers. Frustrating. Inconsistent. Mercurial. Unreliable. Vulnerable. The *Arkansas Democrat* acknowledged the choppy waters for Belinsky in 1961 by labeling him "erratic" before its account of his outstanding performance against the Macon Peaches at Luther Williams Field on July 26. Although the Travelers lost, 7–4, Belinsky recorded 18 strikeouts, including a stretch where six consecutive Maconians whiffed.

Besides his pitching power, Belinsky had the weapon of stamina in his arsenal; he pitched 11 innings. Chuck Daniel spelled him with the score tied, 4–4; Macon scored three runs in the bottom of the 14th inning to win the game. Little Rock began on a down note when Macon went up, 3–0, in the bottom of the first inning, highlighted by two runs scoring on player-manager Jerry Snyder's triple. The Travelers got their first run in the top of the second inning and tied the game in the top of the seventh. Both teams scored once in the 12th inning. The Peaches mounted a two-out rally in the 14th when they got two men on base with a bunt and a single; Lou Skizas's three-run blast earned the victory.[80]

Then a shocking announcement occurred. Belinsky quit baseball. Squashing the hopes of Travelers fans looking for momentum in his scheduled start against the Volunteers on July 31, the lefty pointed northward to

Trenton, reportedly to "enroll in an electronics class." Reasons were vague in the Arkansas press: "Personal problems" and "a misunderstanding with Baltimore farm officials." Belinsky returned to the Travelers after talking with Orioles scout Jim Russo about the situation.[81]

He next faced the Peaches on August 3, going seven and two-thirds innings and striking out nine but getting no decision. The Travelers' offense gave him terrific run support with a 7–1 lead as the eighth inning began, but Belinsky faltered, loading the bases on a bloop single and two walks—the first on four straight pitches and the other with a full count.

Macon chipped away at Little Rock's lead, beginning with a ground ball that scored the second run. After a strikeout, Travelers shortstop Melvin Geho bobbled a grounder that allowed a runner to score, followed by an RBI single closing the gap to 7–4. Belinsky was relieved of his pitching duties; Little Rock scored in the bottom of the eighth, but Macon put up four runs to tie the game in the top of the ninth. The 8–8 tie remained until the bottom of the 14th inning, when the Travelers scored on a pair of errors. After a walk put Dave Nicholson on first, Macon pitcher Phil Clark fielded a ground ball and made a "hurry-up try for a force at second," which went awry as the ball sailed into center field. Nicholson scored because center fielder Donald Ross "kicked it around for a second error on the play."[82]

Hatfield gave Belinsky the ball for the first game of an August 8 doubleheader against the Bears in Mobile. He didn't disappoint—complete game, four hits, eight strikeouts, 3–1 victory. Little Rock took the second game as well, 5–2. Win number eight for the southpaw happened in the second game of a Travelers-Bears doubleheader on August 15. The Travelers won the first game, 2–1, in 13 innings and revived to put nine runs on the scoreboard against five by the Bears as Belinsky pitched another complete game. Further, the left-hander helped his own cause with two RBI and a run scored. The sweep gave the Travelers seven victories in eight games.[83]

Against Shreveport on August 20, Belinsky got back to a .500 winning percentage with a six-inning performance in which he struck out two, walked two, and allowed seven hits. But only one run scored on his watch. The Travelers won, 7–2.[84]

On August 26, he faced the Volunteers and left the game trailing, 6–4, after the fifth inning. The Travelers bounced back to win, 9–7; reliever Robert Walz got credit for the win. Belinsky's next game against the Chattanooga Lookouts on August 30 resulted in a loss, giving him a 9–10 record. Chattanooga dominated with an octet of runs that sent the left-hander back to the bench after two and two-thirds innings and put up four more runs for a 12–1 trouncing.[85]

Belinsky pitched against the Volunteers on September 2 and departed before completing the second inning with the score 0–0; four other hurlers took the hill to no avail as the fellows from Nashville blasted their way to a 10–6 victory. It was a solid season for Belinsky, who topped the Southern League with 182 strikeouts. He pitched 174 innings, had a 9-10 win-loss record, and notched a 3.72 ERA.

There was a sojourn in Hot Springs during the season, prompted by an incident involving Belinsky and Travelers outfielder Bob Walls in a Little Rock club. But they were targets, not instigators. It started off as a night to let off steam. They danced with a couple of women. Walls wore contact lenses, but the smoke in the place irritated him to the point of removing them. When he went to the bathroom with his eyesight failing, he accidentally "brushe[d] into a guy," and that's when the wheels fell off the wagon. The man and his friend approached the ballplayers, mistook them for "Chicago hoods," and told them to leave while one held a knife under the table "inches away from Walls's balls." Belinsky stayed calm, smiled, and decked one of them in the Adam's apple. When he disclosed what happened, Travelers management sent the ballplayers to Hot Springs for 10 days.[86]

Sparked by a 23-14 season-ending run that compensated for a 13-21 record in June, Little Rock's squad finished in third place in the Southern Association.[87] Their fans could look forward to 1962 with pride, hope, and resilience, but without Belinsky. After the season, Baltimore assigned the left-hander to the Rochester Red Wings in the Triple-A International League. Belinsky quit. Again. Harry Dalton persuaded him to get some seasoning in Caracas, Venezuela during the winter. Besides the money, which was more than he made in the minor leagues, Belinsky had women on his mind. "Besides, I hadn't made that South American scene yet and with a good sunburn on my dark skin I could easily pass for a local and make it with all the dancing señoritas."[88]

Dalton's idea worked. After winning his first three games, Belinsky dominated in his fourth game with 17 strikeouts. He got a parrot, named him Loretto, and brought him back to the U.S. Ultimately, his parents took in the bird.[89]

Despite his performance, the southpaw who showed signs of brilliance would not wear an Orioles uniform in 1962, nor would he work elsewhere in the Orioles' organization. Ten days before he turned 25, another team selected Belinsky in the draft of minor league players.

The Los Angeles Angels.[90]

2

"The most pleasant surprise of the 1962 Los Angeles Angels"

Welcome to Los Angeles

When 1962 began, America stood on a foundation of optimism.

President John F. Kennedy entered his second year in office with a major failure behind him—the botched Bay of Pigs invasion to overthrow Cuban leader Fidel Castro—balanced against two successes. The newly created Peace Corps recruited, trained, and dispatched volunteers to assist people in developing countries; John Glenn became the first astronaut to orbit Earth.

Baseball also entered a new era resulting from the fallout of the Continental League, spearheaded by Branch Rickey with a proposed 154-game schedule matching the American League and National League. Even the man who severed baseball's invisible though effective color line by signing Jackie Robinson to a major league contract could not make the CL a reality. It imploded in the summer of 1960 before any team played under its auspices, and caused the AL and NL to boost the number of teams from eight to 10 in each league.

In 1962, the National League introduced the New York Mets and Houston Colt .45s, who changed their name to Astros in 1965; the Mets' moniker harkened back to a 19th-century team. A year before the NL's expansion, the American League added two squads. The Washington Senators moved to Minnesota and became the Twins beginning with the 1961 season. Expansion gave the nation's capital another team, which also used the Senators name. Los Angeles welcomed the Angels, named after a Pacific Coast League franchise that left southern California along with the Hollywood Stars when the Dodgers moved from Brooklyn to LA after the 1957 season.

Dodgers owner Walter O'Malley endorsed the AL expansion and shared Dodger Stadium for four seasons; the Angels played their home games in LA's Wrigley Field in 1961 and in Dodger Stadium from 1962 to 1965 before moving into Anaheim Stadium in 1966.

Gene Autry owned the Angels thanks to a brainstorm of AL President Joe Cronin, who floated the idea in December 1960, as radio stations played Autry's classic Christmas songs—"Frosty the Snowman," "Rudolph the Red-Nosed Reindeer," and "Here Comes Santa Claus." A household name thanks to music, movies, and TV, Autry had ambitions beyond entertainment and began a portfolio of businesses, including radio station KMPC, which had the cornerstone asset of Dodgers radio broadcasts in its programming.

But KFI lured the Dodgers away in 1959, leaving KMPC with a void. Cronin's vision created an opportunity to complement broadcasting games for a new team based in Los Angeles courtesy of major league expansion. Autry could own the team. The entertainer purchased the rights, assembled staff, signed players, and readied the Angels for a 1961 debut. Fans endured the team's eighth-place finish and 70–91–1 record for the inaugural season but recalled some bright spots. LA's batsmen had comported themselves respectably against American League pitchers. Veteran first baseman Steve Bilko hit .279. Albie Pearson placed fourth in the league in on-base percentage and tied for sixth with 96 walks. Leon Wagner finished eighth in slugging percentage and tied for eighth in home runs.

Angels pitchers had their moments, too. Art Fowler and Tom Morgan were in the top 10 in saves in 1961, still an unofficial stat. Ken McBride had the fifth-highest strikeout total, eclipsed by Camilo Pascual, Whitey Ford, Jim Bunning, and Juan Pizarro. The Angels enhanced their 1962 pitching staff by signing Belinsky and three other minor leaguers—George Conrad, Bob Haye, and Félix Torres.[1] Adding Belinsky elevated excitement given his performance over the winter in the Venezuelan League, which produced a 1.91 ERA, 11–4 record, and 144 strikeouts in 131 innings. The strikeout tally set a record. Plus, the Angels needed a lefty. They had two, but one presently had arm problems.[2]

Belinsky's trip to the team's spring training facility in Palm Springs got detoured to the Garden State for a lengthy rest. But that wasn't the whole story. When the left-hander arrived at spring training nine days late, he clarified the reason for going home to Trenton: money. Although Belinsky admitted, "I wanted a longer vacation," he also underscored, "the real reason was a small salary difference with [general manager] Fred Haney." Lounging aside the Palm Springs Desert Inn swimming pool, he fielded questions from Angels reporters like a gifted politician, and they absorbed his words for their copy. Belinsky was a golden offering from the media gods—a handsome, approachable, and entertaining ballplayer who could be a great source for quotes.

Gregariousness fit perfectly with this nascent team looking for amplified media coverage to compete with the Dodgers, especially in a city where personality is a commodity. "Some of the writers say I'm a character, a screwball or a nut," said the Angels' new acquisition. "They could be right because I've got a screwball. And it's a dandy, even if I do say so."[3]

Belinsky described himself as "socially cocky," which some could describe as simply being friendly in social situations. Others might call him downright cocky concerning analysis of his performance and repertoire. Or blunt, at best. "I know this, if I don't make it this year I never will," declared the hurler. "I haven't made the progress I should have in baseball and that's mainly my own fault. But I have all my pitches working now and my control is good. What I've learned in baseball has been all on my own. As far as pitching instruction, I don't think anyone can help me anymore."[4]

Angels manager Bill Rigney noted the 1961 lineup's pitching vulnerability but offered a decent forecast in 1962 due to two factors: the stadium and the players. LA would share Dodger Stadium, which had deeper outfield fences than Wrigley Field. Plus, he gave positive acknowledgment to George Witt, Dean Chance, Jim Donohue, Johnny James, Jack Spring, and, of course, Belinsky. "[O]ur scouts say he is a good one," observed the skipper, who had managed the Giants for five seasons before joining the Angels.[5] Scouts labeled Belinsky's contributions as "great speed and brilliant curve."[6]

The honeymoon didn't last long. Belinsky could grasp a baseball but apparently not a pen to sign his contract. He walked out. Haney knew a thing or two about the combustion that occurs when talent meets ego; he played for Ty Cobb when the legend was a player-manager for the Tigers. But Belinsky hadn't proven his talent yet at the major league level, not even in an intra-squad game. So the Angels GM combatted the southpaw's argument about a clause for a raise depending on the number of wins with a simple explanation: "Before Belinsky left his home in Trenton, he agreed to terms. Now he wants to re-negotiate. I can't. A deal's a deal."[7]

The impasse lasted a couple of days. Haney banned Belinsky from the team, talked with him for reportedly "less than 10 minutes," and quieted the dispute.[8] But all was not copacetic. Belinsky declared his dismay as he offered his John Hancock: "I'm unhappy about the contract but I'm not unhappy about the ball club."[9]

Management may pay attention to the contentment of All-Stars, but not an unproven rookie and especially not a temperamental one. "I don't care whether he's unhappy or not; all I care about is whether he can pitch," stated Haney. "And that's all he should care about now because I never knew an unhappy ball player who was any good."[10]

Gene Autry later offered some insight during a chance meeting on the side of the road when Belinsky suffered a flat rear tire on his bicycle. After pulling over, Autry got out of his car and reportedly advised the rookie like it was a scene from *Leave It to Beaver*, featuring Ward Cleaver telling Beaver to stop complaining about his teachers. "You've got a big chance, son, and I think you ought to forget what's happened and just start from right now," Autry counseled. "You'll never find a man more fair than Fred Haney. And you'll go a long ways before you'll find a manager who'll help you more than Rigney."[11]

Wisdom honed by success came not only from Autry's vision but also the ability to install the right people in the right jobs. Autry believed that Angels management had the capacity to produce a winning team in addition to a profitable one, and Belinsky had the ability to be a highly significant factor if he eliminated the friction. Plus, the left-hander added panache to the team striving for attention in southern California against the esteemed Dodgers, who owned one of baseball's brightest legacies and a new stadium set for a 1962 debut. Belinsky could be a gold mine for the Angels' publicity team.

"We had heard of Bo when we drafted him" said the team's PR chief, Irv Kaze. "We knew he was flaky, and we knew he had been around and would be good copy. We were in direct competition with the Dodgers for tickets, and we knew Bo would sell us some. We had no idea just how famous he would become and what a drawing card he would develop into. After all, my God, he hadn't played in a single major league baseball game yet."[12] But there was a problem. "He never seemed to care about anything," said Kaze. "He had a great arm, he could have been a star, but he wasn't motivated."[13]

Though Kaze saw Belinsky as a valuable source of publicity, which hopefully would translate to ticket sales, a great amount of gamesmanship occurred. Belinsky knew that a good story enticed the press, sometimes at the expense of the facts, especially concerning women. He used a variation on the slang term "broads" to describe them. "So I went along with them," said the southpaw. "When they asked about broadies [sic], I built it up. When they asked about pool, I made out to be the best player that ever picked up a cue. When they asked about my contract, I made it sound like I wouldn't sign under any conditions unless Autry begged me personally."[14]

He got his first opportunity with the Angels when Rigney sent him to the mound for two innings in a seven-inning, intra-squad contest on March 7. Belinsky's opposing teammates hit a "bloop single and drew three walks, but the rookie showed some promise. "His control seems to be better than that for an average left-hander," said the manager. "The walks came on borderline pitches. I don't think he's wild."[15]

Though wildness is important but not crucial during spring training, it caused neither shame nor softening for Belinsky. "Even when I was just starting, I didn't throw this wild," he explained with another doomsday quote regarding his future as a major league pitcher. "My trouble lately is that I have too much stuff. I've picked up some relaxed habits. I'm not saying that's the reason I'm wild, maybe I'm just becoming a wild man. But if I don't make it this year, I never will."[16]

Angels pitching coach Marv Grissom had adjusted Belinsky's technique from stem to stern, maybe accounting for some unevenness in performance given a learning curve that some athletes find steep because muscle memory developed over several years can be deeply embedded. Under Grissom's tutelage, Belinsky gripped the ball and released it with two seams spinning rather than four. His windup changed, too. "I used to bring my hands together and then throw," he explained. "Grissom wants me to swing both arms back in a windup and then throw. He says I'll get more momentum that way."[17]

It didn't have a positive effect immediately. Belinsky lasted seven innings against Houston on March 26 and gave up all the runs in a 7–0 shutout. But he couldn't be faulted for the offense; LA left 10 runners on base.[18] Another outing against the Colt .45s went about as well for the Angels as sales of the Edsel did for Ford. Houston scored nine times during Belinksy's tenure on the mound, which totaled less than two innings in the April 4 game. Los Angeles endured a massive display of offensive power emphasized by homers responsible for a dozen runs in the 20–5 final score. Dave Guisti, Hal Smith, and Norm Larker went yard. Román Mejías did it twice.[19]

Starting the Season

Two weeks later, the Kansas City A's—who had tied for last place in the American League with the Washington Senators in 1961—faced Belinsky on April 18 in his first start as a major leaguer in a regular season game. He had a rocky beginning. In the first inning, Dick Howser drew a leadoff walk, and Bobby Del Greco smacked a double to score him. Jerry Lumpe walked, and Norm Siebern singled home Del Greco for a 2–0 lead. Rigney later revealed that Belinsky stood on the precipice of being yanked. "He was so nervous he couldn't have told you his name," said the manager. "One more hit or walk and he was gone." Belinsky affirmed his unease during the first-inning barrage. "When I looked down and saw Red Witt warming up, I thought to myself, 'Please.... I can't go back to Little Rock.'"[20]

Angels fans among the 7,055 in attendance at Dodger Stadium may have wondered if they made a mistake in selecting the AL squad for investment of emotion, energy, and time rather than the vaunted Dodgers. Why not root for a team with plenty of NL pennants and a couple of World Series titles plus a rich lineage dating back to their NL debut in 1890? True, the Angels had right-hander Ken McBride, eighth in strikeouts in the major leagues in 1961. But the Dodgers had three pitchers in the top ten—Sandy Koufax, Stan Williams, and Don Drysdale. Koufax led with 269, more than 45 above Twins ace Camilo Pascual in second place. Further, Koufax and Johnny Podres tied for sixth in wins with Steve Barber and Lew Burdette.

Worries might have diminished, if not disappeared, in the second inning when Belinsky struck out the side, and he notched two strikeouts in the third. The Angels scored three times in the bottom of the fourth; Belinsky singled home the third run. Because of a blister endured by Belinsky on his pitching hand's middle finger, Rigney sent in Art Fowler to begin the bottom of the seventh inning and protect the 3–2 lead. Both teams remained scoreless for the rest of the game, which gave Belinsky his first major league victory in addition to being the first victory for the Angels at Dodger Stadium. Los Angeles had begun the season on the road with a 3–1 record, then lost the home opener to Kansas City the night before Belinsky's debut.

After Fowler secured the victory, Belinsky dialed the Trenton phone number 393-3318—also known as EXport 3-3318—from the Angels' clubhouse and pierced the quiet of the Belinsky abode. Awake at 2:30 a.m., Ed Belinsky figured that his son would call. Bud Furillo of the *Los Angeles Herald Examiner* transcribed the words of baseball's latest hero as he told his father about winning the game, praised Fowler, and brushed off paternal concerns. "Don't worry, I'm staying clean," said the ballplayer with a carefree spirit. "I'm giving it a good shot this year. Whaddya mean I'll get in trouble with the girls? I told you not to worry."

After hanging up, Belinsky not only told Furillo about the nerves he experienced before the game but also lauded his manager and pitching coach. Given his lackluster performance in spring training, he had something to prove. "Rigney and Grissom have stomachs of iron to stick with me long as they did," said Belinsky. "I'm happier for them than I am for myself. I never listened to anybody in baseball up 'til now. Nobody ever had a better manager and pitching coach than Rigney and Grissom."[21]

Rigney expressed confidence on behalf of himself and Grissom regarding Belinsky's ability while pointing out a question of consistency that hovered before the game. "All we wondered was whether he could get the ball over often enough to pitch big league ball," said the Angels'

2. "The most pleasant surprise of the 1962 Los Angeles Angels"

manager. "Tonight he showed us that he can, and all of us hope that he keeps it up. He can help us plenty."[22]

Belinsky did. For a little while, anyway. He went the full nine for his second victory, a four-hitter at home punctuated by eight strikeouts in a 6–2 win against the Cleveland Indians on April 25. It ended a four-game losing streak for the Angels, who had a 5–2 record before the skid. Furillo answered the statement from an unnamed critic who called Belinsky a "kook" during the winter's minor league draft. "That 'kook' happens to look like the greatest bargain basement buy since the suit with two pair of pants."[23]

The Ohioans worked Belinsky for five walks, including one to Woodie Held leading off the top of the ninth inning. But the lefty responded with the flourish of a movie star signing an autograph in cement on the sidewalk at Grauman's Chinese Theatre, striking out the next three batters to end the game.

His third game, also against the Indians, provided an exhibition of pitchers—five for Cleveland, four for Los Angeles. Belinsky had a 6–1 lead at Cleveland Stadium on May 1 when he faced the home team in the bottom of the sixth inning. After Chuck Essegian's flyout to Lee Thomas in center field, he walked Gene Green, gave up a double to John Romano, walked Held, and hit Tito Francona with a pitch to give the Indians their second run. Rigney called on reliever Jack Spring, who retired the next two batters. Jerry Kindall struck out, and a grounder by pinch-hitter Miguel de la Hoz went to shortstop Joe Koppe, who forced out Francona at second base.

The Angels put up two runs in the top of the seventh for an 8–2 lead, but Spring gave up a two-run, two-out homer to Green in the bottom half. Eli Grba replaced him and got Romano out on a fly ball. Belinsky would still get credit for the win if the bullpen maintained their lead; Cleveland threatened when pinch-hitter Al Luplow belted a two-run blast to make the score 8–6. Ryne Duren relieved Grba, and the pain continued for LA. Don Dillard pinch-hit for Gary Bell—Cleveland's fifth pitcher in the game—with one out and drew a walk, then scampered to second on Buck Rodgers's passed ball.

Fortunately for Belinsky, Duren caught Ty Cline looking for the second out and ended the inning when Bubba Phillips fouled out to Rodgers. Cleveland's submission continued into the ninth, and Belinsky notched his third victory.

The No-Hitter

Asking who threw the first no-hitter in the major leagues on the West Coast might prompt Sandy Koufax as the answer, given his four no-hitters including a perfect game.

When that response proves incorrect, a second guess will likely be Don Drysdale. The fireballer won a Cy Young Award, led the majors in strikeouts three times, and held the consecutive scoreless innings record for 20 years until fellow Dodger Orel Hershiser broke it. But he never threw a no-hitter. Then the responder may figure that an opposing pitcher tossed one against the Dodgers after they planted their flag in southern California in 1958. Lew Burdette? Warren Spahn? Mike McCormick? Jim O'Toole? All good guesses. All wrong.

If told that the achievement belongs to an American League pitcher, rational responses would be Whitey Ford, Mudcat Grant, and Early Wynn. But the honor belongs to Bo Belinsky, who dominated the Orioles on the night of May 5 for a 2–0 victory. Both teams were .500 in the young season. Baltimore stood at 10–10, Los Angeles, 9–9.

Belinsky's 2.21 ERA through three starts indicated a rookie with terrific promise, which he reinforced by starting the game with strikeouts of Johnny Temple and Dick Williams, and Baltimore third baseman extraordinaire Brooks Robinson, who batted .303 that season, grounding out. The Angels scored in the bottom of the first inning when second baseman Billy Moran crossed the plate on a wild pitch by Steve Barber after getting on base with a single and advancing to third when Leon Wagner doubled. Wagner, a right fielder and the team's power hitter, led the 1962 squad with 107 RBI and 37 home runs. First baseman and fan favorite Steve Bilko struck out the first of two times that afternoon, followed by Felix Torres's strikeout to end the inning.

Belinsky's control came into question in the top of the second when he hit Baltimore first sacker Jim Gentile and walked catcher Gus Triandos, who batted an anemic .159 in 66 games that season. Right fielder Dave Nicholson, another Oriole with a sub-.200 average in 1962, grounded into a force out on Triandos. Shortstop Ron Hansen ended the inning with a strikeout—Belinsky's third K of the night.

The Angels added the second run in the bottom of the second inning. Barber—who had gone 18–12 in 1961—walked left fielder Earl Averill and gave up a double to Belinsky's battery mate, Buck Rodgers, which put runners on second and third. Joe Koppe got one of his forty RBI in 1962 by grounding into a 4-5 fielder's choice that scored Averill and retired Rodgers at third. Belinsky moved Koppe to second on a sacrifice bunt, but leadoff hitter and center fielder Albie Pearson ended the rally by fouling out to Gentile.

In the third inning, Williams became a two-time strikeout victim of the southpaw's pitching repertoire. The Angels managed to get one man on base in their half of the third with Wagner's single, but Barber tallied two strikeouts; Billy Moran got caught looking, followed by Torres swinging and missing.

2. "The most pleasant surprise of the 1962 Los Angeles Angels"

Belinsky encountered trouble in the top of the fourth. After striking out Robinson, he walked Gentile and Jackie Brandt, and Torres's error let Triandos reach first safely. With the bases loaded, the Orioles had Nicholson at the plate. Belinsky got his second strikeout of the inning when Nicholson whiffed, followed by Hansen's flyout to center fielder Pearson. Angels fans glanced at the scoreboard to find six strikeouts for the rookie so far. Barber handled the home team in three-up-three-down fashion in the bottom half of the fourth, striking out Averill, followed by Rodgers and Koppe grounding out.

The Angels' lefty looked a little shaky again in the fifth inning when he hit Barber, hardly a batting threat with a .071 average in 1962. But the next three batters failed to get on base. Two outs began the home team's half of the fifth; Belinsky grounded to Barber, and Pearson got caught looking. Moran singled but hopes were short-lived when Wagner flied out to Brandt in center field. Hansen, a part-time shortstop for Baltimore with a .173 average in 1962, jeopardized the no-hitter in the sixth when he crushed a ball to the warning track.[24] Pearson snared it and protected Belinsky's journey toward notoriety. Triandos walked for the second time in the game, but Nicholson struck out for the second time that afternoon. Worries disappeared for LA. At least for the moment.

Earl Averill banged a two-out single in the bottom half of the inning, and Rigney replaced him with pinch-runner Lee Thomas, who played in 160 games that season. Rodgers's grounder to Hansen ended the threat. The Orioles tried to change things up in the seventh inning, when infielder Marv Breeding pinch-hit for Barber, but he got called out on strikes. Hansen and Temple grounded out. In the bottom of the seventh, the Orioles sent in reliever Wes Stock, who retired Koppe, Belinsky, and Pearson on grounders. Barber left the game with a strong performance—seven strikeouts, four walks, and a scoreless game after the second inning. Belinsky eclipsed it.

Belinsky retired Williams on a fly to left to begin the eighth inning. Robinson followed with a groundout to second baseman Moran. Gentile lined to Torres at third base. The Angels fared no better in their turn as Stock retired three in a row. In the top of the ninth, Belinsky struck out Brandt for his ninth K of the afternoon, Moran handled a ground ball by Triandos, and Torres caught Nicholson's foul ball.

The game was over. The rookie had done it. A no-hitter.

"I started thinking about [the no-hitter] in the sixth inning, but I didn't get cautious," said Belinsky after the game. "In fact, I started throwing harder. I wanted to get to the ninth inning as fast as I could because I knew that's what the fans wanted. They were enjoying it as much as I was. This thing's good for me and the [Angels]."[25]

Rigney praised Belinsky by calling his effort "a beautiful job" but also highlighted the involvement of Rodgers. "Not to take anything away from Bo, don't overlook the great job Bob Rodgers did behind the plate," reminded the Angels manager. "He called all the pitches—we made no suggestions from the bench—and Bo shook him off only a few times."[26]

Rodgers was also a rookie, technically. In 1961, he only played in 16 games, but he would play 155 in 1962. "He could challenge anybody with that fast ball," the Angels' backstop praised Belinsky when he died in 2001. "He got the screwball over early, but the fast ball set up everything. When Bo was on, he had that electric kind of stuff."[27]

A touch of revenge accompanied the accomplishment because of the Orioles releasing Belinsky in the off-season and past friction with one of their coaches. George Staller now worked for the Orioles as the third base coach, which gave him a terrific view of Belinsky's achievement. "It couldn't have happened to a nicer team," opined LA's newest baseball hero, who hit two batters, walked four, and struck out nine.[28]

As a pitcher nears a no-hitter, there's a tradition dictating that teammates, coaches, and the manager refrain from talking to him in the dugout lest anything upset the karma of the moment. Belinsky kept his own counsel, as pitchers do in this situation. "Toward the end, when it looked like it might be possible, I kept telling myself, 'Take your time. You're either going to do it or not. Don't hurry this thing. Be careful. You may never get another chance.' But I could not slow down."[29]

Where most ballplayers would prioritize rest to maintain sufficient energy, Belinsky enjoyed his social life and believed it affected his pitching on May 5 in a positive manner.

Bo Belinsky won his first five games in his rookie season in the major leagues. He pitched a no-hitter in his fourth game on May 5, 1962. The Angels beat the Orioles, 2-0 (Los Angeles Public Library, Valley Times Photo Collection).

"The night before my no-hitter, I banged into this secretary out on the Strip," recalled Belinsky. "She was tall and thin and black haired. We had a couple of drinks and I wound up making it with her at her pad. She turned out to be not too b.a.d. [sic]. I got home at four A.M. That night I pitched my no-hitter. After the game I went back to look for her. I couldn't find her. I never did again. She was my good luck charm. When I lost her, I lost all my pitching luck."[30]

Belinsky used Bud Furillo's "Steam Room" column in the May 7 issue of the *Herald Examiner* for an exclusive guest column that he claimed to be original and not the product of a ghostwriter. "This is no spook bit," Belinsky stressed. "Yours truly is putting down these typewriter sounds himself." He showed humility and appreciation regarding the Angels from the front office to the dugout to the field, in addition to noting the importance of Furillo and the *Herald Examiner* regarding his psyche "because this newspaper stuck with me when I was goin' bad."

Readers also got some insight regarding the nickname now prominently used by the press. Back home, Belinsky's tendency to get into neighborhood scraps led to the "Bobo" moniker inspired by the boxer Bobo Olson.

In the wake of the no-hitter, he explained why "Bo" fit him better. "I was just like Olson," he said. "Always taking the count. So let's cool the Bobo bit for now. Bo is more sophisticated. Besides it's easier to spell."[31]

His fourth victory in as many starts proved the potential to be a blue-chip player, which LA sportswriter Braven Dyer had indicated when he described the southpaw as "the most pleasant surprise of the 1962 Los Angeles Angels." Marv Grissom declared, "He could be the best pitcher on our club. His improvement just between his first and second starts for us was amazing. There is no telling how far he can go. It's up to him ... how much he wants to be the best ... how hard he cares to work ... how well he looks after himself. He has all the tools and he's young. He shouldn't miss, if he means business, and I think he does."[32]

In the future, Dyer would have a different view of the ballplayer. Meanwhile, Grissom's words about responsibility could be seen as a warning sign in retrospect.

5–0

The rookie blazed through the White Sox lineup for his fifth win in his first five starts on May 11. Notching 11 strikeouts in seven and one-third innings, Belinsky had solid run support beginning in the bottom of the first inning, when Moran singled and scored on Wagner's double. LA pecked at Juan Pizarro in the bottom of the fourth inning; Koppe hit a bases-loaded single to score two more runs. An insurance run came in the bottom of the fifth when Wagner hit a leadoff triple and scored on Torres's single for a 4–0 cushion.

Chicago put up a run in the top of the sixth inning and another in the eighth. The latter tally forced Belinsky from the game, which ended in a 4–2 win. Nellie Fox led off with a double, then scored as Al Smith's low liner headed straight for Belinsky's right ankle and "took a crazy bounce into right field."[33]

Belinsky's output gave him a 1.72 ERA and hero status for Angels fans, who booed Rigney when he removed Belinsky from the game. "He asked me if I was tired," said the pitcher. "I told Rig I felt I could still throw hard, but some of my pitches were getting away from me. He made the right move." Further, he underscored his appreciation for the fans but reminded them, "It doesn't make any difference to the Angels how we win just as long as we win."[34]

An added boost for his visibility—and potentially his bank account—factored into a conversation with Phil Weltman, one of the most powerful men in show business. Heading the TV department at the William Morris Agency gave him a launching pad to send Belinsky into the stratosphere of celebrity. "The kid's handsome besides being a pitcher and a character," said Weltman. "We'll give him plenty of work if he photographs as well as I think he will. He is very articulate."[35]

In case other teams eyed Belinsky, Fred Haney affirmed his goal of keeping the southpaw with a caveat: "Why, I wouldn't take a half a million dollars for that young lefthander."[36] His next game took place in Baltimore, but Belinsky would have to wait if he wanted lightning to strike twice against his old organization. The O's sent the southpaw from the May 17 game with a 6–1 deficit in the bottom of the third inning, forcing him to explain the falloff from his five-game winning streak and dominance in the previous two contests. "I was mentally tired," Belinsky revealed. Regarding his inventory of pitches, screwball and fast ball being the most prominent, he said, "I just didn't feel like I had my good stuff warming up."[37]

Erasing any thoughts of a slump, Belinsky tossed a two-hit masterpiece against the Red Sox in the second game of a doubleheader on May 20, making him the only Angels pitcher to throw a complete game since the no-hitter. LA's 1–0 victory gave the moundsman his sixth addition to the win column and a four-game sweep of the Red Sox on this part of a 14-game road trip. The following day, Trenton honored the pitcher with Robert "Bo" Belinsky Day and a resolution offering congratulations to him as well as his parents.[38]

2. "The most pleasant surprise of the 1962 Los Angeles Angels"

In less than two months, Belinsky had gone from malcontent to magnificence in the eyes of baseball watchers. But this rise could not be traced solely to Haney, Rigney, Grissom, or even Belinsky himself. If it weren't for Tufie Hashem, a team scout, Belinsky might still be toiling around the minors or perhaps out of baseball altogether. After witnessing the hurler in Vancouver and Venezuela, Hashem consulted with fellow Angels scout Sammy Moses, who got a glimpse of Belinsky with Little Rock. "We agreed that he had a good arm and could throw hard," said Hashem, who credited Haney and his head scout, Roland Hemond, for endorsing his selection. "His improvement in the winter league was quite pronounced, so at the Tampa meeting last December I recommended that the Angels draft him."[39]

Although Hashem saw Belinsky's talent, he admitted that a no-hitter escaped his reckoning. "You have to get so many good breaks for such a performance," stated the scout regarding the rookie's May 5 game. "But Bo proved in that two-hitter at Boston that the no-hitter wasn't a fluke."[40]

Belinsky looked poised to win 20 games in his rookie season. But vulnerabilities emerged. He left his next game on May 24 after five innings with the Angels trailing the Senators, 3–0, at D.C. Stadium; Los Angeles battled back to win, 7–4. Four days later, Belinsky faced the Senators in Dodger Stadium and lasted into the seventh inning. Fowler relieved him with one out and a 2–1 lead. The Senators scored three times in the top of the eighth. Although the Angels went ahead, 6–4, in the bottom of the inning and kept opposing batsmen scoreless in the top of the ninth, Belinsky did not get credit for a victory because the Angels lost his lead and regained it with another pitcher on the mound.

When he faced the Yankees on June 1, Dodger Stadium attendance exceeded 51,000. The 1961 World Series champions recorded a definitive triumph without their star center fielder, Mickey Mantle, as Ralph Terry threw a complete game, struck out eight, and restricted the home team to four hits.

Through eight innings, Belinsky gave up 10 hits, allowed five of New York's six runs, and hit two batters—Moose Skowron and Roger Maris—in the 6–2 loss. Bobby Richardson went three-for-five and scored a run; Skowron hit a two-run single off Belinsky and a solo homer off reliever Tom Morgan. Moreover, Skowron caused a possible omen of bad luck in the second inning when his line drive hit Belinsky "just above the right ankle," the third time that it had happened to the Angels' pitcher, who also got struck in the Washington game on the recent road trip. Belinsky applied a simple explanation instead of citing bad luck. "I just didn't throw the ball good and so we lost," he said.[41]

Belinsky's no-hitter began to look like an anomaly when he got pulled in the top of third inning, trailing the White Sox, 3–1, on June 5. Chicago finished with a 9–5 victory. Recent mishaps hardly provided a reason to start panicking about the rookie, but an item in the *Los Angeles Times* undoubtedly piqued attention by publicizing Belinsky's appetite for distractions off the field, with LA being the site of nighttime opportunities that couldn't be found, at least not to the same degree, in other major league cities.

Rigney took notice, believing these distractions caused Belinsky's downturn of late. Disclosing a behind-closed-doors chat with his star pitcher, Rigney stated, "We agreed especially that on days when he is scheduled to pitch, Belinsky will curtail his outside activities." The Angels' skipper apparently did not go into detail, and if he did, it was off the record because the only activity mentioned was an acting job, albeit "a bit part."[42]

But one could read between the lines and surmise that Rigney meant socializing that went beyond indulgence into excess after hours, enough to impact performance on the mound. It became Belinsky's signature. And his downfall. Less than a week later, Belinsky and his teammate, Dean Chance, made headlines not for pitching achievements but for their nighttime exploits. Early morning, actually. It was the kind of story that every coach, manager, general manager, and owner dreads with fear as substantial as a mudslide in Malibu.

Beverly Hills Cops

On the morning of June 13, southern Californians wiped the sleep out of their eyes and began their routines. Fans of the first-place Dodgers would rather have gone back to bed to forget about the previous night's thrashing by the Milwaukee Braves. Hank Aaron, Tommie Aaron, Gus Bell, Eddie Mathews, and Frank Bolling socked homers, punctuating a 15–2 victory for the National League titans. It was a depressing game but not devastating; Los Angeles had gone 20–4 in their previous 24 games. The Dodgers now had a one-game lead over the Giants and a 7½-game lead over the third-place Pirates.

The Angels fared better. Lee Thomas went yard twice in a 7–5 victory against the Minnesota Twins, putting the fourth-place Angels 1½ games behind the AL-leading Yankees. The Indians and Twins each trailed by a half-game. Fans of the LA teams had reason to be optimistic about winning the pennants in 1962 as they digested the reports in the *Los Angeles Herald Examiner*, *Los Angeles Times*, and other newspapers serving the southern California region. A day later, Angels fans weren't so sure when they read articles about a controversy involving their ace hurlers, which sent them from the sports section to the front page.

At 5:00 a.m. on June 13, Beverly Hills police officers stopped Belinsky, who was driving his Cadillac with Chance and two women in their early 30s. The women lived in the same apartment building on Hollywood Boulevard, but press reports from the two major Los Angeles newspapers neither mentioned whether they were roommates nor how they first met the ballplayers. Belinsky's date, Gloria Eves, bolted from the car and claimed that Belinsky had assaulted them. The *Times* said, "Blood was streaming from a gash over her left eye which later required five stitches, and her dress was blood stained."

Chance and his companion, Bridget Whitaker, backed up Belinsky and said an accident caused the eye injury. Eves sat in the back seat, while the other three occupied the front. For reasons unknown or at least not initially reported, Eves "became belligerent," inducing Belinsky to stop and demand that she leave the vehicle. When she stood her ground—or rather sat it—he tried to "eject her," to no avail. "Her eye apparently struck some object in the car," reported the *Times* in a piece without a byline, citing Belinsky's account to an officer on the scene.

Eves did not press charges. "The whole affair was an accident," said Whitaker to the police on the scene. Belinsky claimed in the Maury Allen book that the women had implored him and Chance to drive them home. Further, he said that Eves doted on him. Belinsky reacted in a less than gentlemanly manner. "Well, one thing led to another, and this girl starts mouthing off about she loves me and will stay with me and wants to cook breakfast and all that bull. I'm really in no mood for that, so I tell her to keep her big mouth shut or I'll throw her out."

When Belinsky pulled over, she refused to get out of the car. The scuffle ensued. "We're on some side street and I lose my temper. I begin pulling her out of the car and she is holding on to the doorknobs. I'm pulling her over the front seat and out the door and she's hanging on to the handle. The next thing I know she smashes her head against the window and cuts herself up pretty good. She's screaming, yelling, carrying on pretty good, and I'm screaming right back at her. Just then the cops hear the noise, and a squad car pulls over."[43]

Belinsky further alleged that she proffered a compromise—no official complaint to the police if he stayed with her for the week. They agreed.[44] The *Times* reported that Belinsky remained silent to the press under orders from Angels management, but Bud Furillo had a quote in the *Herald Examiner* showing humility. "I've made too many mistakes already to make up for the opportunities this ball club has given me," said the ballplayer now under scrutiny for more than balls, strikes, and walks. "I'll do my best to justify them by my pitching."[45]

Rigney fined the pitchers $250 each, then doubled down and declared an increase to $500 for anyone out at that time of night. After that, it would be a grand. Haney talked with the players and updated the press with a statement confirming that the incident occurred at the time reported. It read, in part: "At the time of the injury, a police car was in the vicinity, so the players took the girls to the police. After satisfactory explanation of the injury, the players were allowed to go home."

Their date began when Whitaker and Eves arrived at Dodger Stadium to meet Belinsky. He and Chance took them to a performance by Eddie Fisher at the Cocoanut Grove, a nightclub in the Ambassador Hotel, though they arrived very late and only heard the crooner's final song. Walter Winchell invited them to a party in the hotel. Another gathering followed at the Beverly Hills home of film agent Kurt Frings and his wife, the Pulitzer Prize-winning playwright Ketti Frings. Belinsky asked if the foursome could attend; Winchell needed to get permission from Fisher, who acquiesced.

The incident happened after the Beverly Hills party, during a trip to the Ambassador Hotel so the women could pick up the car that they used earlier in the evening. *Los Angeles Herald Examiner* columnist Melvin Durslag called Belinsky's version of the argument with Eves "a simple disagreement" regarding the route in driving her home. She protested. At that point, he wanted her to take a taxi.[46]

Lest anyone think that booze played a role in the evening's activities, Winchell claimed that the ballplayers "drank nothing but milk at the party that preceded the fracas. I know because I handed it to Bo and watched the two of them toss it down. And I know the girls are both ladies. They each had only a nip."[47] Furillo stuck up for him, too. "Bo is innocent of everything except being out late. Why it's almost impossible to get out of the back seat of his convertible without injuring yourself. Only the other night, I suffered my eighth broken nose trying to leave hurriedly from the rear of the car."[48]

If the media knew harmful details about Belinsky's extracurricular pursuits, they kept a lid on them until this story; indulgences became public, with the *Times* describing Belinsky as "high-living" and accounting for his recent forays into LA's celebrity nightlife. In a four-day span, he had a date ending at 5:00 a.m. with singer Kay Stevens at the Slate Brothers night club; a 7:00 a.m. exit from a birthday party for Connie Stevens, singer and star of ABC's *Hawaiian Eye*; and a cameo scene shot for *77 Sunset Strip*, another ABC show that existed in the same fictional universe as *Hawaiian Eye*. Belinsky played himself.[49]

Times columnist Sid Ziff observed, "It was refreshing to have a character like Belinsky in the limelight until he completely overplayed his hand." True. No longer could off-the-field endeavors be the subject of gossip limited to the clubhouse, press box, or bars. The word was out.[50]

Rigney's lecture had done about as much good as giving a lit candle to the Scarecrow from *The Wizard of Oz*. Another skipper might have punished Belinsky by putting him on the bench; Rigney thought otherwise. Belinsky started the June 14 game against the Twins, the last home game for the Angels before a road trip of 22 games against the White Sox, A's, Twins, Red Sox, Yankees, and Senators. Minnesota managed three runs in five innings, though the left-hander notched seven strikeouts. Los Angeles scored twice with him on the mound. After Rich Rollins singled and Harmon Killebrew walked to begin the sixth inning, Rigney pulled him. Both teams added a pair of runs. The Twins won, 5–4.

In the hopes of tamping down Belinsky's wildfire approach to his social life, the Angels employed Marv Grissom to bunk with the southpaw during the trips to the six AL cities.[51] It would be a challenge to tame him at home, though. Angels teammate Ed Sadowski shared a story about Belinsky offering to pay the air fare for women who wanted to travel from Phoenix to Los Angeles and meet him after they called at 3:30 a.m. It was a fact that the handsome, personable pitcher did not have to pursue female companionship. The women pursued him, attracted by fame or looks or both. "Broads are after him wherever we go, and the trouble is, half these broads are flakey," said Sadowski. "I keep warning him, 'You gotta watch out for the Waitkus bit.'"[52] In 1949, an obsessed woman shot Eddie Waitkus, a first baseman for the Phillies, in a Chicago hotel room. He went there because a note written under a fictional name expressed urgency and an invitation. Waitkus survived. The woman, Ruth Ann Steinhagen, avoided prosecution but was sent to a mental institution.

The Southpaw Rises Again

Belinsky inched toward respectability, if not redemption, in a relief effort in his next trip to the mound. In the first game of a twin bill against the White Sox on June 17, Chance had a 4–0 lead entering the bottom of the sixth inning but gave up a two-run, no-out single to Nellie Fox. Jim Landis then flew out and Floyd Robinson singled, prompting Rigney to call on Belinsky, who walked his first batter and retired the following two Chicagoans on a strikeout and a foul out to first baseman Lee Thomas.

The Angels scored their fifth run when Thomas banged a double in the eighth and Albie Pearson, who had walked, scored from first. Belinsky gave up one run in the bottom of the eighth. Fox led off with a triple; Landis whiffed. Robinson grounded to first baseman Thomas, who tossed to Belinsky for the out and allowed Fox to score. Second baseman Billy Moran fielded Joe Cunningham's grounder for the final out, giving a 5–3 win to the Angels and a save to Belinsky.

Belinsky showed that he could handle pressure when he threw a complete game against the A's on June 21, scattering seven hits and emerging with a 3–1 victory at Municipal Stadium in Kansas City. Los Angeles jumped to a 2–0 lead in the top of the first. In the second inning, Ed Charles and Jerry Lumpe led off with back-to-back singles for the A's, and Haywood Sullivan walked to load the bases. But the rookie hurler retired the next three batters.

In the bottom of the fifth inning, the southpaw walked Gino Cimoli, got the next two batters out, then loaded the bases on singles again by Charles and Lumpe. But he got Sullivan out on a grounder to Félix Torres at the hot corner. Singles accounted for all A's hits; Belinsky struck out six.

The Angels experienced another no-hitter in Belinsky's next game on June 26, but not for the rookie. Earl Wilson blanked them in a 2–0 victory, giving the Red Sox right-hander not only his first shutout in the major leagues but his first complete game in 1962. Belinsky performed well, striking out 10 Bostonians and allowing three hits in seven and one-third innings. Unfortunately, Wilson banged a solo homer, and the other two hits led to the second Boston run.

On the evening of July 4, the Angels occupied first place in the American League standings, with a half-game lead over the Yankees and Indians. Fireworks colored the sky with sparkling lights punctuated by whooshes and booms underscoring the celebration of America's forefathers breaking from the iron-fisted rule of Great Britain in 1776 to establish an independent nation. Metaphorical fireworks took place within the Angels squad a couple of nights later because of Belinsky.

In Oakland for his father's funeral, Bill Rigney left coach Del Rice to helm the team for the July 6 game against Boston, rematching the two no-hit pitchers at Dodger Stadium. Any thoughts of Belinsky settling down evaporated. Quickly. He didn't last an inning. The Red Sox loaded the bases on three walks, and a force out at home resulted from Frank Malzone grounding to Torres. Belinsky walked in a run, prompting Rice to yank his starter; Ryne Duren gave up four more runs for a 5–0 Boston lead before the Angels came to bat. The visitors won, 12–7.

Belinsky added to the misery by making his egress from the pitching mound before Duren arrived—a violation of baseball tradition—plus responding to the boos of Angels fans by "allegedly employing an indecent gesture." Furious, Haney addressed the situation publicly. "He has to realize that he is in the big leagues now," said the general manager, who appeared to be losing patience with the petulant pitcher. Haney also rejected Belinsky's explanation of a sore leg as the problem.[53]

But the press supported the southpaw. One reporter reasoned that a "snapped hamstring muscle" restricted Belinsky's delivery, and another described "a partially incapacitated Bo Belinsky, his pulled leg muscle swaddled in elastic tape."[54] A month later, Belinsky reminded critics and supporters alike that he was capable of great things on the pitching mound when he threw a four-hitter against the Twins on August 11. All the hits were singles; Minnesota failed to move a baserunner farther than second base and suffered five strikeouts.[55]

The Angels, in second place, trailed the Yankees by 4½ games, hardly an insurmountable lead. Belinsky could be the tip of the spear, but his inconsistency manifested itself again on August 15 against the Red Sox in the sixth game of a 17-game homestand, when a commanding 4–0 lead changed to 4–3 in the second inning. Dan Osinski relieved Belinsky; Rigney used Spring and Morgan, too. The Angels won in a squeaker, 5–4. Earlier that day, the rookie's extracurricular endeavors resurfaced because Gloria Eves sued him for $150,000; her complaint included an accusation of "manhandling and mauling" during a "fit of rage."[56] A settlement followed. "My lawyer had to give her a few bucks to get her out of town and shut her up. You just can't trust broads."[57]

Belinsky started the first half of a doubleheader against the Senators two nights later at home and performed better, though not in a dominating fashion as he threw eight innings and tallied five strikeouts, but also allowed three runs on five walks and six hits. Rigney replaced him in the ninth inning with Tom Morgan; Los Angeles won the game in the bottom of the 10th on Wagner's solo round-tripper.

Stamina didn't appear to be an issue in his next game, when he faced the Yankees in Dodger Stadium on August 21, lasting eight and one-third innings. After giving up back-to-back walks in the top of the ninth with one out and New York leading 4–3, Belinsky got sent to the clubhouse. Osinski replaced him and retired the next two batters; Los Angeles tied the game in the bottom of the ninth on an RBI single by Wagner. Duren started the 10th inning, but Rigney replaced him after a walk and two singles resulted in a run. Spring relieved him and gave up six runs. The Angels failed to score in the bottom of the 10th, giving the Yankees a solid 11–4 win.

Chicago scored a quintet of runs in four innings against Belinsky on August 25, propelling Rigney to give him the boot and sufficing to saddle him with the 9–2 loss. He next took the mound for seven innings on August 29 in Kansas City, where the A's led, 4–0, at the time of his departure and tacked on two more runs for a 6–0 shutout of the lads from Los Angeles.

But the Kansas City ball club caused a jolt for Angels fans beyond the box scores in early September when the press identified Belinsky as the player to be named later in LA's half of the trade from mid–July that sent outfielder Gordon Windhorn to the Kansas City A's and brought Osinski from the Portland Beavers—Kansas City's Pacific Coast League team—to Mr. Autry's ball club. Summary: in 1963, Belinsky would wear an A's uniform.[58]

The report revived the Haney-Belinsky friction, causing the latter to call Angels management "stupid" if they believed Osinski to be an even exchange for him. Further, he complained about money owed him. Haney responded, "I think we have done very well by the young man. A short time after he pitched his no-hitter, we tore up his contract calling for $7,000 and gave him a new one for $15,000."

The Angels were in third place but only three-and-a-half games behind the Yankees, making them a viable contender for the AL flag. This distraction, plus Belinsky's headline-making actions, were unwelcome. Rigney summarized, "It isn't healthy for the club."[59]

Thankfully for Angels fans, Belinsky stayed because of a decree from a power higher than Rigney or Autry.

3

Bo and Dean

Staying in Los Angeles

On September 6, Commissioner Ford Frick's office announced that the A's deal needed scrutiny and put the kibosh on it a day later because the initial proposal didn't disclose that the Angels would send a player to Kansas City. As far as Frick was concerned, it was a cash deal.[1]

Coincidentally, Belinsky faced the A's in his next assignment on September 12. He and his counterpart, Orlando Peña, kept each other's team scoreless for the first four innings; Kansas City couldn't manage a hit, while LA notched three. But the A's scored twice in the top of the fifth innings and twice again in the top of the eighth, forcing Belinsky from the game. The Angels scored one run courtesy of Lee Thomas's solo blast in the bottom of the ninth. Final score: 4–1

Belinsky's performance on September 18 disappointed as well. He singled for an RBI off Orioles righty Chuck Estrada, and Moran banged a sacrifice fly in the bottom of the second. But the Angels' 2–0 lead evaporated in the top of the fourth inning, starting with Belinsky's error putting Jackie Brandt on first base. The Baltimore rally culminated in three runs before Osinski relieved with two outs and struck out Estrada looking. The Orioles tacked on two insurance runs to win, 5–2.

Winning his last contest of 1962, Belinsky brought his record to 10–11 for his rookie season. In the first game of the September 29 doubleheader in Cleveland, he blanked the Indians for five and one-third innings, struck out nine, and had a 3–0 lead until they scored a run in the bottom of the sixth inning. The Angels scored another run while holding off the Tribesmen for a 4–1 victory, their final win in their sophomore season and a clincher of third place in the AL. Ending 1962 with three straight losses gave the club a record of 86–76, 10 games behind the first-place Yankees, who won the World Series against the San Francisco Giants in seven games. Rigney declared reasons to be optimistic, including the team's youth, learning, and drive. "There is only one phase of the game in which

I can't ask them for anything more," said the manager. "That's desire, they've got all of that they need."[2]

After Belinsky's rookie season, Myron Cope penned an in-depth profile of baseball's Romeo for *True* magazine. The article's title underscored what even the strongest advocates for Belinsky probably felt: "Bo Belinsky's Dilemma: Baseball or Dames?" A teammate from the left-hander's minor league years said, "I mean, broads are okay two, three nights a week—even five nights a week. But *seven out of seven?*"[3]

Ballplayers deserve to let off steam. Belinsky made it a mission. Cope revealed that Pensacola Dons manager Lou Fitzgerald, who managed Belinsky in 1957 and 1959, monitored the sociable pitcher by building "a network of spies" consisting of nightclub owners who let the skipper know if Belinsky stayed at their establishments past a reasonable hour. Fitzgerald would drive to the place, bring the pitcher home, and reinforce his position as an omniscient, omnipotent force whose powers of deduction Belinsky could never decipher.[4]

Toward the end of November, the Angels agreed to let another hurler depart for Kansas City because the commissioner had prevented Belinsky from being part of the trade for Osinski. Given a choice between righty Eli Grba or lefty Ted Bowsfield, the A's selected the southpaw.[5] To cap off 1962, Belinsky joined fellow no-hit hurlers Bill Monboquette and Earl Wilson as honorees at the National Sports Awards Dinner, an event held by the *Los Angeles Times* in late December.[6]

Notwithstanding the no-hitter, Belinsky had a see-saw rookie season with moments of brilliance. He started out as a disgruntled player in spring training, yet to play an inning in the major leagues; shocked the baseball world with his no-hitter; disappointed parents of kids who were Angels fans with the Beverly Hills incident; had some great games complemented by inconsistency; and remained the subject of trade talk. Haney's declaration of Belinsky's value early in the season had faded. "Evidently the Angels are stuck with Bo Belinsky," wrote Sid Ziff. "Management wants to trade him, but no one has come up with a suitable offer for the no-hit pitcher."[7]

Signs of the Times

Appropriately, Dean Chance saved his pal's last victory in 1962. In the early 1960s, Chance and Belinsky governed southern California like princes in a kingdom where fun equaled currency. They reveled, enjoying success on the field plus the accoutrements, benefits, and indulgences off the field during the beginning of a decade that became increasingly progressive, culminating in the forces of feminism emerging in the late 1960s.

Heroes attracted women consistently, a popular-culture template escalated in 1962 by James Bond pairing with Honey Ryder in *Dr. No*, followed by a string of women in the Bond film series. Television's cultural impact fed into this outlook throughout the 1960s, enhanced perhaps by the youthful, handsome, and dynamic American president assassinated in 1963.

Nearly two years after John F. Kennedy's murder in Dallas, CBS premiered the situation comedy *Hogan's Heroes,* featuring an American colonel leading a group of Allied prisoners in Stalag 13, a prisoner of war camp run by inept, monocle-wearing Colonel Wilhelm Klink in Germany during World War II. It ran for six seasons. Subterfuge was their greatest asset. Fake documents, counterfeit money, firearms, explosives, German military uniforms, and an emergency tunnel below their barracks providing a safe escape from the camp gave them the means to commit acts of sabotage while outwitting Klink, Sergeant Hans Schulz, and their superiors in the German army.

Played by Bob Crane, Colonel Robert Hogan had an ongoing dalliance with Klink's secretary—first Helga, then Hilda—in addition to a variety of women with whom he interacted during missions including attacking munitions factories, kidnapping German military leaders, and destroying trains. Hogan and his men also used Stalag 13 as a way station for escaped prisoners from other POW camps.

But the actor who portrayed Hogan did not believe that he personally aligned with the iconic character he portrayed. "At last, though, I feel safe in confessing that in one respect a more unlikely guy for the role of Hogan would be hard to find," wrote Crane in a guest column in the *San Diego Union* in 1966. "Hogan is, indeed, hip. He's a con man par excellence. I, on the other hand, am at times the kind of pigeon with whom the fictional Hogan would have a field day."[8]

Space provided terrific storytelling opportunities in the 1960s, underlined by the country's fascination with the space race against Russia. Set in the mid–23rd century, *Star Trek* revolved around Captain James Tiberius Kirk and the crew of the *USS Enterprise*—a starship belonging to Earth, a member of the United Federation of Planets.

Kirk hailed from Riverside, Iowa, enrolled in Starfleet Academy, and rose through Starfleet's ranks to lead the Enterprise's voyages during a five-year mission "to explore strange new worlds, to seek out new life and new civilizations, to boldly go where no man has gone before."[9] *Star Trek* premiered in 1966 and lasted three seasons on NBC. The first convention honoring the show took place in 1972, and a Saturday morning cartoon show lasted 22 episodes in the mid-1970s. Movies, TV spinoffs, novels, and a gargantuan amount of merchandising followed.

The captain's swagger gained the affection of females throughout galaxies. Some were humanoids on other planets, and some were Earthlings on their own space journeys.

Couple the romantic exploits of these characters with the portrayal of women in sitcoms, often as accessories evidenced by the gender roles of men, by and large, being breadwinners while women stayed home, kept the house clean, and looked after the children. *Bewitched* and *I Dream of Jeannie* featured female characters who had powers, but often used them to help their significant others. A powerful villainess with ferocious sexuality, Catwoman—played by Eartha Kitt and Julie Newmar—never bested the title character on *Batman*. Lee Meriwether played the feline-inspired character in the first film version.

Against this misogynistic landscape, Bo Belinsky had the focus of women attracted to his fame, looks, and charisma. Companionship—sexual or otherwise—flourished for the ballplayer. Along for the ride, Dean Chance had familial obligations that Belinsky dismissed. "Dean and I were a marriage made in heaven or hell," said the southpaw. "I saw Chance in spring training in 1962 with a wife and kid. Some guys belong with a wife and kid. Dean and me just didn't belong with a wife and kid, especially in Hollywood."[10]

Chance admitted his carousing but acknowledged Belinsky's adeptness. "Nobody made it with girls the way Bo did," stated Chance. "I never learned his secret, but I enjoyed trying."[11]

A farm boy from Ohio and a city boy from New Jersey. Opposites attracted. But they diverted somewhat, too. Chance drank to be social, not to numb, escape, or celebrate. Smoking? Never. He also did not indulge in the adoration from women or respect from men as deeply as Belinsky did. And certainly not as long. Growing up in the Midwest, where doing your job without self-aggrandizement is part of the region's culture, Chance wasn't the type to volunteer war stories of the baseball diamond either during his career or afterwards.

But he abided the courtesies of fans hungry for a tale or two. Whether because of remorse, boredom, shame, growth, guilt, an ethic rooted in his Midwestern upbringing, or a combination of those factors, Chance, unlike his wing man, detoured on a path that reduced socializing, amplified quiet over noise, and reflected a dedication to his craft.

"While they certainly came from opposite backgrounds, they shared some similar interests and characteristics," says Chance's son, Brett. "They were both confident, outgoing, charismatic guys who enjoyed the fruits of fame in LA. Bo was a street-wise city guy, but my dad was also very savvy and had a lot of street sense about him too. I had the impression that their similarities never led to any competition or jealousy between them. Instead they were kindred spirits who enjoyed being together, and their friendship was a loyal one."[12]

In the major leagues, Belinsky had a career 28–51 record, with the no-hitter in 1962 being his standout achievement. Chance debuted with

Bo Belinsky and Dean Chance had a friendship that lasted until Belinsky's death in 2001. Chance won the 1964 Cy Young Award and threw a no-hitter in 1967 for the Minnesota Twins (Los Angeles Public Library, Valley Times Photo Collection).

the Angels in 1961. He pitched five games as a rookie and ended his career with a 128–115 record for a winning percentage of .527. Solid. Respectable. Even overpowering and fearsome in a couple of seasons. Chance had a 20-win season twice, tossed a no-hitter, won a Cy Young Award, got selected to an All-Star team twice, and ended his career in 1971 with a 2.92 earned run average. And he never forgot where he came from.

After winning the Cy Young Award in 1964, the alumnus of Northwestern High School in Wooster, Ohio, okayed a dinner honoring him in his hometown if it financially benefited the school.[13] Chance is in good company regarding his roots in Wooster, the hometown of other notables, including John Dean of Watergate fame; Ohio Light Opera founder James Stuart; Stanley Gault, who served as the CEO for Rubbermaid and Goodyear; Ohio Supreme Court Chief Justice Carl Weygandt; and John Sloane, a 19th-century political giant with Ohio Secretary of State, Congressman, and U.S. Treasurer on his resumé.

From the Family Farm to Baseball's Farm System

When Chance left Wooster after high school to join the Bluefield Orioles of the Appalachian League—a league for rookies—he left behind a tremendous legacy of excellence highlighted by Northwestern winning the state baseball championship and state basketball championship. Chance's teammates in Bluefield included future major leaguers Bob Saverine and Boog Powell. Saverine played in each game of the 70-game schedule for 1959, topping the league in batting average, hits, runs, stolen bases, and total bases.

Powell trailed Saverine by two points in average, hitting .351 to his teammate's .353. Chance led Bluefield's pitching staff with a 10–3 record; his 2.94 ERA stood just a sliver behind the league-leading 2.93 of teammate and Appalachian League MVP Arne Thorsland.[14] The Baltimore Orioles bought the contracts for the four standouts and sent them to the Fox Cities Foxes in the Class B Illinois-Indiana-Iowa League, where Chance continued to show promise in 1960 with a 12–9 record in 26 starts and 15 complete games.

During the 1960 holiday season, baseball fans killed time with distractions until the 1961 season began. They went to movie theaters for action in *The Magnificent Seven*, drama in *Butterfield 8*, and comedy in *Cinderfella*. Los Angeles theater buffs ventured to the Biltmore Theatre on West Fifth Street and enjoyed Bert Lahr's starring performance in *A Midsummer Night's Dream* for the American Shakespeare Festival Acting Company. Three thousand miles away, theatergoers saw Broadway's political fodder in *The Best Man*, *Advise and Consent*, and *Fiorello!*

For real political drama, Americans kept a close eye on news regarding the incoming Kennedy administration, especially the president-elect's choices for the cabinet. Frank Sinatra had the job of planning a celebration on inauguration eve featuring the biggest stars in show business—including Dean Martin, Red Skelton, Gene Kelly, and Tony Curtis—with the proceeds going toward a reported $2 million debt created by the Democratic Party during Kennedy's campaign.[15]

Prime time television offered a diversity of choices in nightly entertainment. Fans of westerns relished an abundance of shows, but baseball followers of a certain age might have gravitated toward former ballplayer Chuck Connors as Lucas McCain protecting the New Mexico Territory town of North Fork in *The Rifleman*. Connors, a first baseman, played one game with the Brooklyn Dodgers in 1949 and 66 games with the Cubs in 1951. He began his baseball career for the Dodgers' Newport, Arkansas, club in the Northeast Arkansas League, playing four games in 1940. He also played in the team's farm system in Norfolk, Newport News, Mobile, and Montreal. With the Cubs organization, Connors played for the Los Angeles Angels of the Pacific Coast League in addition to the parent team.

Viewers who liked intrigue, mystery, and sophistication could watch ABC for private detective shows produced by Warner Brothers and set in Los Angeles, Honolulu, and Miami Beach—*77 Sunset Strip*, *Hawaiian Eye*, and *Surfside 6*—with character crossovers establishing continuity in the same fictional universe. Set in New Orleans, *Bourbon Street Beat* also belonged to this grouping; it aired in the 1959–1960 season.

Need a laugh? *Hennessy*, *Bachelor Father*, *The Many Loves of Dobie Gillis*, *The Andy Griffith Show*, *The Tab Hunter Show*, and *The Jackie Gleason Show* provided comedy. *Naked City* and *Dan Raven* fell into the police drama genre, a TV staple.

Route 66 highlighted various locations across the country as the two main characters—men in either their late 20s or early 30s—traveled in a Corvette, got involved in people's problems wherever they stopped, and helped solved them. Premiering on October 7, 1960, the first few episodes of this one-hour drama, which ran four seasons on CBS, featured actors and actresses who later became stars, including Ed Asner, E. G. Marshall, Edgar Buchanan, Whitney Blake, Walter Matthau, Robert Duvall, Elizabeth Ashley, Robert Redford, and Barbara Eden.

Technological advances revolutionized everyday tasks, exemplified by bank executives learning about a new step in automation—Electronic Recording Method of Accounting (ERMA)—which processed checks at a much higher and cost-efficient rate than bookkeepers could do by hand: 550 per minute versus 200 per hour.[16] Investors studied the announcement of the Chesapeake & Ohio Railway purchasing Baltimore & Ohio Railroad and contemplated the potential benefits of this union; they did the same analysis regarding the Chicago & Eastern Illinois Railroad's rejection of a merger proposal involving the Missouri Pacific Railroad.

But investments, politics, films, TV shows, and other pursuits couldn't outdo the excitement of baseball fans caused by the announcement of expansion in early December, particularly those in southern California and the Washington, D.C., metropolitan area. Dean Chance went to the Angels organization in the expansion draft, ascending to Triple-A ball for the Dallas-Fort Worth Rangers in the American Association. He started 14 games in 1961 but pitched in a total of 63. His record: 9–12 with 14 saves.[17] In his five games with the Angels during September, Chance started four games, relieved in a fifth, and had a record of 0–2.

His first start in the major leagues took place on September 11 against the Twins, a game prompting plaudits and comparisons to Dodgers ace Don Drysdale from sportswriter Braven Dyer. Chance went into the eighth inning with a 2–1 lead and allowed the Minnesotans to tie it. Tom Morgan replaced him with one out and gave up a three-run home run for a 5–2 loss. Bill Rigney remarked, "Chance is going to be all right. He knows how to keep the ball low and he has a lot of confidence. He was in a jam a couple of times but didn't panic. And apparently he's cured his wildness. He walked only one man."[18]

In 1962, Chance came into his own with a 14–10 record, finished third in Rookie of the Year voting, and had the fourth-lowest ERA in the American League behind Whitey Ford, Robin Roberts, and Hank Aguirre. He started 24 games and provided relief pitching in 26. A masterful performance against the Twins on September 10 resulted in a one-hitter that he largely credited to curve balls "breaking sharply." Chance also praised his skipper, unlike the tension that seemed to pulsate with Belinsky by the end of the season: "Bill Rigney is a great manager, and it felt great to be able to win one for him in the pennant stretch."[19]

West Coast living can be seductive. The Beach Boys debuted their first album in 1962, extolling the southern California lifestyle emphasized by beaches, bikinis, cars, and surfing. Although Chance enjoyed the region's social aspects, he returned to Ohio, where he had his family waiting for him. Dean and Judy Chance had married in 1961; Judy gave birth to Brett a year later.

Going home rather than creating a life with his wife and kids in LA made sense. You can take the boy off the farm, but you can't take the farm out of the boy. In an offseason interview with *The Sporting News*, Chance explained that he chose farming to supplement his ballplaying income rather than other endeavors described by the hurler as "get-rich-quick investments we ballplayers hear about so often."

Moreover, Chance had farming in his blood. With more than 80 acres of land, he had the benefit of his father's wisdom; Wilmer Chance owned a farm with 145 acres. A family lineage and the Midwestern work ethic required for farming reflected Chance's approach to baseball. Get up, go to work, repeat. No complaining. Use mistakes and disappointments as learning opportunities.

Gene Woodling saw this work ethic in Chance. A veteran left fielder, Woodling debuted in the major leagues with Cleveland for eight games in 1943, then served in the military for two years; he also played for the Pirates, Yankees, Orioles, Senators, and Mets before retiring in 1962. "He just can't understand it when he gets shelled," said Woodling, who claimed that he scouted the 6'3" righty for the Orioles' organization and helped him secure his first professional contract. "He can't figure out how anyone can hit him. Then he works twice as hard the next time out."[20]

Belinsky and Chance may have been inseparable while teammates, but their output differed as greatly as sunshine and moonlight over the next couple of years. In 1963, Belinsky started 13 games and compiled a 2–9 record; Chance went 13–18 in 35 starts and 10 relief appearances. As Americans began to recover from the shock of President Kennedy's assassination in late November, they had an abundance of cultural options throughout 1964—the New York World's Fair welcomed the first group of visitors that would eventually total more than 50 million; moviegoers delighted in Julie Andrews' cheerful portrayal of the title role in Disney's *Mary Poppins*; and the Beatles dominated Top 40 radio.

Baseball fans had Dean Chance. While Belinsky barely edged .500 with a 9–8 record—including a terrific day against the White Sox on July 9, throwing a two-hitter that yielded a 3–0 shutout—Chance's 1964 season exhilarated though it did not begin on an auspicious note. With two outs in the first inning of an April game against the Tigers, he left because of a blister on his pitching hand.

Chance Finds His Groove

Whatever injury or discomfort he sustained did not have a lasting effect. Chance led the AL in wins, complete games, and innings pitched; led the majors in ERA and shutouts; and won the Cy Young Award in 1964—the youngest pitcher to win the award to date. Chance—who went 20–9 in 1964—shut out the Yankees three times, and his 1.65 ERA ranked second-lowest since Walter Johnson's 1.49 in 1919.

Among his 15 complete games, he threw five two-hitters. His 1–0 victory against the Boston Red Sox on June 2 included 15 strikeouts—breaking a single-game team record of 12 set by himself and Ryne Duren—and overshadowed a fine performance by Jack Lamabe, who only allowed four hits by the Angels. Although the victory ended a five-game losing skid for the team alternately nicknamed Seraphs and Halos in newspaper copy, attendance on this splendid night amounted to an abysmal figure of 3,372 at Dodger Stadium.[21]

Chance had a no-hitter in the sixth inning until Dick Stuart smacked a two-out single; Felix Mantilla got the other Boston hit, a leadoff single in the top of the ninth. But Chance didn't accomplish his feat alone, at least not according to him. "Tom Satriano did a tremendous catching job," praised the right-hander. "We used only one signal for my two fast balls, one of which rises and the other one sinks, but he handled both kinds real well. And when Stuart came up in the ninth, I didn't want to throw him fastballs, but he kept calling for it, and by golly, we struck him out with it."[22]

Despite his exemplary pitching, Chance felt that he had a more effective performance in 1963: "I've pitched only one game better up here. I lost a tough one to the Yankees last year, and that night I felt I could have thrown the ball thru anybody."[23] His comment referred to a game that the Yankees won, 2–1. He pitched eight and one-third innings, allowed four hits and two walks, and struck out five.

On June 6, Chance had another epic outing against the Bronx Bombers at Dodger Stadium. Jim Bouton kept the home team scoreless for 13 innings; Chance surpassed him with 14 shutout innings and had a no-hitter into the seventh inning. In the top of the 15th, Willie Smith took over. The Yankees had two outs with two men on base when Dan Osinski replaced Smith; Elston Howard smacked a two–RBI double for a 2–0 Yankees victory.

Upon learning the news regarding the Cy Young Award, Chance's mom, Florence, revealed her son's disciplined rearing that apparently carried him through his major league career. Chance had responsibilities likely as foreign to his schoolmates as a pork chop to a rabbi at an Orthodox synagogue. They began at 5:30 a.m., when he milked and fed cows on the family's dairy farm. "Basketball and baseball practice always kept him until after supper, but when he did get home, usually around 5:30 or 6, he had other chores to do until about 7:30," said the Chance matriarch.

His duties plus a lack of similar aged playmates—Mrs. Chance said a girl was the only other student in his first-grade class, and no more than 30 students populated the school—forced the future major leaguer "to play with boys much older and bigger or travel almost to the next county."[24]

A regimented schedule may have informed dedication but not modesty for the pitcher with a 51-1 record in high school and 18 no-hitters. A profile titled "The Cockiest Guy in Baseball" in the 1965 edition of *Baseball Yearbook* cites an example of the Angels' offense, or lack thereof, causing a lower victory count in the baseball gospel according to Chance. "One day in Boston I was taken out in the eighth for a pinch hitter," he recalled. "I was getting beat 1–0 and the relief pitcher came in and gave up two runs." Chance surmised, "With any kind of luck, I could be 28–2." However, he also noted the fielding prowess of his teammates, particularly second baseman Bobby Knoop. "But I can thank Bobby for helping me out of a jam many times. When you have a second baseman like that, you can do with less runs, because he keeps down the other team's runs."

Six of his 20 victories in 1964 were 1–0 scores. Yankees shortstop Tony Kubek put Chance on a pedestal that even diehard Angels fans might have looked at askance, comparing him to the powerful southpaw from the other LA squad. "He's a great, great pitcher—probably better than Koufax," opined Kubek. "There's nobody close to him in our league. He throws fastballs, curveballs, sliders, up, down, in and out. What else can a pitcher do?"[25]

A season of accomplishments in 1964 led to an offseason of negotiation over salary. Chance entered the penthouse of the Continental Hotel—also owned by Gene Autry—on a February morning for an announcement that pleased Angels fans looking toward the 1965 season and disheartened their counterparts across American League cities. Bill Rigney, general manager Fred Haney, and team president Bob Reynolds surrounded him at the table in front of the press to confirm another signed contract with the Angels.

Chance reportedly earned $25,000 in 1964. Although neither Chance nor the Angels disclosed the exact figure for 1965, *The Sporting News* estimated it to be "at least $41,000." A profile in the *Saturday Evening Post* placed the salary at $45,000 and cited Chance's ego-fueled declaration. "My God, you could go back further and call your story, *The Most Exciting Pitcher Since Dizzy Dean*," said the pitcher to the article's writer, Myron Cope.[26]

With a clear vision of his job, Chance explained his simple but true plan now that he had resolved the money issue with the front office. "My only goal right now [is] to get off to a good start in spring training," he said. "If I do this, get the breaks and stay healthy, I think the rest will come. I know that last season after I got my raise, I was better able to concentrate on pitching. It should work the same way this time."[27]

Besides his 1964 performance, Chance had a tangible argument for a raise by claiming that attendance figures rose "at least 3,000 more" when he took the mound.[28] But a question arose regarding the potential effect of Belinsky's impending absence after an offseason trade to the Phillies.

Not since Dean Martin and Jerry Lewis broke up their comedy act had Los Angeles endured such a shock from a separation.

With Belinsky moving 3,000 miles eastward to play in a different league, Chance saw the value for his pal's career, respected the other players involved, and mourned the loss not only to the Angels' pitching staff but also to himself. "Sure, I'll miss him," admitted the newly re-signed Angels hurler. "He was my best friend ... and still is. It was a tremendous break for him to be traded to a pennant contender. And it was also a fine break for the young Philadelphia players (Costen Shockley and Rudy May) to get traded to us. I think it was a good trade for both teams."[29]

Besides Belinsky wearing a Phillies uniform, Chance's Ohio roots may have played a role in tempering his boisterousness. Returning to Ohio after the season to tend to his farm and family, Chance encountered fellow Buckeyes who had much less tolerance than LA folks regarding nightlife behavior. They didn't have a puritanical streak as much as a puritanical foundation. "Around here, if you get caught with a case of beer in your icebox, it's as serious as getting caught crawling in someone's bedroom window," explained a resident of Wayne County, Hank Critchfield, a local attorney who tried to soften the pitcher's edges through speech coaching.[30]

Chance tied with three pitchers for second place in the American League with four shutouts in 1965—Denny McLain of the Tigers, Mel Stottlemyre of the Yankees, and Joe Horlen of the White Sox. Stamina did not appear to be an issue as he threw 10 complete games, which tied him for fifth place in the AL with Hank Aguirre of the Tigers, Bill Monbouquette of the Red Sox, Fred Newman of the Angels, and Luis Tiant of the Indians. But more innings on the mound meant more opportunities for opponents—Chance placed 10th in hits allowed and fourth in walks in the junior circuit.

Though not as impressive as his 1964 output, Chance had a strong season in 1965 with a 15–10 record, 3.15 ERA, and 10 complete games in 33 starts. His victory count led the Angels and tied him for eighth place in the American League with four other hurlers—Steve Barber of the Orioles, Eddie Fisher of the White Sox, Mickey Lolich of the Tigers, and Pete Richert of the Senators.

The following year, Los Angeles had a greater cultural impact. *Batman* premiered, showcasing Bronson Cave as the opening to the Batcave. Paul Van Doren opened a store called the Van Doren Rubber Company, later renamed Vans. The newly built Century Plaza Hotel earned the nickname "The Hotel of the Future." Angel Stadium debuted in Anaheim, enticing fans to build the highest attendance in the American League for 1966, but the Angels finished in sixth place with an 80–82 record, ahead of the A's, Senators, Red Sox, and Yankees. Although Chance had a .414

winning percentage in 1966—12 wins and 17 losses—his other statistics were comparable with his performance in 1965: 3.08 ERA, 11 complete games, and 33 starts.

In December, Chance became the third star player in Los Angeles to get jettisoned during baseball's winter meetings. The Dodgers traded two-time National League batting champion Tommy Davis to the Mets and base-stealing authority Maury Wills to the Pirates; these unthinkable exchanges happened just a few weeks after Sandy Koufax announced his retirement, leaving behind a stunning body of work—three Cy Young Awards and four no-hitters, including a perfect game, plus leading the majors in wins three times, ERA three times, and strikeouts four times.

The Angels traded Chance along with a player to be named later to the Twins for Jimmie Hall, Don Mincher, and Pete Cimino. Noting the Angels' need to bolster the offense, Chance figured a trade was possible but not to an AL squad. "I simply didn't feel there was any chance I'd be traded to a contender in this league," said the 26-year-old pitcher. Regarding his 12–17 record and 3.08 ERA in 1966, Chance emphasized that numbers don't tell the whole story. "I guarantee you I won't lose any 1–0 games with the Twins," declared the righthander. "If I come back with a 3.08 ERA for Minnesota, you can bet my record will be better than .500."[31]

The land of 10,000 lakes was good to Chance in 1967; he led the American League in games started, complete games, and innings pitched in addition to reaching a 20-win total for the second and last time in his career, going 20–14. But his effort on August 25 earned him a place alongside Belinsky in the annals of achievements for pitchers—a no-hitter.

Chance had a 16–9 record when he began the second game of a doubleheader at Cleveland Stadium. It seemed unlikely that a no-hitter would happen after the bottom of the first inning. Chance walked Lee Maye and Vic Davalillo, then struck out Chuck Hinton; an error by third baseman Cesar Tovar put Tony Horton on first base. With the bases loaded, a wild pitch sent Maye across the plate. But that was the end of joy for the Indians. Minnesota won, 2–1.

Calmness prevailed for Chance, who explained that the source of maintaining a level approach was his experience, particularly 13 games with a 1–0 score among his career victories. "I don't think I ever was tense," he said. "And I knew it was a no-hitter."[32]

Chance finished the season at 20–14, followed by a 16–16 record in 1968. He brought his ERA down from 2.73 to 2.53—the third-lowest in his career—and increased his strikeout total from 220 to 234. In 1969, his opportunities decreased because of a back injury. He started 15 games, relieved in five more, and compiled a 5–4 record. A Twins-Indians trade in December bundled Chance with Bob Miller, Ted Uhlaender, and Graig

Nettles in exchange for Luis Tiant and Stan Williams. Chance saw more action as a reliever with Cleveland in 1970: 29 games coming in from the bullpen and 19 starts. He had a 9–8 record and a 4.24 ERA in mid–September when the front office sold his contract to the New York Mets, where skipper Gil Hodges limited the righty to three relief opportunities—a total of two innings across three games.

Just before the 1971 season began, New York traded Chance and Bill Denehy to Detroit for Jerry Robertson. The Tigers also used him more often as a reliever—14 games started versus 17 in relief—and released him soon after the 1971 regular season ended. He retired thereafter.

Chance had been part of a glorious era highlighted by expansion, artificial turf, and outstanding baseball. "He liked the challenge of playing against great ball players, and the confidence he had in his abilities allowed him to thrive under pressure," says Brett. "I think he also enjoyed the team aspect of baseball and maintained many friendships with former teammates as well as players from other teams (Mickey Mantle, Brooks Robinson and others). The fact that only one Cy Young was awarded for all of baseball through 1966 made it even a little more special. If he signed an autograph for someone and wrote something below his signature it was usually '1964 Cy Young.'"[33]

> The friendship between Chance and Belinsky endured after their careers ended. Chance had great respect for his pal, who showed terrific generosity even if it impacted his bank account. Bo is a thoughtful guy. He had a lot of good times, but he was always kind, considerate, and understanding. I'm not ashamed to say it. Bo was the best friend I ever had in baseball. He would have made a lot of money if he had been more serious about the game. I always did pretty well with money in baseball, and I always tried to help Bo when I could. He just doesn't know how to hold on to money. Bo is one of those guys if you give him a hundred thousand dollars today, he'll let it slip through his fingers and give you nothing back tomorrow.[34]

One example of Belinsky's selflessness happened with a moneymaking opportunity off the field at Melodyland, located near the entrance to Disneyland. *Damn Yankees* was slated to be showcased during the winter after the 1962 season. Figuring that a big LA baseball name would be a draw, the producers asked Bud Furillo to be an intermediary and get Dean Chance or Don Drysdale. Partial to the Angels, Furillo reached out to Chance. Salary $750 a week for two weeks. Chance countered with a request for double the pay, but only if Belinsky could also be in the show. The producers agreed, but Belinsky didn't display any interest. "That's no money," he told Chance. But when Chance said he'd do it anyway, Belinsky agreed to be in the show to help his pal.[35]

Selecting religion as a foundation gave sustenance later that Dean

Chance could have used during his playing days in LA. Bo Belinsky's path took longer. Alcohol became a fixture in his life. Ever since the incident with Gloria Eves in his rookie season, Belinsky had become a topic of discussion not only for his baseball exploits but also his social calendar. Being a sports hero creates opportunities with attractive women. Being a sports hero in Los Angeles creates opportunities with attractive women who are famous, thereby alluring to millions of men who have only magazines, movie screens, and televisions as vehicles for digesting their beauty. Their fantasies were Bo Belinsky's realities.

For the kid from Trenton, LA was a symphony of women. He strove to play them all.

4

Belinsky's Beauties

A Blazing Romance

Bo Belinsky had his first sexual experience when he was 12, with a 13-year-old girl he met when he visited his grandmother, who lived in an apartment building on Jerome Avenue in the Bronx. The site—an elevator in the building. He never saw her again. And so began his journey of sex.[1]

In the early 1960s, Belinsky's life represented glamor and induced envy. At least that's how it seemed. Millions of males from teenage boys to senior citizens fantasized about the pitcher's array of beautiful, famous, and engaging women. If someone ever creates the Sex Symbols Hall of Fame, his girlfriends and acquaintances would be voted in on the first ballot. Unanimously.

Newspaper readers didn't need to look further than Walter Winchell's syndicated column to learn of Belinsky's travels and travails in socializing, romance, and other postgame activities.

From 1929 until it folded in 1963, the *New York Mirror* served as home base for this powerful, syndicated columnist—who wrote his pieces largely with the help of ghostwriter Herman Klurfeld—entertaining, informing, and titillating through innuendo, gossip, and nicknames. For example, Winchell borrowed from an iconic phrase in a 1961 speech delivered by FCC chairman Newton Minow describing television as a "vast wasteland" and called Jackie Gleason the "Vast Waistband of Television" because of the comedian's weight.[2]

Winchell amplified his connection to the entertainment world when he provided the narration for ABC's *The Untouchables*, a fictionalized version of Elliot Ness going after Al Capone and the mob. Desilu produced the show, which starred Robert Stack and aired from 1959 to 1963.

Bud Furillo had been chronicling Belinsky's exploits in the *Los Angeles Herald Examiner* since the contract rift in 1962 spring training, and he introduced Belinsky to Paul Caruso, an entertainment attorney who hosted a party at his Beverly Hills house where the pitcher and the scribe met.³ Belinsky provided great fodder for Winchell, who didn't let his friendship with the pitcher get in the way of a good story. After going 5–0 in his first five games, Belinsky lasted two and two-thirds innings in his loss on May 17, then pitched a complete game for a victory against the Red Sox. His next two games resulted in a no-decision and a loss to the Yankees, followed by five more no-decisions. Winchell's June 17 column featured a related question and answer. "How come Bo Belinsky's in a slump? *Simple story: 'Bo Meets Girls!'*"⁴

In the same column, Winchell used his trademark sarcasm with another question and answer. "Why don't you help your friend, pitcher Bo Belinsky, by playing 'lose me'? *I got a laugh in the press box with: 'I'm dropping Bo Belinsky—he's giving gossip columnists a bad name!'*"⁵

Winchell didn't just match Belinsky with the business side of show business. There was quite a bit of the show side as well. Dean Chance remembered a road trip that ended with the team's plane arriving in southern California at 3:30 a.m. and his tireless pal scampering out of the airport with new companions, probably aspiring actresses given Winchell's connection to Hollywood. "We get off the plane and there's Winchell waiting in the lobby with three of the best-looking girls you ever saw in your life. Bo doesn't even wait for his bags. He just gets somebody else to pick up his suitcases and takes off into the night with Walter and the girls."⁶

Belinsky's notoriety earned him three mentions in Winchell's column on July 9, 1962, the first alluding to the car accident in Beverly Hills with a statement: "They are saying: 'He has a Million Dollar Arm and a Ten Cent Head!'" Then, Winchell dinged Furillo's reaction to the horrible performance against Boston on July 6, when Belinsky got yanked in the first inning, by comparing the sportswriter to Jack Paar, the host of *The Tonight Show* known for crying on camera. "Bo Belinsky's Boswell Bud Furillo (of the *Herald-Exam*) began to weep when Bo knocked himself out of the box in the 1st round after forcing in a run via 4 walks…. 'Aw, c'mon,' we comforted, 'cut the Paar cry baby bit. Thatz showbiz.'" Winchell noted that fellow gossip columnist Hedda Hopper had attended her first baseball game, which appeared to be the game that the Angels lost to the Red Sox, 12–7.⁷

Winchell allowed Donald Freeman, Radio-TV Editor of the *San Diego Union*, to interview him and write about it in Winchell's *Mirror* column. Freeman relayed Winchell recounting his first meeting with Belinsky. "Like a big kid he said, 'Mr. Winchell, you going to put me in The Untouchables?' I said, 'Bo, you are untouchable. You're also unbelievable!'"⁸

Belinsky ruined his chance and earned a new nickname from Winchell. "We now call him Schmobo because, after keeping our promise to get him into 'The Untouchables,' he never showed up…. Why? 'I had to start taking my singing lessons!'" But Winchell also praised Belinsky's pool skills and suggested a contest against Jackie Gleason to benefit the Damon Runyon Cancer Fund. A week later, Winchell claimed that Gleason had left a message for the scribe to call him. The match never happened.[9]

Being connected to Winchell had its advantages. The columnist wrote that Lindy's sent the pitcher "two fat salamis" because of his friendship, which apparently led to after-hours socializing. According to Winchell, Belinsky dismissed any negative impact fostered by journalists. "Bo told a friend of mine you shouldn't be depressed because some sports writers scold you for keeping him up until half past 9; that the sports writers are 'all good gheezers' and that 'if it weren't for them, I'd still be mentioned only in the Trenton, N.J. phone book.'"[10]

Winchell underscored Belinsky's extracurricular activities in his August 6 column for the *Mirror*, highlighted by another spelling of the nickname more in line with someone enjoying popularity with women. "Overheard at Del Mar's swelegant Namara Hotel (Del Mar, Cal.): Let's go to see the Angels game tomorrow afternoon and see what Beau Belinsky looks like in the daytime!"[11]

The Winchell-Belinsky connection apparently caused some raised eyebrows among Angels executives, whom the writer mentioned in his August 16 column. "Angels' ballteam brass reportedly warned Bo to 'cut out hanging around with the Winchell speedy set or you and Dean Chance and Winchell will suddenly find yourself back in Dallas!' (Talk about Freedom of Assembly! What's happening to this country???)."[12]

But Belinsky wasn't the only baseball topic in 1962 for Winchell. In his August 22 column, he described William Frawley, aka Fred Mertz in *I Love Lucy*, as a fan who avoided going to a Dodgers game because he didn't like the "immense crowds" going to or leaving Dodger Stadium, even though he lived close. "He flies to San Francisco and watches it on TV at the Mark Hopkins Hotel ... attired in pajamas, slippers, with a nip in one hand and a blonde in the other."[13]

In the summer of 1962, Winchell chronicled Belinsky's romances. Regarding Belinsky's social life, he used a misspelling of either his own or Klurfeld's derivation—or a phonetic breakdown of Belinsky's speech—in quoting the pitcher about his critics. "What's with those stoopitts in New York? I read where I was dating this and that dame. I never heard of them or the places I never went at!"[14]

Belinsky became a means to an end for some Hollywood folks looking to ride his coattails of publicity. "These agents and producers were always trying to get me to take out their newest girls," explained the ballplayer. "We'd go to some joint, the owner would pick up the tab, there would be an item in the paper the next day, and everybody would be happy."[15] Somebody who worked for Hollywood Newsreel asked him to go out with an emerging actress named Tina Louise, whom Winchell mentioned in his July 18 column; he called the pitcher "Baseball's No. 1 Lady-Killer" and noted actress Lita Leon Preston's link to him followed by dropping Louise's name. Winchell advised LA's latest lothario, "He wants to make-like-the-leadingmen-in-the movies. Look, kid. Actresses are also Ladies! Make like a Gentleman. You may win a Gal—and a Game."[16]

Belinsky warranted the nickname "Beau" again in Winchell's July 25 column, explaining that the pitcher and Louise enjoyed night spots in the Cocoanut Grove section of LA with another woman. Fame as a ballplayer and a bachelor made him a target of criticism, which Winchell not only acknowledged but also deflected. "He'll never fling another no-hitter doing that!" the columnist quoted an unnamed critic. "Oh, poo to yoo, that's the way the Bo bounces."[17]

A month into Belinsky's relationship with Louise, Winchell called it "a blazing romance" and took credit for introducing the ballplayer to the redheaded actress, who embraced her boyfriend at the dugout after his four-hit, 3–0 victory against the Twins on August 11—the first notch in the "W" column for the lefty in nearly two months, since beating the A's, 3–1, on June 21. Looking for a quote, Winchell said, "It looks like you like him." Louise responded, "Like him! I love him."[18]

A statuesque woman standing around 5'9" who had measurements of 38–25–37 thanks to an intense discipline regarding exercise and calisthenics, Louise began her acting career on the stage in the early 1950s. Her first on-screen role occurred in the 1956 episode "Johnny August" of the *Studio One* anthology series. In recounting the episode for the *New York Times*, Jack Gould noted Louise's sparse dialogue and compelling beauty. "But Miss Louise commanded the most attention—particularly when she was on camera, saying nothing."[19]

Later that year, she joined the Broadway musical *Li'l Abner*—based on Al Capp's rural-set comic strip of the same name—in the role of a sultry, voluptuous character named Appassionata von Climax. Noted theater critic Brooks Atkinson called it "a genial, busy, good-looking show with a number of excellent songs and jovial performers."[20]

Louise won the 1959 Golden Globe Award for Most Promising Newcomer—Female for her performance in the film *God's Little Acre*. Her films spanned genres: *The Trap* (thriller), *Armored Command* (war), *For Those Who Think Young* (beach party). In addition, she made the rounds as a guest star on TV shows including *Tales of Wells Fargo*, *Checkmate*, *The Real McCoys*, *Route 66*, and *Burke's Law*. Her most famous role began in 1964—movie star Ginger Grant on *Gilligan's Island*. It lasted three seasons on CBS and became a staple in TV syndication during the 1970s, but she did not appear in any of the three reunion TV movies that aired on

NBC from 1978 to 1981, nor did she provide the voice for Ginger in the Saturday morning cartoons *The New Adventures of Gilligan* and *Gilligan's Planet*.

A UPI feature article on August 31, 1962, dispelled any notions about the hurler's unavailability for southern California's eligible women, even though the word "engagement" had been used to describe their relationship. "I needed an engagement like Custer needed Indians," said Belinsky.[21]

That same report undoubtedly surprised Angels fans when the pitcher described other American League cities as potential destinations for his career, using their nightlife opportunities as a barometer. The top choices were obvious: New York, Boston, Chicago. Next up were Minneapolis-St. Paul, Detroit, Washington, and Cleveland. Kansas City and Baltimore trailed because they "don't show me much in the nightclub department. On the other hand, I've seen some sharp looking dames in both towns, so what the heck, it all evens up, I guess."[22]

Winchell could set up Belinsky with the finest-looking women from Santa Clarita to Santa Ana. But there were other sources for the ace, who had built up his contact list thanks to Winchell and socializing at nightclubs that Hollywood types frequented. Belinsky's fame would be a boon to actresses needing publicity, so the people approaching the Angels' star might have had an ulterior motive, though that that didn't matter much to the 26-year-old. "I wouldn't take out a broad without checking her references," said Belinsky. "Most of the times the broads I dated all were touted by friends of mine. Hollywood agents, directors, producers, friends of Winchell, newspaper people, guys like that, responsible, serious people."[23]

Belinsky still had a job to do on the baseball diamond. Haney agreed to bump up his salary from $6,000 to $8,500 for the season. He got a bonus of a different kind when a car dealership offered a free car if Belinsky set aside time every Saturday during Angels homestands for the rest of the season to sign autographs. His choice: a "candy apple" red El Dorado Cadillac. He got the vanity license plate to read BO.[24]

According to Belinsky, the Angels played a shell game that wound up costing him more than the Cadillac's sales price of $3,000 when Autry promised he wouldn't have to sign the autographs or pay for the car. A bill arrived for payment, bewildering Belinsky. Haney explained that the $2,500 salary bump should cover the car. Final price tag when all was said and done: $3,200.[25]

As spring training began for the 1963 season, San Diego sportswriter Jack Murphy suggested that Belinsky might be fodder for a trade and highlighted the Red Sox as a potential suitor. Colorful and good for copy, Belinsky heightened the Angels' publicity though it mattered little to Haney and Rigney; Murphy described them as "obviously weary of his extracurricular hijinks."[26] They might have taken solace when Belinsky claimed that another actress "has calmed me down."[27]

All About Mamie

Mamie Van Doren acclimated to celebrity like a beaver to wood, so dating Belinsky seemed like a natural pairing. Born in 1931, the aspiring actress then named Joan Olander dated singing star Eddie Fisher in her late teens and later got engaged to former boxing champion Jack Dempsey. There was a massive age gap; Dempsey was in his mid–50s. A marriage never happened.[28]

It had taken her a few years to break into stardom. A deal with Paramount tanked because she looked too much like Marilyn Monroe, so she became an actress at Universal-International, known informally as Universal, and received a new moniker inspired by the First Lady—Mamie Eisenhower. Van Doren had bit parts until getting cast in 1953's *Forbidden*, starring Tony Curtis. An audition for a singing scene led to her being in the studio's array of actresses. "She wrapped up the role in 10 minutes and signed a studio contract three hours later," wrote entertainment reporter Harold Heffernan.[29]

Despite her beauty, talent, and curves that seemed to be infinite, the road to success in Hollywood proved challenging. Sisyphean, almost. She lost a job to Gloria Grahame, fired her agent, and got roles at Universal that were not as meaty as the ones given to her peers. The studio embraced the Monroe factor, looking at Mamie Van Doren as solid competition without giving her the diversity of roles that Monroe enjoyed. Consequently, Van Doren fell under the category of either a dumb blonde or a girl from the wrong side of the tracks.[30]

Jayne Mansfield got cast after Van Doren turned down a role in *Will Success Spoil Rock Hunter?* They were grouped together as Hollywood began using the slang term "Three M's" to refer to the three blonde sex symbols—Mamie, Mansfield, Monroe (or Marilyn). Van Doren ascended to fame in the late 1950s, playing sexually charged characters.

In *High School Confidential*, appearances are deceiving. This 1958 film centers around Russ Tamblyn as Mike Wilson, an undercover narcotics cop using the persona of Tony Baker, a loudmouth student, at Santa Bello High School in southern California. Posing as Tony's aunt and landlady for the scheme, Van Doren's character wants to seduce him. "You're looking for excitement?" she inquires as she takes a bite of his apple. Her analysis of high school girls is blunt: "That's why I worry. Thinking of you coming up against those young, tight sweaters."

Jerry Lee Lewis's "Boppin' at the High School Hop" opens *High School Confidential* against a scene of the students outside, waiting for school to start. Slang is sprinkled in the movie's dialogue. One character says, "I'm putting it down." Another character responds, "I'm picking it up." Where a phrase about a cookie crumbling might have acknowledged futility in the past, *High School Confidential* has a modern take: "That's the way the bongo bingoes." Instead of saying that someone is a "square"—a derogatory term of the era on par with "boring"—a character used the term "L-7," which denotes the letter and number that can form the shape.

Hollywood had begun to represent beatniks in the late 1950s, most popularly by Bob Denver's character of Maynard G. Krebs in *The Many Loves of Dobie Gillis* on CBS. In *High School Confidential*, Philippa Fallon plays a beatnik poetess who gives a recitation backed by a band at a student hangout.

Van Doren's portrayal of an academic goes against her voluptuous, sexually charged image in the 1960 comedy *Sex Kittens Go to College*. Dr. Mathilda West is a new professor at Collins College with an IQ of 298, 18 languages in her repertoire, and 13 degrees, including Doctor of Philosophy and Doctor of Constructive Anatomy. Her allure causes the college's football captain to faint when she asks him to kiss her on the cheek.

Reflecting the emergence of computer technology, there's a computer named Thinko with the "first name" of Sam, an acronym for Sequential Auxiliary Modulator. Westinghouse's Elektro is Thinko, built in the late 1930s and showcased at the New York World's Fair in 1939, joined by the robot dog Sparko a year later. When *Sex Kittens Go to College* premiered, America had begun the dawn of the space age, which is mentioned. President Eisenhower authorized the formation of NASA in 1958 on the heels of the Russians launching the first satellite on October 4, 1957—Sputnik.

Martin Milner plays George Barton, the college's public relations director and Dr. West's potential love interest. Although he's better known for serious roles in the TV dramas *Route 66* and *Adam-12*, Milner does a fine job as a comedic actor, particularly with a bit of dialogue that's a wink to the audience—he says that Dr. West looks like Mamie Van Doren. Louis Nye, who delighted millions as a regular performer on *The Steve Allen Show*, plays a professor. Tuesday Weld had some TV success as the title character's crush on *The Many Loves of Dobie Gillis*; she plays a Collins student. Jackie Coogan shot to fame as a child actor with Charlie Chaplin. In *Sex Kittens Go to College*, he plays a major donor to Collins.

It is revealed that Dr. West was once a stripper named Tassels Montclair; she considers leaving Collins and going back to her former career. George steals a fire engine, chases after her, and proposes marriage before she leaves. Ever the publicity seeker, he convinces her that nuptials will help boost her notoriety.

In the 1957 film *Untamed Youth*, Van Doren and Lori Nelson play prisoners on a Texas work farm run by a crooked businessman whose reach extends to the sheriff's office. Their characters, Penny and Jane Lowe, are arrested on trumped up charges of hitchhiking and skinny dipping, then sent to the farm, where they join other young folks in forced labor. The farm owner has seduced and married the judge who sentences the youths, so his bases are covered, but her son discovers the truth about the operation—which includes a coverup of a female prisoner who dies from being overworked—and convinces the judge to turn on her husband.

Van Doren has a chance to show off her singing skills with four songs: "Like a Rolling Stone," "Oobala Baby," "You're as Slimy as a Salamander," and "Calypso Song." Her rendition of "Oobala Baby" represents the sex appeal of rock and roll in the late 1950s, combining her body language with lyrics of sexual innuendo that are as subtle as a tsunami. *New York Times* film critic Abraham Weiler described Van Doren's singing performances as accompanied by "a variety of torrid gyrations that are guaranteed to keep any red-blooded American boy awake. Nothing else in this picture can make that claim."[31]

In 2024, Van Doren recalled the wardrobe that she and Nelson wore for *Untamed Youth*. "I believe I was the first woman to wear blue jeans on the big movie screen. They brought me a full skirt and I told them to give it to Lori Nelson. Then they brought me a pencil tight skirt.... I said how can I move in that. I saw these old pair of blue jeans.... I tried them and never took them off. Rolled up the cuffs.... The executives had a fit but after they saw the rushes they agreed with me. My dance movements fit perfectly."[32]

The *Los Angeles Times* highlighted Van Doren's undeniable sexuality and praised the bombshell's singing but unfairly disrespected her acting without mentioning that an actor is only as good as the script. "Pretty Mamie couldn't act her way out of a little white lie, but with her other extravagant attributes ... who cares?" wrote *Los Angeles Times* film critic Geoffrey M. Warren. "Whatever she lacks as an actress she more than makes up for as an entertainer. Her show-closing calypso number is tops in any class."[33] Van Doren had other outlets for her vocals, illustrated by a 1957 photo with a caption explaining that the 26-year-old performer wore "a $12,000 rhinestone trimmed gown" while performing at the Riviera in Las Vegas.[34]

A buxom presence can be striking on screen, but also a danger for a long-term career. Actors get placed into boxes quite easily by producers, studio executives, and casting directors who want reliability rather than risk, so they get hired for roles that are similar without any inclination toward their potential beyond typecasting. *Sex Kittens Go to College* parodied Van Doren as a professor because nobody would have accepted her in a straightforward portrayal plus her character's secret maintained an edgy, lusty side to her on-screen persona.

Van Doren had no illusions about the ruthlessness of the Hollywood machine. She utilized sexy wardrobe as part of a career strategy. "A girl has to do something to set her apart, but I don't intend to be this type forever ... look what it did for Marilyn Monroe!" she said in 1957. "Seriously, I want to get in and do some real acting some day—not just the 'body' type. I tried to look like Marilyn when I first aimed at pictures, but not any more. We really don't look alike, you know—only our figures, maybe."[35]

She also revealed details about her boudoir—black sheets on a round bed—which must have kindled the imagination of her male fans. "I don't like anything that's square, and black makes me feel sexy."[36] Two years later, she noted her success and the importance of B-movies in establishing her career. "I've been learning and accomplishing a great deal," stated Van Doren, who had also made a guest appearance as herself on the sitcom *The Bob Cummings Show*. "I'm confident I'll be able to handle dramatic roles in big pictures now. I'm ready for them." Again, she emphasized the necessity of evolution for an actor. "There comes a time in a girl's life when she has to switch from glamor girl to actress. If she doesn't do it she's dead."[37]

Van Doren had a supporting role as the younger girlfriend of a once popular actor in *The Girl in Black Stockings*, a murder mystery about a serial killer at a spa. Her character is also one of the victims in this 1957 offering filmed at Parry Lodge in Kanab, Utah. It starred John Dehner as the sheriff trying to find a serial killer. Dehner, a character actor, worked steadily from the 1940s to the 1980s appearing in some of prime time television's biggest hits, including *Hogan's Heroes*, *Get Smart*, *The Rockford Files*, *Hawaii Five-O*, and *Hardcastle and McCormick*.

In *Teacher's Pet*, Van Doren plays a nightclub performer and the girlfriend of Clark Gable's character, the editor of the *New York Evening Chronicle*, boasting a circulation of 500,000. Van Doren sings in a nightclub scene but doesn't appear until about halfway through this 1958 film; she has some funny lines about how you can't know a person by the way they look and where would she be if she just read books. Doris Day co-stars as a journalism professor and competing love interest for the hard-nosed editor. In addition to Van Doren, the supporting cast for this 1958 film includes Charles Lane, Nick Adams, Jack Albertson, Harry Antrim, and Marion Ross. Van Doren reportedly got paid $20,000 for her performance. Length of work: two weeks.[38]

Teacher's Pet had two A-list stars in Gable and Day. Even though Van Doren couldn't get roles in more such films, she found work throughout 1959. Set in New York City, *Vice Raid* depicts narcotics, gambling, and prostitution operations owned by an organization called the Syndicate.

Van Doren shared top billing with Richard Coogan in this B movie. Another chance to showcase her singing chops as a nightclub performer emerged along with solo top billing in *Guns, Girls, and Gangsters*, set in Las Vegas before New Year's Eve but filmed on location in Newhall, which is part of Santa Clarita, California. Van Doren also got an opportunity to sing in the 1966 film *Las Vegas Hillbillys*; country singer Ferlin Husky played her love interest.

There was no lack of suitors for the curvy blonde who could use either her body, voice, or eyes to create a sexual tone. Van Doren married

Bo Belinsky and Mamie Van Doren were a celebrity couple who provided great fodder for sports reporters and gossip columnists. They're doing the Twist, a popular dance in the early 1960s (Associated Press).

bandleader Ray Anthony in 1955; they divorced in 1961.[39] Anthony suggested that his ex-wife go out with Belinsky after he had attained fame because of the no-hitter. She said no, but Winchell called her while he and Belinsky were at the Peppermint West, a hot LA club. Belinsky got on the phone and cajoled her to join them. "When Winchell introduced me to Bo, I felt a strong tug of attraction," admitted Van Doren. "There was that immediate ignition that I'd felt before between myself and a man. I knew this would be the beginning of something, but I didn't know what."[40]

Belinsky exaggerated his serenity during 1963 spring training, staying out past curfew with Chance and Van Doren. Rigney fined the pitchers, who played pool to let off steam. Even Perry Mason wouldn't be able to convince the Angels skipper that they didn't violate the curfew rule but overslept because the Riviera Hotel operator didn't call them, which caused them to miss the start of the next day's practice.[41]

Attending her boyfriend's next start and occupying a seat in "a front row box" attracted the attention of Braven Dyer, who called her Belinsky's "No. 1 fan" in his lead paragraph describing the game for the *Los Angeles Times*. Belinsky went six innings and got tagged with the 9–3 loss to the Houston Colt .45s. He had a 3–2 lead going into the sixth inning, but the opposition tagged him for two runs, one unearned. Still, he drew praise. "I thought he was a working pitcher out there today and I liked the way he reared back and got out of that jam (nobody out, two on and two runs in) in the fifth," said Rigney.[42]

On April Fool's Day, Belinsky revealed that he and Van Doren were engaged. So much for the pitcher prizing his freedom to prowl at nightclubs, bars, and anywhere else the fairer sex congregated. But who could deny being smitten with a gorgeous actress possessing an amazing figure plus the intangible qualities of poise, loyalty, and personality? "I like her a lot," said the ballplayer who had fallen victim to Cupid's bow and arrow. "In fact, I'm mad about the girl. She's my kind of woman. Things are too unstable right now to think of a wedding date."[43]

His revelation surprised Van Doren because she thought they were going to make a joint announcement in Los Angeles when the Angels ended spring training with a series against the Dodgers. Fault did not rest exclusively with Belinsky. He had believed that the reporters would keep the couple's secret until an official disclosure. Rankled, he declared a boycott: "From now on, it's going to be 'no comment' on all subjects."[44]

Van Doren and Belinsky may have been attractive, famous people with great physical chemistry between them, but their approaches to life were about as different as a Cadillac and a Corvette. Belinsky was fine with the engagement. Setting a wedding date, not so much. It became a see-saw relationship with breakups and makeups.[45]

When Van Doren and Belinsky connected, it seemed like a match made by the publicity gods. Gorgeous actress. Handsome athlete. Both were based in southern California. Van Doren credited—or blamed—him for arranging publicity when they went out. "If we had dinner at some quiet place, almost miraculously photographers appeared."[46] Belinsky disregarded a common guideline that athletes and entertainers restrain from sex before a game to preserve energy. Spending it on a pleasure will have a negative impact, even as a satisfying outlet with a woman whose beauty and sex appeal were as certain as a sunrise. Or so the theory goes.

"Bo had no such constraints," explained Van Doren in her 1987 memoir. "In fact, Bo left some very good work there indeed. Making love all night was part of the ritual for him. He seemed to try to drive himself to exhaustion. His pitching performances began to show the effects of his life-style [sic]. As the season went on, it became obvious that the early promise of his pitching career was not being realized."

But Belinsky had competition beyond batters on other AL teams—his girlfriend's fame. Belinsky enjoyed the spotlight as well, but Van Doren's stardom commanded a brighter one, providing catnip for photographers, reporters, and gossip columnists. It led to distrust, which Van Doren sourced to his imagination. "The kind of publicity that you get when you're a so-called sex symbol is hard for any man that's serious about you to live with," she explained. "There's the implication that you're always available. It's part of the image. Other men think of you as their personal property because you have so often been the object of their fantasies."[47]

Engaged

When Belinsky wanted to signify his adoration by buying an engagement ring, he asked Judy Campbell, ex-wife of Van Doren's fellow Universal actor Bill Campbell, to help him, despite protestations from the actress. Van Doren didn't want a third wheel. Among the glitterati and gossip mongers of Hollywood, news circulated that Campbell had bedded President Kennedy, though the public did not learn about the association with JFK until the publication of her 1977 memoir. Van Doren recalled Belinsky saying, "I told her that if Jack Kennedy came sniffing around you, I'd make him real sorry."

Further, she said that Campbell got "a big discount" from Marvin Hime & Company and described the purchases as "a prodigious amount of jewelry too. According to Bo, it was all charged to a secret account and paid for by the thirty-fifth President of the United States."[48] But in Allen's book, Belinsky said that he got a deal to pay off the $2,000 bill for the ring "over a long period of time" on one condition—he tell the press where he bought it.⁴⁹

What should have been a joyous occasion was anything but in the environs of the Angels organization. Undeserved and unprovoked, Van Doren became a target of scorn from the press and the front office. While they put Van Doren in their crosshairs, they didn't have the full story of her impact on the pitcher. "Actually, I was trying to coax him into getting enough rest," she said. "Or cut down on his heavy smoking or his drinking."

Belinsky lacked discipline and dedication. More than physical ability, baseball requires patience, study, and preparation; those concepts were not in his vocabulary. Van Doren recollected, "All the other things, the things a pitcher needs to build his career on, like running or practicing his pitches, Bo hated. He neglected all the fundamentals and did as little as he could get away with."⁵⁰

Anna Belinsky had a theory on the source of her son's romantic troubles with Van Doren. "They were jealous," said the matriarch. "That's right, I think the Angels brass, Rigney and Haney and Autry and all of them, were jealous of Bo having such a glamorous movie actress for a girl friend. That's what I think."⁵¹

In 1965, Belinsky publicly confirmed the shenanigans of his overseers during his time in an Angels uniform. They told the pitcher about Van Doren's potential to distract him from his job and then race to the bombshell like bees to flowers. "But every time I would introduce Mamie to them, their goddam tongues would hang out, from [club owner] Gene Autry on down. Everybody wanted to take a nip at her. Oh, it was fast and furious action."⁵²

Belinsky confirmed the hypothesis and detailed the hypocrisy of his bosses years later in Maury Allen's 1973 biography of him. "We had a couple of parties with the club—players, wives, officials—and I brought Mamie to them. Every time I look up there's Rigney or Haney or Autry getting her a drink and being real friendly to her and acting like she was with them. Then the next day they would tell me she was bad for me, bad for the club, bad for baseball. If she was so bad for baseball, why didn't they stay the hell away from her?"⁵³

Their relationship status was only volatile on days ending in the letter "y." A broken engagement freed Belinsky, who paired with an older woman reflecting sophistication, culture, and wealth in addition to being a member of one of America's most well-known families. Ricky duPont "pursued Belinsky with vigor" and accessed a new world for the son of a TV repairman from Trenton. Belinsky had enjoyed the glamor of LA, but duPont traveled in circles available to a slim percentage of the population.

"I didn't know people had this kind of money until I met Ricky," said the ballplayer. "She really opened my eyes to things. Here, I thought it was a big deal to be riding around in a Cadillac. Her chauffeurs rode around in Cadillacs when they went for the groceries."[54]

Van Doren and duPont were aware of each other because the newspapers reported on their connections to Belinsky, though neither woman was keen on these stories fit for a soap opera. Plus, Belinsky had another dilemma—he wanted Van Doren to return the engagement ring. While he toiled in American League ballparks during 1963, Van Doren worked on different stages in a touring performance of the musical *Silk Stockings* with Lee Grant, including a stint presented by the Storrowton Music Fair at Exposition Park in West Springfield, Massachusetts. It became the focus of an argument that broke the Belinsky–Van Doren pairing. Belinsky believed that his fiancée was having an affair with the teenager whose job entailed driving her from the hotel to the theater and back to the hotel. Van Doren denied it, then realized Belinsky had been having her watched.

Belinsky got support in his quest to get the ring; duPont financed a private detective to monitor and record Van Doren. A tape recorder in her room documented a dalliance. "When I heard the tape, I knew I would get my ring back, get that jeweler off my ass, and get Ricky quieted down," said Belinsky. "It was just getting too much."[55]

Though he had been rumored to expand his acting exploits with Van Doren in a film titled *Pirate Girl*, his raising the Jolly Roger no longer looked viable. Neither did their coupling. On June 24, the news broke that the ballplayer and the beauty had parted ways. Though he did not give details, Van Doren negated the veracity of claims regarding infidelity. "Unfortunately, Mr. Belinsky was given some false information," explained the actress. "It was so petty, so simple. But he was hurt. He thought I was dating while on tour with the show, and it just wasn't true."[56]

A letter from Paul Caruso explained that litigation over the ring would necessitate playing the recording for a judge, but Belinsky still cared about Van Doren and didn't want this situation to escalate further, nor did his relationship with duPont present a viable future. He felt claustrophobic juggling two women who wanted to be with him. "It wasn't that I was mad at Mamie or was going to run off with Ricky. It was just that I didn't like the idea of being obligated to any woman. I had to be free like a bird to fly my own way."[57]

It had been that way for Belinsky ever since Trenton. Van Doren returned the ring by mail, but the duo met up again and again. Their bond didn't die with the ending of the engagement. In fact, Van Doren visited the Belinsky home on Hewitt Street when she was in the area for several years after the split.[58]

Hawaii

Seeing the buxom blonde as a distraction, Angels management had pressured Belinsky to end the engagement after he compiled a 1–7 record and they demoted him to the Triple-A Hawaiian Islanders in the Pacific Coast League. It didn't sit well with his fiancée. A report about the couple at a restaurant near Dodger Stadium stated that Van Doren "looked as if she had been crying."[59]

Belinsky packed his bags and headed for Honolulu. He cheated on Van Doren, inspiring her to break up with him. She alleged that he got revenge by calling the police and claiming that she overdosed because of the breakup. Then she mailed back the engagement ring. A post-breakup conversation led to makeup sex, which led to another engagement.[60]

Van Doren refused to let the latest rift sideline her socially. She adored Belinsky but focused on her future. "I really was in love with Bo, but no one took us seriously because we were engaged on April Fool's Day," said the actress. "I'm still not over Bo, but the only way to forget a man is to find another one."

Athletes were in contention. She wanted "an outdoorsman" but excluded actors and musicians from her search. Been there. Done that. Van Doren had been married to a bandleader. Her future male companion also needed to be an American. Regarding age preference, she had none. Her range was "between 18 and 90 as long as he's healthy and likes to swing." Millionaires could go to the top of the list for the buxom bombshell. "It would help if the guy is rich, too," she added.[61]

There appeared to be a détente between the former lovebirds in late July, when Van Doren flew to Washington state for an Islanders game against the Tacoma Giants. Her willingness to see Belinsky augured optimism for those who wanted to see another celebrity romance. "So many terrible things were said about us when we broke up," said Van Doren. "I felt terrible. When Bo asked me to come here and talk to him, I caught a plane."[62]

Whether it was the emotional impact of seeing his ex-fiancée, the skill of Tacoma's batsmen, or a combination therein, Belinsky got shelled. His numbers staggered the Islanders' fans, who must have wondered if he could handle Triple-A lineups: two innings as a relief pitcher, five runs, and five hits including three home runs. Tacoma won, 16–6. But his social life provoked equal—if not more—attention from the press. Belinsky underlined the status quo of his relationship with Van Doren. "She's a doll," he declared. "But we're just good friends. No reconciliation. No re-engagement. We just know each other and that's it."[63]

They were done. Countermanding her earlier affirmation about curing lovesickness with another relationship, Van Doren declared, "Just say I'm through with men. They're bad for me and I'm bad for them." Venting further about Bo the beau, she joked about needing to fulfill Belinsky's request to return the engagement ring: "I somehow got the feeling that if I didn't, he might have cut off my finger, or worse, made me take over the payments."

Her personal barbs were understandable. Then she went further by attacking his ballplaying prowess, comparing Belinsky the pitcher to Belinsky the paramour: "If Bo could only pitch strikes like he pitches woo, the Angels would have been in first place by now. I think we got engaged after our first date, know what I mean?" Still, she had a soft spot for him. "You can't help but like the guy," Van Doren admitted.[64]

There didn't seem to be bitter feelings with the Belinsky clan, either. When the actress opened in the musical *Wildcat*, Belinsky's sister and grandmother traveled from Trenton to see the performance in Westchester. Baseball obligations did not permit Belinsky to go, but he did call her.[65]

Van Doren's ban on the entertainment industry as a feeder for eligible suitors did not last long. Substituting for Winchell, Frank Quinn reported that the star dated her leading man, Bob Holiday, who later starred in the musical *It's a Bird.... It's a Plane.... It's Superman*. Quinn also revealed that Belinsky had been "paying off those private eyes whose report led to his bustup with Mamie," thereby casting more doubt on her claim of chasteness while they were 6,000 miles apart during her previous stage stint.[66]

Fellow gossip scribe Sheila Graham concurred that the Van Doren–Holiday romance on stage reflected the romance off-stage. "Mamie is not that good an actress, although her reviews have been good," wrote Graham. But the ex-fiancé wasn't out of the picture. Not entirely, anyway. "Mamie still gets an odd call or two from former beau, Bo Belinsky."[67]

The fall of 1963 was a stellar time for Hollywood. Gidget went to Rome; Allied prisoners of war attempted a great escape; Cleopatra got her due as a ruler; Clay Spencer saw his namesake leave the family's mountain in Wyoming to attend college; and Professor Ned Brainard followed his discovery of flubber with an invention that could change the weather. Though Van Doren could not get regularly cast in A-list movies like *Gidget Goes to Rome*, *The Great Escape*, *Cleopatra*, *Spencer's Mountain*, and *Son of Flubber*, she refused to let the heartbreak over Belinsky curtail her show business activities, either in performing or promoting. She appeared on *The Tonight Show*, for example.[68] But Winchell reported that she was "upset" about the press reports regarding her romance with Holiday.[69]

Return to LA

Back with the Angels, Belinsky got credit for a 6–5 win over the Boston Red Sox, led by Bill Monbouquette looking for his 20th win of the 1963 season on September 10. AP's report on the 10-inning game indicated a restoration of Belinsky's relationship with Van Doren. Or some form of it. The lead paragraph contained the statement that "Bo's back and Mamie's got him—and Bo got Monbo in the process." AP described the shapely actress as the hurler's girlfriend with a status of "on again—off again."[70]

A month later, southern California's press pushed aside Belinsky's baseball exploits to focus on the Dodgers-Yankees World Series. Sandy Koufax set a World Series record for a pitcher with 15 strikeouts in LA's 5–2 victory in Game One. A 4–1 victory in the second game put the National League ball club halfway toward a sweep of the New Yorkers.

But even the World Series couldn't eclipse coverage of Belinsky's social life. Van Doren and Belinsky had reconciled, with marriage in their future, when the October 5 edition of the *Los Angeles Times* reported the relationship to be kaput. This time, Van Doren ended it. Her description was as vague as Belinsky's back in June. "I had my blood test, wedding gown and everything," she explained. "But I found something out this morning ... we had a discussion ... that was it."[71]

Whatever the two meant to each other, it did not propel them to the altar. Van Doren announced the latest outlet for her charm, physique, and presence—performing "a modified striptease" as part of a touring show in Washington state to raise money for the Republican party. She would remain somewhat clothed during the finale; six shows were scheduled. "I wear a little leotard underneath," said the brazen blonde. "It's nude color. It always gets a gasp."[72]

Despite the allure that Van Doren would provide, the show's producer disapproved. "I was just about flabbergasted when I read about Mamie's plans in the paper today," revealed LeRoy Prinze. "She's not going to strip [in] any show that I produce nor that the Republicans produce."[73]

A few days after Van Doren's announcement and the subsequent cancellation, Belinsky offered his opinion. It was neither kind nor necessary. "What'd she say a thing like that for? She ought to try to get rid of that impression ... no class."[74] He had his own show business concerns. Beginning in mid-November, Belinsky appeared for five weeks in Las Vegas. His act at the Silver Slipper with comedian Hank Henry put him in a city that thrived on excitement. But Belinsky denied that he sought celebrity beyond the baseball diamond. "Some people said I'm going Hollywood. I'm not the type to go Hollywood. It's the cash."[75]

Las Vegas offered two lures for Belinsky in addition to greenbacks, initially a salary of $1,000 for one week plus an option for another week of performances: women and gambling. "I always managed to hit Vegas all through my career," said Belinsky. "Even when I lived in Hawaii I would catch a flight back to Los Angeles every so often and jump on the plane for

Vegas. I would gamble for a few days, make some of the clubs, make some of the broads, jump on the night plane back to L.A., get the next plane to Hawaii, and be out surfboarding before anyone had missed me."[76]

Aftermath

Interviewed by Sid Ziff during the winter, he opined again about his former love. No pain. No remorse. Plenty of blame. "Yeah. What about Mamie? I'd like to know myself. She gets around pretty good. But I don't want any more ties. I wasn't taking too good care of my condition. Love plays funny tricks with you, like losing your appetite, etc." He used the Custer-Indians line again, described by Ziff as being capped "with a dismal sigh."[77]

But there was another side to Belinsky, according to Van Doren. In 2024, she responded to an update on X (formerly known as Twitter) from the author of this book, updating his followers on the manuscript's progress. "When I broke up with him he pulled a gun from his pillow and was going to kill me." It wasn't the last time that Belinsky would brandish a gun with a significant other.[78]

Rigney praised the pairing with Van Doren. "Belinsky made a lot of mistakes," he said. "His worst one was in not marrying that blonde. Mamie was smart, she was good for him. He was too dumb to know it, he was just so damn dumb, that guy."[79]

In 1966, the unmarried Van Doren got pregnant but didn't disclose the identity of the father. She recounted her choices in her memoir: keep the baby, get an illegal abortion, or marry someone quickly and convince him the baby resulted from early consummation. While she pondered what to do, Dean Chance asked her to go out with another baseball pitcher—Lee Meyers, who came from a wealthy family reportedly making him the eventual inheritor of a $2 million bounty.[80] His grandfather used to own the women's magazine *McCall's*. She was 35. Meyers was 19. Van Doren and Meyers married in 1966 but divorced in 1969; she had the abortion.

A UPI story in July 1966 claimed that the pair dated for two years before getting married in Boise. "To be honest, it was because it's the only place you can get married as a minor without parental consent," said Van Doren. Regarding the wealth, Meyers squashed further conversation. "We don't want any publicity on the money deal," he declared. "We married for one reason—because we love each other."[81]

When they got hitched, Belinsky offered his congratulations. "I wish them all the luck in the world," he said. "Marriage. That's a fine thing. Not for me, of course, but it's a fine thing."[82]

Meyers joined the Angels' organization in 1964, playing for the team's farm system in the Arizona Instructional League and in the Midwest League. He went to the Cubs and played for their teams in Wenatchee, Tacoma, Dallas–Fort Worth, and Lodi in 1965–1966; the Athletics and Phillies organizations employed him for his last year as a pro ballplayer in 1967. He ended his career with a 22–40 record, having never played in the major leagues. Meyers died in 1972 of injuries resulting from a car crash in Huntington Beach. The *Los Angeles Times* stated, "Mr. Meyers reportedly swerved to avoid colliding with another car that had cut off his vehicle."[83]

Belinsky had also been linked with Ann-Margret, Connie Stevens, and Juliet Prowse, among others in his Hollywood romances. "I think the only girl from those days he really loved was Mamie," said Dean Chance. "I think a lot of them loved him, though. There is no question in my mind that Tina Louise was in love with Bo. If Bo had asked her to marry him, she would have given her movie career up in a minute for Bo."[84]

Still, Van Doren and Belinsky remained friends; she even showed up to support Belinsky at a press event for the publication of his biography in 1973 and an Angels Old Timers game in the 1980s.

5

Aloha!

Spring Training, 1963

In 1962, Bo Belinsky had been the toast of the town. The no-hitter launched him into the stratosphere of fame, while his postgame lifestyle branded him more as a mischievous pleasure seeker than a mean-spirited troublemaker. Even the incident with the Beverly Hills police didn't seem to have sustaining negative traction regarding his reputation. His relationship with Van Doren provided terrific stories for the press, but there was controversy surrounding the southpaw in 1963 before the couple even met in the spring.

Belinsky did not need to make a new year's resolution. Haney and Rigney made it for him when they sent a missive in January strongly encouraging him to tone down his off-the-field activities or risk being booted. Sid Ziff used Belinsky's "bone-headed performance at a recent sports banquet" as a rationale for doubtfulness concerning a "promise that he would turn over a new leaf."[1]

Angels management must have had confidence in Belinsky's ability to adjust because his salary got a boost to $13,500.[2] Belinsky projected a 20-win season and revealed that he'd been playing tennis to build up his left pinky finger, which had been broken.[3] It seemed that the détente between Belinsky and Angels management teetered on fracturing when he missed the February 10 reporting date for spring training in Palm Springs and the following day's roll call where the players got into their 1963 uniforms for the first time. He arrived, albeit while the team was already on the field. His explanation: illness.[4]

A week later, Belinsky's tardiness eclipsed any thoughts of a clean slate. Neither the consequences of a late night nor a refutation of authority caused the half-hour delay in his arrival at practice. Police had stopped Belinsky for speeding; he got a warning instead of a ticket. It revived distrust for Rigney, who declared, "I'm going to have a chat with Mr. Belinsky. All winter I've been reading about the new Belinsky, but so far he's the same Belinsky as he was the second half of last season."⁵ But Rigney covered for his headline-making pitcher after a missed lunch appointment with Ziff. "It's nothing unusual," said Rigney. "He probably got distracted."⁶

In his first spring training game of 1963, Belinsky started for the Angels' regulars against the rookies in an intra-squad game showcasing several hurlers. Rigney's newbies tagged the lefty for two singles and three walks during his two-inning tenure on the mound; Belinsky got one strikeout but allowed no runs in the regulars' 6–1 victory. His tactics changed because Rigney saw him "tipping" his curveball. "We've got Bo gripping the ball on the seams now," said Grissom. The pitching coach also praised, "I thought he pitched well. You wouldn't expect much more considering he's trying something new."⁷

Belinsky's travails with the Angels had become national news. An Associated Press article in early March cited the pitcher's superficiality, an ongoing concern reflecting an avoidance of the discipline necessary to combat the inconsistency evident during his rookie season. It created a question whether the no-hitter amounted to a fluke or his social pursuits interfered with his potential. The latter seemed more likely. "I like fun," declared the Trenton native. "I like people. I like going to night clubs, taking out dates, staying out late. In order to be an outstanding player, you've got to be a loner, avoid meeting hep people, give up good times, deny yourself of lots of pleasures. It just isn't worth sacrificing my fun, my youth, and my personality unless you make real dough. That's why I set my aim on being a $40,000-a-year pitcher."⁸

Rigney endured the bluster, blarney, and bloviating. He had a left-hander who could help the Angels be competitive for the AL pennant but saw the required energy being funneled into Belinsky's nightlife rather than his craft. The intra-squad game provided a peek into a possible shift in priorities. "He wants to do it," explained the Angels' skipper in an article syndicated by the North American Newspaper Alliance. "But how badly does he want to? Wanting it and doing it are two different things. I figure him for one of my four starters now, but I've got four other left-handers on the staff and maybe they want a place more than Belinsky does."⁹

Staying at the Riviera Hotel on East Palm Canyon Drive, where he roomed with the notorious hurler, Albie Pearson had an insider's view of Belinsky's lifestyle. Married for nine years at the time, Pearson observed that his stability might have been a factor in the Angels pairing them, with the hope of lowering Belinsky's social temperature. In a *Times* article with Braven Dyer's byline but consisting entirely of quotes from Pearson, Belinsky received plaudits for his generosity as well as his potential.

"Bo is unselfish," stated Pearson, a five-year veteran of the majors and the AL leader in runs scored in 1962. "If you're his friend, he'll do anything for you. Bo's problem won't be the opposite sex. It'll be his control on the mound. If he can control his pitches as well as he does the girls, man, he'll win 40 games for us."[10]

Pearson hit a bullseye with his forecast about control being a key factor for Belinsky. In his first 1963 spring training start against another major league squad—a 5–1 loss to the Cleveland Indians at Tucson's Hi Corbett Field—the left-hander received high praise from Rigney: "What I liked best was his control. He didn't walk a man and had plenty on the ball. If he can keep that up, he's one of our starters." Belinsky limited the Tribe to four singles in his three innings of pitching, and though two runs scored on his watch—both unearned—no batsman got to first base on a walk. Two Clevelanders struck out.[11]

In his next start, Belinsky faced the San Francisco Giants on March 15 in Phoenix, their home turf for spring training. Again, he showed consistency. The National League champions, who lost the previous year's World Series to the New York Yankees in seven games, recorded no walks against the left-hander, nor did they score off him. A contributor of four solid innings in the 18–2 victory, Belinsky gave up one hit in his occupancy of the pitching mound at the original Phoenix Municipal Stadium; Harvey Kuenn had the honors. Excited by his performance, Belinsky relished a chance to pitch against the World Series champs. "Bring on those Damn Yankees," he challenged. "I just wish we were opening the season tomorrow and I was going to pitch against them."[12]

Belinsky proved equally effective in his next opportunity on March 20, extending his streak of no walks to 11 and two-thirds innings until Lou Brock's pass in the third inning in an Angels-Cubs game. Chicago scored an unearned run, but the Angels' lefty shut out the opposition for six innings and left the game with a 2–1 lead; relief pitcher Lee Brewer and the other Angels protected the victory.[13]

The southpaw bared strength, steadiness, and momentum during these three outings, with a 2.00 ERA topping the Los Angeles staff. Angels fans were justified in believing that Belinsky had taken a path toward determination instead of debauchery for the 1963 season. If the hurler kept this focus and ignored the social distractions that were surely tempting but also destructive, he might just propel the Angels into the first division. All was heavenly, until it wasn't.

The incident with breaking curfew reinforced the image of Belinsky as a fun-loving ballplayer who didn't take his craft seriously. Angels GM Fred Haney had also been at the bar, watching Belinsky and Chance play pool, which ended "a few minutes before midnight" and, according to the pitching duo, did not prevent them from getting back to their rooms before the team's midnight curfew. Amounts of the fines were undisclosed. "That blankety-blank convention at the hotel has everything loused up," said Belinsky. "You can't get a phone call through for hours. No, I'm not going to worry about the fine. It's only a game, you know."[14]

But the Riviera combatted the story, beginning with the chief operator stating that phone records proved someone in Belinsky's room answered the requested wake-up call at 8:30 a.m. Further, the hotel manager dismissed the claim about phone lines being busy and noted that no member of the Angels' organization had complained during spring training.[15] Years later, Chance offered another take. "We forgot to put in a wake-up call, and we got up an hour late. By the time we got to the park, we were about two hours late for the workout."[16]

The next day, Belinsky threw six innings against the Houston Colt .45s and left the game with a 4–3 deficit, which amplified to a 9–3 loss. He had a 3–2 lead going into the sixth inning, but the opposition tagged him for two runs; one was unearned. Though he gave up eight of Houston's 13 hits, Belinsky earned compliments from his skipper. "I thought he was a working pitcher out there today and I liked the way he reared back and got out of that jam (nobody out, two on and two runs in) in the fifth."[17]

Belinsky and Chance missed another baseball outing—the Baseball Writers' dinner for the Los Angeles ball clubs, emceed by Bob Hope at the Hollywood Palladium a few days before Opening Day. A crowd of "more than 1,000" enjoyed Hope's comedy plus other entertainers. Claiming car troubles—the gas tank on Chance's Chevrolet "ran out of gas on the freeway"—they missed an array of awards, including teammate Leon Wagner named the "Player of the Year" for the Angels and the troika of Tommy Davis, Maury Wills, and Don Drysdale sharing that recognition for the Dodgers.[18] Indeed, they topped the major leagues in 1962. Davis led in batting average, Wills set a record with 104 stolen bases, and Drysdale notched the most wins plus the Cy Young Award.

Rigney could not punish the pair, financially or otherwise, because the dinner did not fall under the jurisdiction of a team event. Hope pointed to Belinsky's absence and social reputation with humor: "The Angels had a little trouble finding this place, but Belinsky gave them directions—then went back to his other sport."[19]

While some, perhaps many, in the Palladium audience found humor regarding Belinsky, his antics did not amuse Angels management. The *Times* cited Haney plus minority owners Bob Reynolds and Leonard Firestone being "fed up with his efforts to get publicity."[20] But when the Angels faced the Dodgers for the Los Angeles City Series to close out spring training, Belinsky's press coverage extended only to his performance—a solid three innings that yielded two strikeouts, two hits, one walk, and no runs. He also committed a balk. The Angels won 3–0 but didn't score until the bottom of the sixth inning.

Those who thought that Belinsky would wring publicity from his latest effort against LA's vaunted NL team—who had tied the Giants in 1962 and forced a three-game playoff that the Giants won—would be disappointed by his response regarding the victory. "I really couldn't care less. The main thing is our club is working right. My arm feels good, and I'll be ready for the White Sox next Thursday."[21]

Ladies and Gentlemen, Your 1963 Los Angeles Angels

Belinsky looked at the big picture, which Angels fans hoped would be a team competitive enough to improve the 86–76 record from 1962 and win the AL pennant. They opened the season by splitting a two-game series against the Red Sox at Dodger Stadium on April 9–10. Belinsky started the next game against Chicago on April 11 but left after six innings with his team trailing, 3–1; neither team scored again. He struck out five but walked four.

A story having nothing to do with curveballs and strikeouts described a criticism that came from a power higher than the Angels' front office or LA's sports media. Trenton's diocese opined on the comings and goings of the man nicknamed the "playboy pitcher," even though he wasn't a practicing Catholic, and labeled him "a person of limited consequence" in its newspaper, *The Monitor*. America is a free country, so the Catholic church can criticize however it sees fit. But attacking a hometown boy who was a non-Catholic for his personal behavior just gave him more attention, which is what the church lamented in its statement. "It is the personality of Bo Belinsky, his arrogance and boastfulness, together with his exploited romantic interests, that make the average reader of newspapers a little tired of seeing his name in print."[22]

Another rebuke came from someone well-known in the baseball community. Rube Marquard—whom the Baseball Hall of Fame inducted in 1971—pointed out the financial consequences that extracurricular endeavors will create for the two hurlers making headlines. "I'm afraid these two young men [Belinsky and Chance] don't realize that they're just throwing their money away. When they can't win regularly—and it always happens to those who follow the night-life crowd—they'll find that these associates will drop them like a hot stove. And then later they'll wonder why their salary was cut."[23]

Ziff provided some cover in his *Times* column by invoking another pitcher nicknamed Rube—George Edward "Rube" Waddell, inducted into the Hall of Fame in 1946. "Rube had a phenomenal record on the days when he could be found. This was not easy, as he might be out fishing, or in a saloon, at a fire or in a lady's boudoir." Ziff also wrote, "[Connie] Mack used to say in all the years he managed nobody gave him the trouble Waddell did."[24]

Belinsky's control seemed fine in his second game, which took place on a road trip in Kansas City. In the first game of a doubleheader on April 19, the lefty allowed one walk and seven hits in six and one-third innings, but also gave up two solo home runs. The Angels began the game with Albie Pearson hitting a leadoff homer against Orlando Peña. Athletics first baseman and cleanup hitter Norm Siebern cracked one in the bottom of the fourth inning to tie the game at 1–1; Rigney sent in Art Fowler after George Alusik slammed a solo shot in the bottom of the seventh. Kansas City scored another run; LA scored once in top of the eighth. The A's won, 3–2.

A game against the Washington Senators on April 23 resulted in no decision for the southpaw, who left trailing, 3–1, after six innings. The Angels tied it when Leon Wagner and Ed Sadowski hit solo home runs in the top of the seventh; Joe Koppe pinch-hit for Belinsky and got a single, but Pearson's grounder to pitcher Don Rudolph ended the rally. The Angels put up two more runs and beat the Senators, 5–4, in 10 innings. Control was good—he struck out five and allowed one walk.

Saddled with another loss against the Orioles at Baltimore's Memorial Stadium on April 27, his record went to 0–3. The Angels trailed, 4–0, when they went to bat in the top of the eighth inning. After Ed Sadowski crushed a two-run homer, George Thomas pinch-hit for Belinsky but struck out. No subsequent scores happened, giving the Angels a 4–2 loss.

On May 1, Belinsky's first win of 1963 happened at home. He went the full nine innings against the Yankees in a 5–3 victory, restoring confidence with a four-hitter and nine strikeouts. The Angels leapt to a 4–0 lead in the bottom of the first inning courtesy of George Thomas's grand slam, which knocked Ralph Terry out of the game and caused Yankees manager Ralph Houk to bring in Jim Bouton.

Pitching perfectly through four innings—no walks, no hits—Belinsky whiffed Tom Tresh to begin the top of the fifth, then walked Elston Howard and allowed a single by Roger Maris. A wild pitch moved the runners ahead one base. Belinsky loaded the bases with a walk to Harry Bright, and Tony Kubek's sacrifice fly to left field scored Howard for the Yankees' first run of the game. The Angels scored another run in the bottom of the fifth. The Yankees added a run in the sixth and another in the ninth.

Joy was short-lived. On May 5, Cleveland led, 4–1, when Willie Kirkland doubled to lead off the top of the eighth inning at Dodger Stadium. Art Fowler replaced Belinsky, who received his fourth loss of 1963. A rally for the home team notched two runs in the bottom of the ninth, but Cleveland won, 4–3. Belinsky's next three outings hardly inspired confidence. Lasting three and two-thirds innings against the White Sox on May 11, Belinsky got pulled with the Angels behind, 4–0. LA's batsmen later scored twice but lost, 4–2. Rigney bounced him after two and one-third innings with the Angels trailing, 7–1, in the first game of the May 15 doubleheader at Fenway Park. The Red Sox won, 9–3.

Belinsky's tenure got truncated quicker in the south Bronx when the Yankees scored five times in the bottom of the first inning and three times in the second. He did not make it to the Yankee Stadium pitching mound for the third inning. New York won, 10–4, and handed Belinsky his seventh loss. The reason for the 1–7 record and 6.43 ERA was a mystery worthy of Sherlock Holmes's talents to decipher. "The last three times he's started, we've been in trouble early," said Rigney. "I can't figure it out. He looked so great in spring training. Everything he pitched was low. He rarely walked anyone. You wouldn't believe a pitcher could turn so bad."[25]

Standoff

Rigney sent Belinsky to the bullpen and dismissed reports of trades or demotions to the minors, but Braven Dyer reported that Rigney had been talking to the Indians about the troubled left-hander.[26] Just in case the Angels' manager et al. decided to let Belinsky find his focus in the minors, the Hawaii Islanders had a locker designated for him.[27]

It was solid thinking. In a few days, Belinsky received his transfer to the 50th state along with Ken Hunt, who played outfield and first base. Whatever caused Belinsky's troubles—whether distractions caused by his romance and engagement with Van Doren, a sophomore slump, a lack of discipline, a need to hone talent, or a combination of these and other factors—Rigney hoped that Honolulu could be a balmy solution. "The reason this is being done is because we want these fellows to go back and play," said the Angels' skipper. "Just as soon as this lefthander [Belinsky] plays the way he can, he'll be back with our club."[28]

Belinsky had gone from exaltation to exile in a little more than a year. If anyone wondered what he thought about the season and this latest decision by the Angels, they didn't have to wait long. The day after the story hit the newspapers, Belinsky had a byline in an Associated Press feature revealing his insights about the move, the Angels' offense, and his capability. "But I still don't think it makes any sense," said the Islanders' new pitcher. "Sure, I'll admit I was wild my last three starts. I walked 13 guys. But I started nine games for this club this year, and they got me one run or less in eight of them. That doesn't help much either."[29]

Belinsky spoke the truth about the Angels' scoring. His losses illustrate the lack of offense.

April 11: White Sox won, 3–1
April 19: Athletics won, 3–2
April 27: Orioles won, 4–2
May 5: Indians won, 4–3
May 11: White Sox won, 4–2
May 15: Red Sox won, 9–3
May 19: Yankees won, 10–4

Then Belinsky suggested voluntary retirement. Haney responded with force and clarity: either go to Hawaii or risk getting put on a list of disqualified ballplayers, which meant a ban from playing for a professional team. But Belinsky did not suffer a lack of confidence from his bosses regarding ability. Haney, Rigney, and pitching coach Marv Grissom selected Hawaii for their ace to regroup and hone his skills so he could add value to the Angels. "I believe Bo is a big league pitcher," declared Haney. "But he has to go down and start pitching."[30]

The Angels' general manager boosted his position by making a formal request to baseball commissioner Ford Frick for Belinsky's disqualification. If granted, the team's salary obligation to Belinsky would cease; Haney emphasized to the press that the Angels didn't reduce Belinsky's salary with the move.[31]

In addition, Haney notified AL President Joe Cronin and Minor League President George Trautman of the disqualification. When they met on May 28, Belinsky declared his refusal to go to the Islanders, and he reiterated his stance when they met two days later, which coincided with the end of a player's window of 72 hours to report where assigned. Still, Haney remained flexible. He offered the pitcher an extra 24 hours but clarified that the reassignment was neither retributive nor permanent.

Belinsky needed to focus. Hopefully, the serene sunshine of Hawaii could replace the bright lights of the Sunset Strip and put the southpaw on a track of making a highly significant contribution to the Angels. It was up to Belinsky. "If he would devote one-third of his thoughts to baseball, he would be able to help us and help himself," opined Haney. "We're not doing this to punish him. If he showed he was back in the groove after pitching a few games, he'd be back with us in 24 hours."[32]

Believing that his fame could translate to a lucrative career in show business, Belinsky miscalculated the impact of his obstinacy. In the *Citizen-News*, an LA newspaper, Coy Williams reported that the pitcher's suspension plus salary absence caused a public clamor, with the common thread being repulsion at this latest initiative apparently spurred by an inflated ego. The most popular comments were "he had it coming" and "hope that's the last of Mr. Belinsky."³³ *Los Angeles Times* columnist Jim Murray gave a more pointed account with sarcasm lacing his June 3 column. "The Honolulans were delighted and offered Bo a grass skirt, but Bo was holding out till they put Esther Williams in it," wrote Murray. "Besides, Bo tried to play the ukulele but, as usual, lost his control along about the fifth chorus and Art Fowler had to finish up for him."³⁴

Murray's *Times* colleague Sid Ziff disclosed that Angels pitching coach Marv Grissom said that Belinsky's problem was a lack of concentration. "Maybe he had other things on his mind," said Grissom. Whatever the reason, Belinsky was no longer his problem. The team had games to play, opponents to study, and more than half a season remaining on the schedule. "He's not with the Angels any longer," Grissom reminded Ziff. "I've quit worrying about it."³⁵

Haney didn't ignore the Belinsky issue entirely. On June 3, he met with the malcontented hurler, but the conversation didn't move either party from their respective positions. Belinsky remained intractable in refusing to play for the Islanders. Whether to impress or bluff Haney with non-baseball topics to show he was in demand, Belinsky's orations fell on unwilling ears. "He talked about 101 deals in which I have no interest," said the general manager. "I told him when he decides to play baseball, then come to me and I'll listen."³⁶

Belinsky got some publicity when the *Citizen-News* printed a photograph of him flanked by Walter Winchell and Lionel Hampton, who was in LA to perform at Basin Street West from June 7–9. The caption read in part, "Hamp made it to town to bid Bo Belinsky and Walter Winchell bon voyage."³⁷

He had been making $15,000 a year playing baseball. Being based in Los Angeles plus Van Doren's connections and his previous dabbling on screen could open doors for an acting career, which had reportedly been under consideration. Picking up a baseball again seemed about as likely as Jed Clampett puttering around his Beverly Hills mansion in a three-piece suit with a pocket watch rather than his raggedy clothes and hat. A restaurant proprietor who claimed Belinsky to be "my dearest friend" affirmed that the Angels' decision made the pitcher "pretty bitter."³⁸

Belinsky appeared at the Peppermint West nightclub and got a plaque from legendary actress Ginger Rogers, marking his new entertainment career. Gossip columnist Hedda Hopper reported that he wanted to handle public relations for celebrities.³⁹

The Hawaii Islanders

In late June, Belinsky agreed to go to Hawaii but sent "an emissary" to request a workout with the Angels first; Haney rejected the proposal. Belinsky's path back to the majors went through Honolulu or not at all. "When manager Irv Noren informs me that Bo is in shape to pitch, then, and only then, does he go back on the payroll," explained Haney.[40] But the Angels' general manager hadn't received a formal notice—or an informal one—regarding Belinsky wanting to play baseball again, either from the pitcher himself or from Paul Caruso, his attorney.[41]

It took another three weeks for Belinsky to agree formally, underlined by the caveat of needing Noren's certification of readiness to draw a salary. For Haney, who met with Belinsky about returning, it was about time that the headline-making pitcher accepted his fate in baseball or left the sport for good. "I think the boy is coming to his senses," said the GM, who also expressed his view of Belinsky's social life interfering with the potential to be a solid contributor. "Control has been his problem, but that also may be due to his off-field activities."[42] Moreover, Haney observed that Belinsky's delay in reporting to Hawaii wasted time that he could have used to study, work, and improve. "Too bad he didn't decide to go to Hawaii when we first tried to send him.... He might be back here now."[43]

Angels fans hoped that Belinsky could work out whatever problems plagued his performances, as did the team's leadership, while the pitcher began to take the move in stride. Or appeared to. "They tell me there are 30,000 gals in bikinis in Hawaii," said the pitcher, satisfying the press and its readership craving a good quote.[44]

Given his statement, even if delivered tongue-in-cheek, it would be logical to believe that Hawaii's social aspects posed a danger, especially when UPI reported that he landed toting "a pool cue and with a full schedule of night club dates." If one needed reassurance in the Angels' and Islanders' front offices, not to mention among their fan bases, Belinsky tried to allay concerns about his dedication, approach, and expectations. "I really am not here to fool around," stated the hurler. "I hope to work myself back into shape within the next 10 days, and if I can pitch earlier, fine. The main thing now is that I take it slow and easy and don't hurt myself. Remember, I haven't pitched in two months."[45]

Following the precept of doing as the Romans do when you're in Rome, Belinsky absorbed himself into a staple of Hawaiian culture by learning how to surf. He also restated his priority of getting back in shape and ingratiated himself to Hawaii by declaring, "It's a fabulous place. I just wish I'd come here two months ago. The people are great."[46]

Hawaiians embraced their new baseball star, who brought excitement, prominence, and notoriety to their baseball team. Maury Allen wrote, "He was received as a conquering hero, wined and dined by the owners of the club, local politicians, business executives, industrialists. He was invited to shoot pool in the homes of millionaires. He was treated like a Hollywood celebrity. He was interviewed almost daily. He was introduced to most of the island's important people."[47]

Belinsky got his first chance to pitch as an Islander on July 28 during a doubleheader against the Tacoma Giants. It was brutal. In the bottom of the seventh inning of the first game, Noren called on Belinsky—who hadn't pitched in a game since the drubbing by the Yankees on May 19— and watched Tacoma score five runs, all earned, on five hits, including two homers with a man on base and one solo clout. In the eighth inning, Belinsky dispatched the offense in three-up-three-down fashion; Tacoma swept the twin bill, 16–6 and 4–3.[48]

With his trademark nonchalance—or a veneer of it—Belinsky did not make a big deal of his first outing for the Islanders, nor did he show disappointment. "I had a little something on the ball and got it over the plate," shared the southpaw. "After all, I hadn't pitched for nearly two months." If anyone doubted his drive, Belinsky's declaration of intent clarified the reason for being in Hawaii and the desired result. "My main concern is to get back to the big time. This is a pretty good league, but the minors ain't for Bo."[49]

If the path back to the Angels or another major league squad proved to be a dead end, Belinsky said he'd be "a beach boy."[50] Also a relief job, his next appearance occurred on August 1 against the Seattle Rainiers; he began in the fifth inning after Seattle's offense racked up six runs, and he gave up an additional score in the 7–4 loss.[51]

Belinsky faced the Rainiers again when he made his first start for the Islanders on August 5 and delighted his teammates with a 1–0, complete-game, five-hit victory. In this battle of the cellar dwellers in the PCL's five-team Northern Division—Hawaii was in fourth place, 17 games behind the first-place Spokane Indians while Seattle trailed by 20½ games— Belinsky proved that he had the mettle, endurance, and skill for going nine innings and getting the ball in the strike zone or fairly close to it.[52] Though he maintained the goal of rebounding to the major leagues, Mr. Autry's team did not look like a probable destination. "My relations with the Angels will never be good under the present setup," revealed Belinsky.[53]

In his next start—his first game at Honolulu Stadium—nearly 11,000 people crowded into the ballpark for a nighttime contest on August 10. The Islanders fans got their money's worth. Belinsky blanked the Portland Beavers for five-plus innings, ending his tenure with two outs and a 3–1 lead in the sixth inning to obtain his second PCL victory; Hawaii tacked on seven runs after Belinsky's departure for a 10–1 final tally.

Anxiety hovered over the home team when Belinsky began by loading the bases with two singles plus a walk. Portland had two outs, but Haywood Sullivan's "hot liner" hit the left-hander's glove and led to a force out at second base. Belinsky walked another batter later, struck out six, and allowed seven hits. All in all, a favorable outing.[54]

Belinsky held the Beavers scoreless for five innings in his next start on August 14, allowing three hits and recording six strikeouts. Portland got three runs in the top of the sixth; a bases-loaded single scored two runners, and Belinsky's wild pitch allowed another to cross the plate. But Hawaii, also scoreless through five innings, rallied for a 7–3 victory thanks to a grand slam by Bobby Knoop plus Bob Perry's 2-for-4 day comprised of a solo homer and a two-run single with the bases loaded.[55]

In a home game against Tacoma on August 19, Belinsky went five and one-third innings. He had a 5–0 shutout in the sixth when the Giants scored a trio of runs; Noren summoned Hal Griggs, who gave up a run to reduce the lead to 5–4. Hawaii won, 8–7, in 11 innings for their ninth victory in a row and 14th in the last 15 games. But excitement went beyond obtaining a victory in extra innings. It gave the team second place in the Northern Division.[56]

Hawaii won the next three games before Spokane ended the winning streak at 12 games with a 4–2 defeat on August 23. Belinsky's star power lifted attendance, partially responsible for the Islanders having not only the highest attendance of any PCL team, but also any team throughout the minor leagues. League president Dewey Soriano was happier than a pork-loving vacationer at a luau as he visited Honolulu, reportedly planning for the league's 1964 season. "This man has a tremendous arm and there's no question he can pitch in the major leagues," praised Soriano, who recalled watching Belinsky's 1–0 victory against the Rainiers in Seattle. "I admired his statements after that game in which he praised his teammates for fine support. I think that game actually started Hawaii's comeback."[57]

The Islanders were 15–3 in their last 18 games when Belinsky and his cohorts took the field for the final home game on August 26, which preceded a 20-game road trip to finish the 1963 season. With nearly 17,000 people watching him—reportedly the largest attendance at Honolulu Stadium since World War II—Belinsky pitched a four-hit shutout against Spokane, the Northern Division leader by 12½ games. All four hits were singles. The Islanders gave the southpaw offensive support with 10 hits and six runs.[58]

Called Up

Three days later, Belinsky received notice that the Angels wanted him back, with a reporting date of September 9. Though he had proved his value to Haney et al., the southpaw preferred another team and figured that Rigney would put him in the bullpen. "I just don't want to play with them," shared Belinsky. "I'm not knocking the club that pays me, but the way things have happened, I feel it's best they make a deal with someone. I can help some club."[59]

The Islanders used him again before he headed back to Los Angeles, beginning with the first game of a doubleheader against the Oklahoma City 89ers on the season-ending road trip. He pitched a complete game for the 5–1 victory and did it with what the press described as a broken nose suffered "in a minor auto accident in downtown Oklahoma City." He had 10 stitches. Eli Grba pitched a complete game in the second contest and won, 9–1.[60]

With a three-game winning streak, Belinsky took on the San Diego Padres at Westgate Park. This clash of PCL goliaths ended in a 3–0 shutout of the Islanders, giving the Padres their 13th win in the last 16n games.[61]

Belinsky said aloha to the Islanders and returned to the Angels. Rigney tapped him to start the September 10 game at Dodger Stadium against the Boston Red Sox, who were mired at 70-76, in sixth place and 25½ games behind the first-place Yankees. LA stood deeper: 64–82, in ninth place and 31½ games out of first. Control did not appear to be a factor for Belinsky, who recorded four strikeouts, one walk, and eight hits before getting pulled in the top of the ninth inning with a 5–1 lead after Román Mejías and Carl Yastrzemski hit back-to-back singles. Rigney brought in Art Fowler to squash a Boston rally before it could do any damage.

A four-run cushion should have been enough to preserve a win for Belinsky in his first outing after rejoining the Angels. It wasn't. Frank Malzone singled home Mejías, and Dick Stuart walked to load the bases; Red Sox skipper Johnny Pesky put in Jim Gosger as a pinch-runner for Stuart.

Dan Osinski offered his relief efforts; Lou Clinton's two-run double scored Malzone and Yaz, which closed the gap to 5–4. Gosger scampered to third base and tied the game when he scored on Bob Tillman's ground ball to Angels shortstop Jim Fregosi. Clinton took third. Osinski gave an intentional walk to Geiger to set up a double play; a ground ball by pinch-hitter Russ Nixon to first baseman Charlie Dees forced Gary Geiger out at second base. Felix Mantilla struck out to end Boston's rally. The Angels won in the bottom of the 10th inning on an RBI single by pinch-hitter Lee Thomas; Bob Duliba got credit for the win, having pitched the top of the 10th.[62]

Belinsky drew far bigger crowds in Honolulu than the 4,649 who showed up at Dodger Stadium, but the lackluster attendance did not appear to bother him. Angels insiders and followers found a psychological adjustment in the hurler regarding his situation. "I don't have anyone to blame but myself," said Belinsky in reviewing the game.

Hawaii's aura of friendliness had affected him. There seemed to be less pressure and more joy for the pitcher whose exploits off the field required a scorecard to keep track of women, headlines, and antics. "They gave me the decent treatment," explained Belinsky. "They played up the playboy angle but they weren't nasty about it. They didn't bring out the bucket and splash me with mud. Then when the record crowds started coming out, I just had to come through."[63]

Belinsky lasted five and one-third innings in his next appearance, a home game against Cleveland on September 15; Los Angeles faced a 4–3 deficit when Belinsky departed, then allowed two more runs for a 6–3 Indians victory and Belinsky's eighth loss of the season for the Angels. On September 19, the Angels played their last home game of 1963. Belinsky got his second Angels win with a complete-game, 7–2 triumph against the Orioles in front of a measly attendance of 476.

The Yankees pounded Belinsky early in his next opportunity. He started off well at Yankee Stadium on September 24, striking out Tony Kubek and getting Bobby Richardson on a foul out to third baseman Felix Torres. Then he loaded the bases on Tom Tresh's walk, Mickey Mantle's single, and Roger Maris's walk, followed by Elston Howard crushing a three-run triple and scoring on Joe Pepitone's bunt single for a 4–0 lead.

Rigney kept the lefty in the game; New York scored again in the bottom of the fourth inning. Frank Kostro pinch-hit for Belinsky to lead off the top of the sixth and banged a single for naught as Whitey Ford retired the next three batters. The Yankees scored three more times, while Leon Wagner provided the only run for the visiting team, a solo homer to lead off the top of the ninth. The 8–1 loss put Belinsky's major league record at 2–9 for 1963.

Whatever antagonism may have existed between Belinsky and the Angels' management appeared to lessen greatly, if not disappear, when he became the first player on the squad to grab a pen and sign his contract for the following season, reportedly for the same salary he received in 1963. Belinsky offered a humble, realistic appraisal of his value: "They could have cut me 25%. It would have been justified. I really appreciate it."[64]

During the off-season, Belinsky broke his nose. Again. This time, it happened when he went surfing in Hawaii. The vacationing pitcher got "tossed off his board" and it smacked him, causing him to worry about the possible impact of surgery on his singing because he had been working on an act for Las Vegas.[65]

That turned out to be a minor matter in 1964. To use a surfing analogy, Bo Belinsky had the equivalent of a wipeout to his reputation.

6

Basebrawl

Looking Forward to '64

Once asked what he did in the winter, baseball legend Rogers Hornsby replied, "I look out the window and wait for spring."

Living in a warm weather state like Florida, Arizona, Nevada, or California presents a bonus opportunity for kids to satiate their baseball appetites by playing Wiffle ball during the national pastime's annual slumber between the World Series and the date when pitchers and catchers report for spring training. But winter's chill forces millions of fans to find catharsis elsewhere. Tabletop simulation games like Strat-O-Matic, which debuted in 1961, perpetuate conversations during the off-season.

Baseball stories were not totally foreign to sportswriters, whose attention turned toward basketball, football, and hockey during the winter. Belinsky's saga made the newspapers in mid–January of 1964 when Al Wolf graced the *Los Angeles Times* with a comment about the odds being 6–5 for the southpaw finding his way to Palm Springs for the initiation of the Angels' spring training on February 17. A recap of Belinsky's 1963 experience followed, with a jibe here and there making Wolf's piece sound like a script for a comedian.

While highlighting a positive stint with the Islanders and the 4–1 record, he suggested that Belinsky worked at a high level because he brought in crowds, which meant leverage for his salary. Wolf had a faulty thesis because Belinsky signed his 1964 contract for the same salary that he received in 1963.[1]

Also, Wolf underscored Belinsky's social life, always a fertile topic for baseball scribes. During his time with the Angels, the pitcher had at least four roommates, apparently because nobody could sustain living with the phone constantly ringing. Sarcasm dripped from Wolf's solution like water from a melting icicle: Haney and Autry could room with Belinsky. "After all, Gene and Fred won't have to pitch the next day."[2]

Later in January, the *Times* published Belinsky's comments from an interview with Sid Ziff showing that the "playboy pitcher" was a thoughtful roommate, aware of and apologetic for the pressure that his social life brought. "I'd only check in a couple of hours after he'd be asleep," shared Belinsky of his pairing with Albie Pearson. "And there were a few phone calls, too. But I felt guilty with him. I told him he'd be better off with someone else."

Ziff's piece also recounted Belinsky's five-week engagement at the Silver Slipper in Las Vegas. "I did skits with some of the 'burly' comedians, sang a little baseball parody, and did a little soft shoe," said the southpaw. "It was good experience, and they gave me good money."[3]

Baseball's upcoming season would be a welcome dose of normalcy for a country emotionally shellshocked by the assassination of President John F. Kennedy on November 22, 1963. Two days later, millions of TV viewers saw Jack Ruby's murder of Kennedy's presumed assassin, Lee Harvey Oswald, in the basement of the Dallas Police Department's headquarters, which housed the city jail, as detectives escorted Oswald for transport to the county jail.

As the calendar turned to 1964 five weeks later, the 35th American president received a posthumous honor when Idlewild Airport in Queens, New York, was renamed John F. Kennedy International Airport, known colloquially as JFK.

Whether by providence or design, Hollywood released an array of presidential-themed movies in 1964. *Dr. Strangelove (or How I Learned to Stop Worrying and Love the Bomb)* offered a comedic narrative on the danger of nuclear war, countered by a sobering story in *Fail-Safe,* based on the 1962 novel by Eugene Burdick and Harvey Wheeler. Fletcher Knebel and Charles W. Bailey authored *Seven Days in May*—another 1962 novel that inspired a 1964 film—revolving around a military coup d'état in the U.S., starring Kirk Douglas and Burt Lancaster. HBO's 1994 remake, titled *The Enemy Within,* starred Jason Robards and Sam Waterston.

Gore Vidal scripted *The Best Man,* based on his Broadway play concerning a battle between a U.S. senator and a former Secretary of State for an unnamed party's presidential nomination. Scandal, mutual disrespect, and behind-the-scenes maneuvering emphasize the drama. For comedy, Fred MacMurray and Polly Bergen played a fictional First Couple in *Kisses for My President*; Bergen's character was the first female president.

Contrary to FCC chairman Newton Minow's 1961 declaration that TV was a "vast wasteland," prime time offered compelling, thought-provoking choices in the early 1960s. *The Defenders* and *Route 66* each ran four seasons. *East Side/West Side* revolved around social workers in New York City, with cutting-edge stories about statutory rape, post-traumatic stress in soldiers, blockbusting, age discrimination, and child abuse, among others. It only lasted the 1963–1964 season.

6. Basebrawl 93

Dr. Kildare and *Ben Casey* competed for fans of the medical genre. Comedy stalwarts like Jack Benny, Red Skelton, and Lucille Ball had successful shows bolstered by decades of fame. But if they wanted to poke fun at LA's American League team at the beginning of 1964, they would have serious competition in the Angels' organization. Crowds enjoyed the humor of executives and players in what the press described as "a good-will tour" visiting 25 cities in "the southern half" of California to shore up support for the upcoming season and help raise money for a local charity at each stop. "And they are acquiring additional polish each time they get to their feet," reported Braven Dyer in the *Times*.

Barry Latman—a newcomer to the Angels, courtesy of a December trade with the Indians for Leon Wagner and a player to be named later, who turned out to be veteran Joe Adcock—"keeps his listeners in stitches" and "has a lot of poise." Rocky Bridges got complimented as "a riot." Buddy Blattner, a former major leaguer in 1942 and 1946–1949, served in the navy for three years during World War II and became a baseball radio announcer after retiring from playing. He joined the performances, as did radio personality and future Honorary Mayor of Hollywood Johnny Grant.

A joke about Belinsky got printed but was not credited to anyone: "Bo Belinsky was a life guard and head waiter in Hawaii and a blues singer in Las Vegas during the off-season. Now the big question is whether he's going to be a pitcher again or maitre d' [sic] at the Stadium Club."[4]

Belinsky might have relished being included in the fun and perhaps even laughed at the jokes spotlighting him. But frolicking had faded, according to the hurler. Responsibility took its place. He told Ziff, "The talent is there. If there was no talent I'd give up. I still haven't found the right combinations. I'm too easily distracted. And I think I may be giving something away, tipping off the batters. I don't know what it is but I'm going to find out. Whatever it is, I'm going to have them show a little more respect."[5]

Defying nonbelievers who bet against him, Belinsky showed up to Palm Springs on time for the Angels' spring training in 1964 and declared his accountability, though he also noted other factors besides talent affecting his goal of winning 15 games. "It's up to me how well I do this season," stated Belinsky, who admitted that he had been out of shape and suffered control problems in 1963. "Defense counts a lot, and I'm not knocking our guys when I just remind you that we weren't the best fielding team in the American League."[6]

Indeed, the Angels placed ninth out of 10 AL teams on defense.

Belinsky started the March 10 game—his first in 1964 spring training—and threw two innings. Each squad used four hurlers in the Indians'

9–7 victory over the Angels. Cleveland had a 3–0 lead in the first inning when Wally Post—who would only play in five games in the 1964 regular season, his last in the majors—hit a three-run homer off Belinsky. The southpaw otherwise "pitched effectively" in his two innings on the mound.[7]

Toward the end of spring training, another outing against Cleveland turbocharged his appeal for those who might have been skeptical regarding statements of a new and improved approach. Belinsky allowed three hits in six innings and got credit for the 6–0 win, prompting Marv Grissom to praise the change in Belinsky's mental and physical prowess. "Belinsky has worked much harder this year," observed the Angels' pitching coach. "He's in better shape and getting much better action. His attitude is improved, too."[8]

With confidence and composure, Belinsky showed no fear. "Bring on the Dodgers," he stated. Even if uttered in jest, his words represented quite a challenge considering the Dodgers' sweep of the Yankees in the previous year's World Series. But he got his wish. A day before Opening Day, Belinsky started the Angels-Dodgers exhibition game and pitched the way a chef at a restaurant with two Michelin stars prepares a meal. Splendidly. He gave up one hit in five innings—a fourth-inning single by Frank Howard—and a couple of walks as he benefited from the Angels putting a quartet of runs on the scoreboard before he left the game. In the sixth inning, they got another run for a 5–0 victory.

Belinsky's control plus the failure of the first 10 Dodgers batters to get the ball out of the Dodger Stadium infield gave a sense that hard work, introspection, and determination could put the left-hander on track for a solid season. Don Lee threw three innings in relief and struck out four. Bill Kelso took over in the ninth, loaded the bases on a pair of hits and a walk, and retired Jeff Torborg on a popup to secure the blanking.[9]

The Angels looked like a team of substance in 1964. "Our defense is our biggest improvement this year," said Rigney. "We're going to be stronger in defending it … and how did you like Bo? If he pitches like that, he's going to win. He's going to win big."[10]

But there was always a good chance of carelessness off the field. After a dinner date in his hotel room, Belinsky caused havoc in the middle of coitus with his latest conquest. With the table so close to the bed, he accidentally kicked it over with his right leg. Dinnerware sprayed over the floor. Broken glass, too. The hotel maid was upset, to say the least. So was the hotel management. Rigney fined Belinsky $500.[11]

In his Belinsky biography, Maury Allen recounts a story that took place in Boston during the 1964 regular season, resulting in another $500 fine, but it's most likely a mistake or misunderstanding regarding the year. When a fire forced his teammates to leave the Somerset Hotel in the middle of the night, Belinsky arrived to find them on the sidewalk after he spent several hours with one of his paramours. Rigney fined him for breaking curfew. There was a fire in 1963, not 1964. Though three fire alarms occurred during their stay in 1964, they were tests of the alarm system.[12]

A New Season

Opening the 1964 season on the road, the Angels split a two-game series against the Senators. A trip to Detroit resulted in another two-game split, an outcome repeated when the Tigers went to Los Angeles a few days later. The Angels lost the home opener, 6–4. Belinsky started the second game, giving a decent but not overwhelming performance: eight hits in eight innings, one run, two walks, and five strikeouts. With the score 1–1 and runners on first and second with two outs, Rigney pinch-hit for Belinsky in the bottom of the eighth. Félix Torres whiffed. Detroit scored a run in the top of the ninth, but Los Angeles rebounded with a pair of runs in the bottom half to win, 3–2.

Humility eclipsed hubris after the game for Belinsky. "All in all, I guess I ought to be satisfied with the way I pitched, but when you don't win after pitching eight innings you don't feel too good," he said.[13]

Bill Monboquette started for the Red Sox in a deeply disappointing game for LA on May 19 at Fenway Park. Belinsky gave an amazing performance: a 3–0 lead and a four-hitter through eight and two-thirds innings. But Dick Stuart worked him for a walk after facing a 1–2 count and went to third on Tony Conigliaro's double.

Bill Rigney brought in Barry Latman to pitch. A walk loaded the bases; Bob Tillman left for pinch-runner Earl Wilson. Latman hit Román Mejías with a pitch, which scored Stuart and advanced the other runners.

Boston skipper Johnny Pesky took out Bob Heffner—who had replaced Monboquette in the top of the ninth—and put in Dalton Jones to pinch-hit; Don Lee took the mound, hoping to save Belinsky's second victory of 1964. Instead, Jones's double emptied the bases for a 4–3 Boston victory and heartbreak for Angels fans, who found comfort in Dyer's description: "This was far and away Belinsky's best effort of the season. He looked like the Bo of 1962 when he hurled his no-hitter. It was a crime that he couldn't even get a win after pitching as well as he did."

Dyer also noted that a line drive smashed by Carl Yastrzemski connected with Belinsky's right shin, but the pitcher "recovered quickly."[14]

Pouring on the plaudits again when Belinsky went the full nine innings in a 4–1 home game victory against the Twins on May 27, Dyer wrote, "Belinsky pitched like the Bo of 1962." He struck out eight with no walks while scattering seven hits in the 4–1 triumph; Minnesota's only score came from Harmon Killebrew's solo bash in the second inning. Additionally, Mamie Van Doren went to the game with Belinsky's sister and got labeled an "ex-flame."[15]

Belinsky had a 3–3 record so far in 1964, not domineering but a far cry from the 1–7 record that had sent him to Hawaii. On June 17, he got his fourth victory. Holding a 4–2 lead against the Senators at DC Stadium in the eighth inning, Belinsky gave up a triple to Ed Brinkman and an RBI single to John Kennedy before Rigney called upon Don Lee for relief. The Angels tacked on an insurance run in the top of the ninth for a 5–3 final score.

It would seem to the average observer that Belinsky had delivered on his promise to focus on ballplaying because stories about his social life diminished in number, importance, and interest. Except for the throwaway mention about Van Doren at the Twins game and a few other items, strikeouts overshadowed sex symbols as the foundation for reporters' accounts of Belinsky's life in 1964. But he revealed that he still appreciated his postgame lifestyle as a stress release.

On the surface, playing in the major leagues has enormous benefits, such as fame, money, and adoration. But there's also a terrific price. Disruption, for example. Players uproot their lives in February for spring training and spend approximately six weeks in Florida, Arizona, or California before settling in their team's city for the season. For many players, their residences are temporary. Plus, they're away for half the season. When it ends, they return to their permanent home and stay there for the winter until spring training begins and the cycle repeats.

By the mid–1960s, the players had to confront physiological adjustments because of baseball's evolution. Planes had replaced trains for going on road trips. Night games became more prominent. There was also the time that players must dedicate to work out, practice, strategize, and rest. Baseball's daily burdens caused Belinsky to recoil like a Slinky. "It just isn't worth it, I've learned, to sacrifice my youth and personal ways to be a major league ball player," revealed the 27-year-old. "If the management doesn't like me being out at a party, let them get rid of me. I'm just sick and tired of catering to the ball club."

Money did not concern him. Belinsky said that even a $20,000 salary boost wouldn't change his mind. "I just wanted to relax," he explained. Hawaii presented itself as a desirable destination, which the unhappy hurler made known to Haney.[16]

But there may have been another reason triggering Belinsky's request for a trade or a demotion to the Islanders. It happened a few days before the Washington game; Rigney tapped him for relief pitching at Tiger Stadium in the second game of a doubleheader on June 14. The Angels led, 4–2, in the bottom of the seventh inning. Latman gave up a leadoff single to Mike Roarke and a walk to Bill Bruton, who pinch-hit for Mickey Lolich. Jerry Lumpe's bunt single loaded the bases.

Belinsky took over and retired George Thomas—pinch-hitting for Gates Brown—on a grounder to shortstop Jim Fregosi for the first out, but Roarke scored. Al Kaline drew an intentional walk, a good idea considering he had the second-highest batting average in the American League in 1963. But any thoughts of a double play ended when Belinsky walked Norm Cash, allowing the second run to score. Don Lee relieved Belinsky and gave up four more runs; Detroit won, 6–4.

Belinsky felt disrespected by being told to pitch in relief. Petulance abounded. Boundaries of behavior that he agreed to—and which seemed to be working, as proven by some fantastic efforts on the mound—began to feel restrictive to the sociable ballplayer. "But with my personality, why should I turn into a square," opined Belinsky. "I'm a single guy, and I can do what I want without those down-the-nose looks from club officials. From now on, if I want to be seen with 10 blondes I'll be seen with 10 blondes, and I don't care what they think. In fact, I think I'll walk into the park Friday night with a blonde on each arm."[17]

Bacchanalian desires fell by the wayside after a Father's Day victory at Dodger Stadium elevated his record to 5–3 with another showcase of dominance, stamina, and control in his eight and two-thirds innings against the Indians. He had nine strikeouts and yielded two walks and six hits in a 4–1 victory. The Angels faced Jack Kralick, a fellow member of the 1962 no-hitter club, and broke a scoreless tie in the bottom of the fifth inning, when a barrage of singles and two errors by Indians backstop John Romano led to a 4–0 margin.

Belinsky benefited from one of the errors and made an error of his own. With runners at the corners in the bottom of the fifth, he whiffed and got lucky when Romano tagged him "about 20 feet from the plate" but dropped the ball, which allowed Buck Rodgers to score from third base for one of the Angels' quartet of runs. Belinsky was supposed to square off and bunt. "Yeah, I missed the signal," he admitted. "And I sure would have been sore at myself if I had lost, say by one run."[18]

At 29–37, the Angels were in eighth place. The Yankees and Orioles were tied for first place, but the victory over Cleveland turned Belinsky's obstinacy to optimism: "We're not looking for the first division now. We're looking for the pennant." Not since Dr. Jekyll and Mr. Hyde had there been a transformation of this magnitude. "At the time I said I wanted to go back there, I felt I couldn't stand the grind of losing the close ones the way we were," reminded the hurler about returning to Hawaii. "I had nothing against anybody on the club. ANGELS? I just thought my health was in jeopardy. I felt sick. I couldn't keep my food down. But now we're becoming a different kind of ball club."[19]

Belinsky wasn't exaggerating. Los Angeles had lost 15 games by a one-run margin, including a three-game series at Fenway Park. But something changed in June—the Angels had begun the month at 16–29 and ended it at 35–41. Their Father's Day victory was the fifth in an 11-game winning streak.

Blanking the A's through eight innings on June 26 guided Belinsky to his sixth win, a 1–0 victory in the first game of a Dodger Stadium twin bill. After Ed Charles singled and Rocky Colavito walked to begin the top of the ninth, Belinsky got support from Bob Duliba, who retired the next three batters and recorded his fifth unofficial save. Bobby Knoop's sacrifice fly scored Rodgers in the bottom of the fifth for the Angels' sole run; LA won the second game, 6–0.

Belinsky commanded with his seventh win—a two-hitter against the White Sox at home on July 9. The Angels won, 3–0. Hitless through 14 batters, Chicago got its first hit in the top of the fifth inning when Ron Hansen singled with two outs; Jerry McNertney banged a single in the sixth. Belinsky showed tremendous control, walking two batters—Don Buford and Mike Hershberger—though some might have doubted it when he began the game by hitting Buford with a pitch on his helmet.

Despite the performance, Belinsky offered a somewhat muted appraisal. "I didn't feel that I was extremely strong tonight," he said while also acknowledging Dodger Stadium as a factor. "But I had adequate stuff, not extra special. I'm luckier in this park than in many others. Yes, this is where I got my last shutout."[20]

Indeed. His last blanking happened almost two years before, a four-hitter against the Twins on August 11, 1962. Dyer described Belinsky as "the reformed (?) playboy," indicating that the pitcher could not shake his reputation despite the recent outstanding pitching.[21]

There was no question mark in Sid Ziff's reporting about an off-the-field conflict between the "playboy pitcher" and Angels management regarding past fines totaling $750. Belinsky wanted the money back but said that he'd settle for $500. He didn't believe that Fred Haney would increase his salary in the middle of the season even though he topped the Angels in wins. "I don't want a raise," said Belinsky. "I just want something back that they took out of my pocket."[22]

Belinsky lost his next start, a July 14 contest kicking off a three-game homestand against the Tigers. He threw five innings and left the game for a pinch-hitter in the bottom of the fifth; Detroit had scored three times. LA's offense provided no run support for the southpaw but scored twice in the bottom of the sixth. Each team scored once again for a final Detroit win, 4–3. The Angels won their next six games in a row, lost the July 20 matchup against the White Sox in a 9–0 trouncing, then won three straight, beginning with a 2–0 victory at Comiskey Park. Both runs occurred on Belinsky's watch, which lasted six innings, so he got credit for the win and boosted his record to 8–5.

At Municipal Stadium in Kansas City on July 25, the final score of 18–2 seemed more appropriate for football than baseball. Belinsky showed masterful form in this crushing defeat of the A's—a complete game, eight strikeouts, five hits, three walks. The Angels batted around the order in the top of the first inning and scored six runs; Joe Adcock and Bobby Knoop both hit bases-loaded doubles, scoring all runners.

It was Bo Belinsky's last victory of 1964. The next three games that Belinsky started resulted in shutouts of the Angels. He gave up three runs in five innings against the Yankees, who tacked on two more tallies to give Jim Bouton a complete-game, 5–0 victory at Dodger Stadium on July 29. Also at Dodger Stadium, Baltimore scored four times before Belinsky left in the sixth inning with the Angels scoreless on August 3; LA allowed three more runs for a 7–0 final. Belinsky and rookie Indians hurler Luis Tiant each threw a complete game on August 11. Max Alvis cracked a three-run homer in the top of the ninth inning to break a scoreless tie, give Cleveland a 3–0 win, and register Tiant's fifth victory on his way to a 10–4 season.

Displeasure resurfaced. Belinsky declared that he wanted to leave baseball and floated ideas about getting "something stable" in the corporate world. With a 2.86 ERA and 9–8 record, he disclosed that he felt most comfortable on the mound. "It doesn't bother me when I'm pitching," said the left-hander in a piece by AP writer Charles Maher. "I can go out there and give 'em my best shot every time. But in between games it eats away at me."

Haney offered a lukewarm response, at best. "That's entirely up to Bo. He's got to run his own life. I think it's up to each individual to decide for himself what's best for himself and make his move accordingly."[23]

The Angels were 60–57. In fourth place, they stood 13½ games behind the first-place Orioles, so it was improbable but not inconceivable that they could catch up if the pitching came through, especially if Belinsky could pitch more games like the two-hitter against Chicago. Baseball followers from Torrance to Tarrytown devoured his latest utterance. He clarified that he was "not giving up baseball right now." But his resolve couldn't have been sharper: "I do intend to get out as soon as I find something with a future."[24]

The Slap Heard Round the World

An earthquake happened, metaphorically speaking, when Belinsky decked Angels beat writer Braven Dyer. An indefinite suspension followed. Belinsky claimed that Dyer provoked him. Dyer was 64 years old, more than twice the age of the 27-year-old pitcher; it happened in Belinsky's Washington hotel room during a mid–August series against the Senators. But the facts were in dispute. Dyer claimed Belinsky invited him to his room for clarification about the scribe's story regarding quitting baseball, while Belinsky denied that he proffered an invitation.

According to the hurler, Dyer taunted him on the phone. A "hot argument" followed, and Dyer went to confront Belinsky in his hotel room. "Well, I was in the bathroom brushing my teeth when I heard a knock on the door. I opened the door and there was Dyer in his shirtsleeves with his fists clenched like he was ready for a fight."[25]

There were other factors. After the loss to the Indians on August 12, the Angels and their beat writers flew to Washington for a series against the Senators, arriving at the Shoreham Hotel at 1:30 a.m. "Many of the writers, including Dyer, were fighting the lingering effects of too much drink and too much jet lag," wrote Maury Allen. But Belinsky and Chance took a detour to grab "a late dinner" before getting to the Shoreham about 90 minutes later. At 3:30 a.m., the phone rang in the room shared by the two hurlers.

Dyer wanted to follow up on the quote about Belinsky quitting in Maher's article. Belinsky denied that he said it. Dyer persisted in wanting a story for the *Los Angeles Times*. The time of night, the jet lag, the frustration of the loss to Cleveland, and Dyer's nudging ignited Belinsky's fury. "Look, Dyer, I've had enough of your shit for three years. You've never liked me and you've been ripping me ever since I got here. Now I don't want to put up with any more of your bullshit again. Just stay the fuck away from me. If you ever come within two feet of me again, I'll put your face in the toilet bowl and flush it."[26]

Challenge accepted. Dyer went up 30 minutes later. Belinsky opened the door, Dyer moved into the room, and the two stood nose to nose. "I threw the glass of water in his face," said the pitcher. "He was getting close to me, and I didn't want to have to hit him. I thought that might sober him up and make him leave."[27]

There, the stories diverge. Belinsky claimed that Dyer went to the ballplayer's bag, grabbed a bottle of hair tonic, and attempted to hit him with it. That's when he slugged Dyer, who said that he went to the room at Belinsky's request because the Angels' ace wanted him to change a story he had already written and filed about quitting. That's when the threat about the toilet bowl happened, but Dyer went to confront him instead of attributing the comment to stress. According to the sportswriter, he never had a bottle of hair tonic in his hand.

Belinsky slapped Dyer instead of punching him. But it caused significant damage. Whatever the source of the provocation, it led to a clash resulting in Dyer suffering a black right eye and six stitches in his left ear. Belinsky alleged self-defense, claiming that Dyer "grazed his cheek" with something that he "grabbed" from the ballplayer's toilet kit. UPI reported that "he shoved Dyer away with the palm of his hand but that Dyer hit the bathroom wall and fell unconscious."[28] Allen wrote, "Blood was gushing from his ear and the side of his head."[29]

The incident prompted Rigney to state that he wanted to jettison Belinsky, a fine proposition with the pitcher: "If they're going to suspend me without pay, fine. Let them give me my release. It was something out of my control."[30] When Belinsky returned to LA, he doubled down on the virtue of his actions. "I don't think I could have behaved differently if the situation happened again."[31]

He had a point about the coverage by the press and treatment by the Angels' management.

> Nobody wanted to hear my side of the story. All they were interested in was the fact that I had flattened Dyer. Nobody cared that he had come to my room. I didn't go to his. Nobody cared that he had been drinking on the plane and I hadn't. Nobody cared that Dean saw the whole thing and could have told them what happened. Nobody asked him. All anybody seemed interested in was getting me suspended and out of town as fast as possible.[32]

Belinsky had been making a solid contribution until the Dyer incident: a 9–8 record with a 2.87 ERA. To take the edge off the suspension, he found solace in socializing. There were always women willing to date the guy who had been with Hollywood's most desirable actresses. But Ricky duPont played an especially effective role. "She really helped me out of my depression," said Belinsky.[33]

Haney extended a reprieve, of sorts. Using his authority as general manager to make a Solomon-like decision, he removed the suspension but sent Belinsky to the Islanders. This left Belinsky only one option—play in Hawaii or don't play at all. He no longer was the Angels' problem because Haney's maneuver, which allowed the pitcher a 72-hour window to resolve his fate, put him under the Islanders' jurisdiction. Further, Haney had satisfied a rule about suspensions getting removed "within 10 days. While Belinsky claimed through his attorney that he wanted a formal hearing in front of baseball commissioner Ford Frick, he lacked justification."[34]

Belinsky refused to return to Honolulu, incurring another suspension by the Angels.[35] A proclamation followed: he would don a uniform for "anyone in the major leagues." But there were no takers. His future in baseball remained doubtful, even improbable by some accounts.[36]

Romantic exploits, occasional flourishes of baseball greatness, and a devil-may-care aura had always made Belinsky good copy for the press. Whether he could contribute on the mound was a matter of opinion for managers and executives, but he remained confident that his skills warranted placement: "I still feel that I'm a major league pitcher."[37]

Belinsky faced another hurdle beyond the potential to perform. Given the incident with Dyer, he could be too much trouble to handle. Obstinate in the wake of the fracas, Belinsky persisted in maintaining his major league status as the team revealed an artist's depiction of Angel Stadium set for a 1966 debut in Anaheim to give the squad a home and, in turn, solidify its identity. No longer would they have to bunk with the Dodgers in Dodger Stadium.[38]

Life went on. Prime time TV saw the debuts of *Gilligan's Island*, *The Munsters*, and *The Addams Family*. Disney's *Mary Poppins* premiered, earning 13 Oscar nominations and winning for Best Actress, Best Film Editing, Best Special Visual Effects, Best Original Song, and Best Original Score. Radio stations with a Top 40 format played hit songs from The Beatles, who had released three albums since making their first appearance in America on *The Ed Sullivan Show* in February.

The Angels ended the season in fifth place at 82–80, trailing the AL champion Yankees by 17½ games. Baseball got another exciting World Series—a seven-game affair between the Cardinals and Yankees. St. Louis won its first of two World Series titles in the 1960s, Yankees skipper Yogi Berra got fired, and Cardinals manager Johnny Keane replaced him, to the shock of baseball insiders who expected him to stay in St. Louis.

Belinsky found baseball employment. Sort of. He and Dean Chance portrayed ballplayers in *Damn Yankees*, originally slated to star Bert Lahr at the Melodyland Theater in Anaheim. When Lahr got influenza before the show's premiere, Eddie Bracken took over the role of Mr. Applegate, aka the Devil.[39]

Uncertainty regarding Belinsky's baseball career lasted through November.

7

Philadelphia

A New Team

December 1, 1964, was an exciting day for sports fans in the City of Brotherly Love.

In the midst of a mediocre 40–40 season, the Philadelphia 76ers came within a basket of defeating a dominant Los Angeles Lakers team. Final score: 118–117. Villanova handled the University of Scranton with ease, notching an 88–42 victory. St. Joseph's beat Fairfield, 95–64. In football, the hopes of Eagles fans raised when Notre Dame's quarterback, John Huarte, disclosed that he liked the team as a landing place. Ultimately, he chose the Jets in the AFL.

Baseball's winter meetings began on this first day of December. Phillies fans from Berwyn to Bellmawr followed the developments with great anticipation boosted by the team's outstanding feats in 1964—Jim Bunning's perfect game, 19-8 record, and 219 strikeouts along with Chris Short going 17-9, Johnny Callison knocking in 104 runs, and Dick Allen winning the Rookie of the Year Award. The 1965 season heralded promise, indeed.

Philadelphia sighted Bo Belinsky, looking to improve the pitching roster after a heated three-way pennant race ended with tying the Reds for second place, a game behind the Cardinals. Although the Angels initially balked at releasing him,[1] he remained a target when it seemed unlikely that the Phillies would acquire the Mets' Alvin Jackson or the Astros' Ken Johnson.[2]

As post–Thanksgiving thoughts and conversations turned to upcoming vacations, trips, and employee bonuses for the holiday season, baseball conversations remained focused, passionate, and hopeful. At a Philadelphian's core is an impenetrable loyalty in sports, reinforced in the off-season through conversations about past glories, present challenges, and future possibilities throughout corner bars in the Kensington neighborhood, finished basements in the Main Line suburbs, and conference rooms in Center City.

Philadelphians are a prideful lot. But realistic, too. News of the Phillies seeking Belinsky caused curiosity, at the very least. How would a fellow known for the high life in Hollywood fit with the storied history of baseball in a city with a puritanical streak? The trade happened, sending Belinsky to the land of cheesesteaks and two minor leaguers from the

Los Angeles Herald Examiner sports reporter Bud Furillo holds a copy of his newspaper detailing Belinsky's trade to the Philadelphia Phillies (Los Angeles Public Library, *Los Angeles Herald Examiner* Photo Collection).

Phillies' farm system to the City of Angels—southpaw pitcher Rudy May and first baseman Costen Shockley.

Playing for the Phillies meant playing closer to his hometown; a little more than thirty miles separate Trenton from Philadelphia. Belinsky admitted that he thought he'd be heading for Kansas City, but this deal sending him 3,000 miles eastward put his fate on a different track with more value. "This means I'll finally be playing with a pennant contender," said the southpaw. "This may also be the boost I really need in my baseball career."[3]

The strength of the Phillies' squad inspired Belinsky. "It will be a lot different playing with a contender," he observed. "You know, you give it that little extra effort. It's not that I didn't break my back for the Angels. But this new arrangement might bring out something else in me." Friction between the pitcher and the Angels' front office manifested in Belinsky discovering the trade because a newspaper reporter reached out to his parents rather than an Angels representative calling him directly. He declared a policy of silence regarding his former employer. "I'll show the Angels a little more courtesy than they showed me. I'll be courteous by avoiding talking about them. People don't know the aggravation I've had the last three years. They should have called me to tell me about the trade."[4]

Had Belinsky's reputation plus the Dyer incident caused any distress in the Phillies' front office, it appeared to be minimal and fleeting if it existed at all. Phillies skipper Gene Mauch affirmed, "All I care about is his background as a pitcher and everyone tells me he can throw hard. We didn't trade for his troubles. We traded for his pitching."[5]

Dean Chance, who had recently won the Cy Young Award, chimed in regarding his pal. "Bo gets along with everybody. I've never heard him knock a player, and I've never heard a player ... knock him. But there always seemed to be a bad image. I know he's happy with the trade because he said he wasn't going to pitch for the Angels—and I don't think the club wanted him. I think he can help the Phillies. As a matter of fact I'd like to see him win 20, and I think he can."[6]

Living in Philadelphia might calm, or even tame, the wildcat known for his postgame socializing in Los Angeles plus the black mark created by the incident with Dyer. *Los Angeles Herald Examiner* columnist Melvin Durslag broke down the ballplayer's penchant for partying versus the headline-making scuffle that undoubtedly put him on the trading block and injured his standing. "To those who knew Belinsky, this came as a shock, because for all his failings, he had no reputation for violence," stated Durslag. "He was a drifter whose prime charm was gentleness." Moreover, he quoted the pitcher on the financial impact: "That affair ruined me financially. I had $30,000 worth of side deals that were canceled because of the bad publicity."[7]

While baseball fans looked forward to 1965, the holiday season also provided its annual aura of reflection. It had been a year of change. A revolution, in some respects. When 1964 began, Americans were still dazed by the events five weeks prior resulting in the assassination of their 46-year-old president in Dallas and the shooting death of his alleged murderer two days later in a police station.

Lyndon Johnson took the oath of office, fulfilling his duty to carry the torch of John F. Kennedy's political leadership. His speech to a joint session of Congress five days after Kennedy's murder commended the previous president on his work involving civil rights and urged passage of a new bill: "We meet in grief, but let us also meet in renewed dedication and renewed vigor. Let us meet in action, in tolerance, and in mutual understanding. John Kennedy's death commands what his life conveyed—that America must move forward. The time has come for Americans of all races and creeds and political beliefs to understand and to respect one another."[8]

Congress passed the 1964 Civil Rights Act on July 2, 1964. United States Surgeon General Luther Terry certified what had been common knowledge—cigarette smoking is hazardous to one's health—in the first statement from the federal government on this topic, which prompted warning labels on cigarettes. The United States Supreme Court upheld the right to criticize politicians without censorship in the landmark case of New York Times Company vs. Sullivan.

A joint congressional resolution labeled the Gulf of Tonkin Resolution authorized President Johnson to use military action in Southeast Asia, beginning an escalation of the Vietnam War. Barry Goldwater set a new standard for conservative politics when he ran on the Republican ticket for president. LBJ beat him soundly, winning 486 of 538 electoral votes and more than 61 percent of the popular vote. But Goldwater's campaign cast the die for Republicans, evidenced by Ronald Reagan running on a conservative platform and winning the California gubernatorial race two years later.

The World's Fair in Queens, New York, highlighted the space program with an exhibit called Space Park featuring Aurora 7, the capsule piloted by NASA's Project Mercury astronaut Scott Carpenter—the second American astronaut to orbit Earth. Other attractions included a full-scale model of an X-15 plane, a replica of the Telstar I communications satellite, and the Lunar Excursion Model that would be used in the Apollo Moon landing missions. Elsewhere in New York City, Harlem endured race riots lasting nearly a week.

Cassius Clay had 5–1 odds in his heavyweight bout with Sonny Liston, who gave up at the beginning of the seventh round.[9] Clay later changed his name to Muhammad Ali.

Shea Stadium debuted. The Yankees fired Yogi Berra as manager after the World Series loss to the Cardinals.

As 1965 began, Belinsky continued to make the rounds of LA Walter Winchell reported in his syndicated column that the pitcher had a nose job and "stags it nightly at Patsy D'Amore's Villa Capri," a popular Italian restaurant in Hollywood.[10] Durslag's feature on Dean Chance mentioned the kinship between the two ballplayers and their escapades. As roommates with the Angels, they conquered southern California's party lifestyle, though Durslag admitted that it was unknown which one led the other on this bacchanalian path. The difference between them was in their respective approaches to pitching. Chance was a "dedicated competitor." Belinsky wanted to play but didn't let winning or losing tap his emotions.[11]

Philadelphia Inquirer sportswriter Allen Lewis acknowledged the baggage of Belinsky's reputation in addition to the difficulties of Dick Stuart, another acquisition. But he also acknowledged that Mauch counted on the duo to perform; their output plus the team's diversity of talent could give the Phillies a legitimate shot at the pennant. Lewis praised the skipper for knowing how to best use his players, particularly those who had the ability to play multiple positions.[12]

"They aren't kids," said the Phillies' helmsman in addressing the Stuart-Belinsky potential for misbehavior. "They're at an age when I'm not going to change them. They'll do it themselves, if they want to." Mauch pointed out that Stuart faced tough competition in Frank Thomas for the first baseman job. Belinsky got the same treatment. "If he pitches better than some of our others, then he'll help us. If not, he just doesn't pitch."[13]

Belinsky filled the space caused by the Phillies trading Dennis Bennett to the Red Sox for Stuart, who threw some verbal jabs, including a crack about paying more in taxes than Bennett's salary. Stuart also praised Belinsky's screwball but noted Bennett's fastball and curveball.[14] The Stuart-Bennett feud accelerated. Bennett opined that Stuart sought personal glory rather than team gain. "The Phillies are a team ball club and he's an individual, and I just can't see him fitting in with that type of club," stated Bennett.[15]

Stuart later claimed that the tax comment was a joke. "In fact, the Boston writer who talked to me said that I probably paid more in income tax than Bennett got in salary, and I just laughed, and said, 'Yeah, that's right.'"[16] Meanwhile, Mauch believed that Belinsky would match the 12 wins that Bennett compiled in 1964.[17]

The Angels seemed to get the worst of the Belinsky deal when Shockley didn't report to spring training and hinted that he might leave baseball. A new round of negotiations would be needed to make the Angels whole if this came to fruition.[18] Fortunately for all parties involved, Shockley and the Angels achieved a détente.[19] He had a .414 batting average in spring training toward the end of March, but only played 40 games for the Angels in 1965 and then retired from baseball.[20]

Belinsky's view of Mother Nature affecting playing conditions got a mention by Durslag in a column about Dodgers lefty Claude Osteen, who credited "evening moisture" as creating a favorable field for pitchers at Dodger Stadium because it "offer[ed] resistance to the batted ball." Durslag underscored the lack of scientific evidence and a similar void for Belinsky's claim of a jet stream in the evening giving balls hit to center field an extra boost.[21]

Strength and Strive in '65

Some positive news emerged during an intra-squad game in early March, when Belinsky, Dallas Green, and Ferguson Jenkins did not allow a run.[22] Four days later, Belinsky blanked the Mets for three innings and gave up a hit and a walk as Philadelphia won, 1-0. UPI sportswriter Joe Gergen used the word "new" to describe Belinsky in his piece; newspapers used that label in their headlines.[23] Belinsky admitted, "I was calmer than I thought I'd be. I liked those goose-eggs, but my arm isn't completely strong yet."[24]

His next outing did not go as well. Ray Herbert started for the Phillies, who jumped to a 1-0 lead against the Tigers in the top of the first inning courtesy of Johnny Callison's solo home run. In the bottom of the fourth, Detroit notched two runs. Clay Dalrymple, who cracked four home runs during the 1965 regular season, went yard with two men on base in the top of the fifth inning to make the score 4-2.

Belinsky relieved Herbert and tossed four innings as well, allowing two runs. Bill Roman, a Tigers rookie, smashed a solo round tripper in the bottom of the sixth to reduce the Phillies' lead to one run. In the top of the eighth, Detroit put two men on with Roman's leadoff single and Mickey Stanley's bunt. Ruben Amaro, Philadelphia's shortstop, fielded Ray Oyler's bunt attempt—which hit the ground and vaulted like an Olympic high jumper past third baseman Tony Taylor—and stepped on the bag for the force out of Roman.

Or so the Phillies thought.

The umpire, Lee Weyer, called Roman out and then switched his decision to safe. Mauch protected Amaro by getting the "enraged" infielder away from Weyer and took his place in screaming. But there was more than distress at the call. Mauch and Weyer had a history; during an Astros-Phillies game in 1964, Mauch "bumped" him. Philadelphia's manager argued with another umpire about Weyer's call, and then the home plate umpire intervened. Mauch's tirade continued and led to his ejection.

With the bases full of bengals, Willie Horton's sacrifice fly scored Roman and Belinsky's wild pitch advanced the runners. Amaro fielded Jackie Moore's "high bouncer" and got Moore out at first while Stanley scored to give Detroit a 5–4 victory.[25]

Belinsky started against the Twins in his next effort but left the game in the fourth inning with a pulled muscle in his back.[26] Tempering doubts about his potential on April 2, he tallied eight strikeouts in a 3–2 victory—including striking out the side in the sixth inning—against the Braves, playing without slugger Hank Aaron, sidelined while recovering from an operation on his left ankle. Belinsky pitched six innings and threw 89 pitches; Milwaukee scored both of their runs on seven hits off him.[27] "I'm not a strikeout pitcher," said Belinsky. "The most I ever had was eleven in one game. I'm average, nowheres [sic] near Koufax or Chance."

Admitting another factor—tiredness, undoubtedly due to the 21 pitches he tossed in the first inning—Belinsky showed humility in his self-assessment. "I'm fumbling around in my glove," said the pitcher. "I don't have a grip on the ball, and then I'm trying to grip it while I'm in my windup. That comes from rhythm. I can get by with what I've got now, but I want to get better."[28]

Still, the "playboy" persona stuck. Ad copy for the *Inquirer*'s 1965 baseball preview extolled its appeal for Phillies fans. "Why? The answer is easy. As easy as it is for Maury Wills to steal second ... or Bo Belinsky to catch the eye of a pretty blonde behind the dugout. This big, separate section, you see, provides page after page of features, facts, figures, photos, rosters, records, rundowns, stories, sidelights and schedules."[29]

In the guide, Belinsky's reputational baggage received attention. "There are some possible morale problems, a few of which bloomed late last season. There might be others created by the addition of Stuart and Belinsky, each of whom has been known to hit the headlines for more than winning games."[30] But Dean Chance calmed his running buddy's reputation as a ladies man by citing Belinsky's comments about an active social life: "Bo answered, 'If I had half the action I'm supposed to have, I'd be dead.'"[31]

In his first regular season start for the Phillies on April 18, Belinsky got charged with the 6–2 loss against Sandy Koufax and the Dodgers at Connie Mack Stadium. They lost again to the Dodgers with Belinsky next on the mound, managing 10 hits in the 9–3 defeat at Dodger Stadium on April 24.

Belinsky threw four and two-thirds innings in the second game of a May 2 twin bill against the Braves. His prospects looked more promising than the odds of Ben Casey diagnosing his latest patient correctly when Philadelphia's offense pounded Hank Fischer for four runs in the top of the second inning. Belinsky contributed an RBI single and scored on Dick Allen's triple off reliever Clay Carroll. But the glory was temporary; Milwaukee tied the score in the bottom of the second. Both teams scored a run in the third inning. The Phillies notched their sixth run when Allen doubled home Ruben Amaro; Tony Taylor's solo bash in the top of the fifth made the score 7–5.

Mauch pulled Belinsky after he gave up solo homers to Felipe Alou and Aaron in the bottom of the fifth. Philly added three runs for a final score of 10–7 and a sweep of the doubleheader. One of Belinsky's counterparts from the trade got some attention that week—a UPI feature said that veteran star Joe Adcock mentored Costen Shockley. "What a guy that Joe is," said Shockley. "I guess you'd say he took me under his wing this Spring when I came to camp and has taught me plenty about baseball."[32] Shockley smacked a grand slam in a 7–1 win against the Red Sox.

Going into the game against the Cardinals on May 8, Belinsky had the burden of making Phillies fans forget about the previous night's submission to Bob Gibson, who tossed a one-hitter. Fulfilling his mission, Belinsky headed for baseball immortality with a potential second no-hitter on his resumé after keeping the sons of St. Louis hitless for five innings. "Yeah, I thought about a no-hitter," he admitted after the game. "When you've got one in the sixth inning, you've got to go for it."

Belinsky began that inning with a 1–0 lead. Fortunes changed faster than it takes to eat a cheesesteak at Pat's. After walking Bob Uecker, he fielded Curt Simmons's grounder to force the future Miller Lite endorser at second base. Ruben Amaro made an error that allowed Phil Gagliano to get to first base safely, and Lou Brock punctured the hope of the Phillies getting a no-hitter for the second year in a row with a one-out single to score Simmons.[33] Belinsky threw a wild pitch that advanced the runners, and Curt Flood's sacrifice fly sent Gagliano across the plate for the second St. Louis run.

Philadelphia scored three times in the bottom of the sixth and added three more runs an inning later for a 7–2 lead. Belinsky gave up a single to Uecker and walked Tito Francona, pinch-hitting for Steve Carlton; Jack Baldschun relieved his teammate. St. Louis scored six runs; Philadelphia tied it, 8–8, in the bottom of the ninth and won on a bases-loaded walk. "My body wasn't tired, just my arm," explained Belinsky.[34]

At a luncheon honoring Gene Mauch, the Phillies' skipper squashed any doubts about his left-hander's comportment. "I think Bo Belinsky is one of the classiest fellows I've ever seen in my life."[35] But it made great copy to label him. Often, writers and editors called him "the controversial pitcher."³⁶ His name graced the newspaper in another way when retail giant Gimbel's used Belinsky's "baseball round-ups" in advertisements for Philco televisions; Belinsky appeared on Philadelphia's WIBF-TV, which debuted on May 16, 1965, with the Phillies broadcasts as a cornerstone of its programming.³⁷

His first win as a pitcher in the senior circuit happened with a 2–1 decision in St. Louis on May 17, earning a front-page blurb in the *Inquirer*. Belinsky threw a five-hitter with seven strikeouts in a complete game with good control; the Cardinals managed two walks, both on full counts. His next outing took place on May 22 in Cincinnati, a disaster. The Phillies racked up two runs in the top of the first inning, but Belinsky gave up a quintet of runs during the home team's turn. He loaded the bases with a walk to Pete Rose, Tommy Harper's bunt single, and another walk to Vada Pinson. Frank Robinson drew a third walk, which scored Rose. Deron Johnson's sacrifice fly scored Harper, and Tony Pérez bashed a three-run homer into the Crosley Field stands for a 5–2 lead.

Reds lefty Joe Nuxhall gave up a run in the top of the third when Callison hit a leadoff homer. With the score 5–3, Pinson responded with a leadoff homer in the Reds' half, and Robinson got to first base with an infield single. Belinsky left the game. Final score: Reds 9, Phillies 4. Belinsky's 1965 record to date: 1–3. But the Phillies had been cloaking a major story from the public—Belinsky pitched with a cracked rib that he suffered during spring training.

It traced back to the April 2 game against the Braves. Belinsky said that the injury happened in the fifth inning, when "all of a sudden I could feel it tighten up on me." But the news leaked after Belinsky confided in Chance, who told an LA scribe about his buddy going on the disabled list. At first denying the news, the Phillies said the crack had healed. It could have been much worse. And no one knew or appreciated that more than Belinsky. "I'm just glad that nothing worse happened, that the rib didn't splinter or something like that."

The *Inquirer* reported, "He complained about it at the time, but it was believed to be a strain of some sort, and no X-rays were taken until this week." The impact remained, according to the pitcher once again described as "controversial" by the newspaper. "I don't know how much it affected my pitching, but I know there were times when I was short-arming the ball and not throwing naturally," said the southpaw. "I'm glad I didn't hurt my arm."³⁸

Mauch used him as a reliever for the next few games. He pitched two innings on June 1, two innings on June 5, one-third of an inning on June 6, and three innings on June 15. Belinsky enjoyed an exemplary return to the starting rotation with 10 strikeouts and six hits in a complete-game, 7–1 victory over the Astros at the Astrodome on June 20—the second half of a doubleheader. Again, Belinsky showed the control of a surgeon, walking one batter. But he also hit one. Philadelphia took the first game, 3–2.

Belinsky pitched next on June 25, a 4–1 loss to the Giants at Candlestick Park, bringing his record to 2–4. But he bounced back with a 7–1 win, courtesy of an explosive offense highlighted by three home runs against the Cardinals on June 29. Tony Gonzalez banged a homer to start the bottom of the fourth inning; Johnny Callison homered with Cookie Rojas on base. Dick Stuart's three-run shot in the bottom of the eighth stretched the lead to 7–1. It wasn't just the offense that supported Belinsky. "They made some great plays behind me," he observed. "That makes a pitcher keener to win the ball game."[39]

Mauch gave him the responsibility of starting a Phillies game on a day that Philadelphians celebrate with a deeper pride than anyplace else in the United States: Independence Day—an annual reminder of the gathering in Philadelphia of representatives from 13 colonies meeting, debating, and ultimately declaring independence from Great Britain on July 2, 1776, then ratifying their decision two days later. But the 189th anniversary of that historic event would not be joined by a celebration involving baseball. Belinsky gave up four runs to the Reds at Connie Mack Stadium before leaving in the sixth inning with one out. Philadelphia had scored once when Alex Johnson began the bottom of the fourth inning with a triple and scored on Amaro's single.

Burdette finished the game for the Phillies; Nuxhall threw a five-hitter for the Reds and recorded nine strikeouts in his 4–1 decision. Control eluded Belinsky like a legal victory eluded Los Angeles County District Attorney Hamilton Burger on *Perry Mason*, a disappointing outcome considering the southpaw's fine effort against the Cardinals a few days prior, inspiring the *Inquirer*'s Allen Lewis to discern that Belinsky threw "too many pitches outside the strike zone to be effective. He was behind too many hitters and, when he had to come in with a pitch, the Reds teed off."[40]

Belinsky tossed three scoreless innings in relief in the Pirates-Phillies game on July 6 at Connie Mack Stadium. He began the top of the sixth with the Pirates leading, 8–1; Philadelphia rebounded for three runs in the eighth inning, but got no further in the ninth, giving the visitors from western Pennsylvania an 8–4 win. Mauch called on the lefty for relief again in the second inning of the Giants-Phillies game on July 10, after the San Franciscans hammered Ray Culp for four runs in the top of the first. He did a formidable job of keeping the visitors quiet, leaving in the bottom of the sixth for a pinch-hitter. It gave Belinsky eight consecutive scoreless innings, a bright spot in an otherwise dismal day as the Giants tacked on three more runs against Jack Baldschun for a 7–0 blanking.

Belinsky started against the Cardinals on July 18, boosted by the Phillies' 14–7 victory a day earlier marked by 22 hits, including Callison's grand slam. Callison gave Belinsky a one-run lead in the top of the first with a solo home run, but Lou Brock's leadoff home run and Dick Groat scoring on a passed ball put the Cardinals ahead, 2–1. Belinsky maintained that score until the bottom of the sixth, when Tim McCarver hit a one-out homer. Burdette, Baldschun, and Gary Wagner combined relief efforts and prevented St. Louis from adding more runs, but Philly's bats failed to produce another score.

Pitching in relief again on July 21, Belinsky faced the top of the Cubs' order in the bottom of the 10th inning with the score tied, 7–7, at Wrigley Field. After retiring Glenn Beckert on a fly ball, he gave up the winning run on a sequence that ignited revelry on Chicago's North Side— Don Landrum singled, Billy Williams walked, and Ernie Banks hit a game-winning single.

In a doubleheader against the Mets at Shea Stadium on July 25, Belinsky started the first game and left in the bottom of the second inning after giving up four runs. The Phillies lost the game, 8–1, but won the second game. Despite his pitching efforts and lack of headlines indicating controversy, Belinsky's social reputation emerged as a descriptor in New York's *Daily News*, where Red Foley called the southpaw "the playboy of the Western world."[41]

Mauch gave him a passport to the bullpen for an indefinite term after the Mets game, his fourth consecutive loss. Philadelphia's manager didn't have a cure for the lefty, as the source of the problem could not be identified. "Whatever is wrong, he'll find out in the bullpen, because that's where he's going to be," stated Mauch. Belinsky admitted, "I'm tired of making explanations."[42]

When the August issue of *True—The Men's Magazine* hit the newsstands, Phillies fans either found delight or disgust in Belinsky's words about the team's heartbreaking end to the 1964 season; Myron Cope's article, "A Dialogue Between Baseball's Bigmouths," focused on Belinsky and Dick Stuart. Belinsky declared that he could have relieved the burden for the Philadelphia squad by drawing attention. "You know what I hadda done last year if we were that close to the flag and taking a nose dive? I would have gone out and got some big blonde and punched her right out, at Broad and Market. I would have knocked her right on her can and made the headlines in World War II print. Take the pressure off everybody, you know? In those last days, those ballplayers just didn't know what was happening. They needed a fall guy to take the heat off them."[43]

Justifying sex before a game rather than afterwards, Belinsky also argued that he was too tired when his pitching duties were finished and revealed that he wondered about the wisdom of this postgame paradigm. Fans, journalists, and insiders likely had the same concern. "I try to squeeze this extra curriculum in, but it doesn't work entirely, because after I party with a girl I'm on my way to the ball park and I'm thinking, 'What the hell did I do? Do I have enough energy to go two innings, three innings?' Just thinking about it shakes me a little."[44]

Mauch called on Belinsky to relieve Culp in a Cubs-Phillies game at Connie Mack Stadium on August 3. Taking the mound in the eighth inning with a 2–0 deficit, he retired the first two batters before Ernie Banks got a base hit and Ron Santo walked, but escaped further damage with Vic Roznovsky's grounder. Baldschun replaced him in the top of the ninth, notching two strikeouts plus a groundout. A rally for the Phillies did not occur, though. Belinsky also closed out the Phillies' 4–3 win on August 5, getting Billy Williams out on a fly ball to center fielder Adolfo Phillips.

In San Francisco, Mauch tapped the southpaw to take on the Giants in the bottom of the fifth inning with the Phillies trailing, 2–0, on August 13. Belinsky did fine, striking out two of the seven batters he faced. Alex Johnson pinch-hit for Belinsky in the top of the seventh inning and started a three-run rally; Gary Wagner kept the Giants to their deuce of scores, and Belinsky got credit for the 3–2 win.

Two nights later, Culp had a 4–1 cushion against the Giants going into the bottom of the third inning at Candlestick Park. He surrendered four runs; Belinsky relieved him with one out and retired the next two batters. Hal Lanier hit a leadoff triple off him in the bottom of the fourth to begin a four-run rally. Bill Henry singled home Lanier and got forced out at second by Matty Alou's ground ball to Phillies shortstop Bobby Wine. Alou stole second base, followed by Jim Davenport striking out, Willie Mays drawing an intentional walk, and Willie McCovey getting on base because Belinsky fielded a bouncing ball and threw wide of Stuart at first base. All three runners scored, McCovey coming around thanks to another error.

Johnny Callison's throw from right field to Phillies catcher Pat Corrales was on target, but the umpire called Mays safe at home while McCovey sprinted to third base. Corrales made an errant throw to Dick Allen, described by Bill Conlin in the *Philadelphia Daily News* as "off the box seats, about a mile past Allen."[45] McCovey scored.

Mauch kept his reliever on the Candlestick Park mound with the damage of the fourth inning totaling four more runs for the Giants and a 9–4 lead. After Len Gabrielson's leadoff home run an inning later and Tom Haller getting to first base on Belinsky's second error, Art Mahaffey relieved the lefty. But San Francisco's offense could not be stopped; McCovey's three-run bash in the sixth inning and Matty Alou's two-run double in the seventh increased the score to 15–4. Mahaffey stayed through the seventh inning, and Burdette closed out the eighth for a decidedly miserable afternoon.

Against the Reds on August 21, Belinsky took over for Baldschun with no outs in the top of the 11th inning at Connie Mack Stadium after Leo Cardenas's RBI single put the visitors up, 2–1. He got pinch-hitter Don Pavletich out on a grounder to Allen, then walked Tommy Harper and Pete Rose in succession to load the bases. Bobby Wine fielded Vada Pinson's ground ball, fired to Corrales for the force out, and Corrales responded in kind by nailing Harper at third base for a double play. The Phillies did not score or even threaten in the bottom of the eleventh.

During the same homestand, Belinsky took the mound in relief on August 25 against the Astros. With the score 3–3 at the end of five innings, he got the call to pitch in the top of the sixth and began by plunking shortstop Eddie Kasko. Houston scored two runs, one on an error charged to Belinsky and another on a wild pitch. The Astros won, 7–6, but the two innings for the left-hander didn't reflect a true accounting of his performance. Not one Astro clocked a ball to the outfield off Belinsky. He had a strong repertoire. "I'm disgusted with myself," he revealed after the game. "It would be different if I didn't have good stuff. I was throwing as good as I've ever thrown in my life. The man had confidence in me, bringing [me] into a 3–3 game."[46]

Mauch deferred to Belinsky when the Dodgers chipped away at the Phillies' 4–1 lead in the top of the third inning on August 27. Ray Herbert gave up two runs, leaving Belinsky a no-out, men-on-second-and-third situation; Belinsky loaded the bases by hitting Jim Lefebvre. Wes Parker grounded into a force out at home, but John Roseboro's single added two more tallies—Lou Johnson and Lefebvre.

The Dodgers scored another run in the fourth inning thanks to Johnson's sacrifice fly, which made the score 6–4. An inning later, Maury Wills doubled home Parker and Roseboro with one out. Lew Burdette took over for Belinsky and retired the next two Dodgers. Philadelphia notched a run in the bottom of the fifth to make the score 8–5, but Los Angeles responded with another tally in the top of the sixth when Lefebvre's double sent Johnson home from second base. Callison's solo home run changed the scoreboard to 9–6. Philly bounced back with two runs in the bottom of the ninth but couldn't overtake LA's lead.

Belinsky started on September 6 in the first game of a doubleheader against the Cardinals at Busch Stadium. He pitched six innings, allowing eight hits and four runs. When he left the mound, St. Louis had a 4–2 lead. Philly lost, 10–3. Belinsky received his next and last assignment of the 1965 season in the second half of a twin bill against the Mets, entering in the top of the fifth inning, facing a 2–0 deficit. He showed decent control—Kevin Collins and Ed Kranepool struck out looking, but Greg Goossen's two-out homer gave the Mets their third run. Mauch pulled his lefty for a pinch-hitter in the bottom of the sixth; New York continued blanking Philadelphia's offense until Tony Gonzalez's RBI double in the seventh inning gave the home team its only score of the game. Jim Hickman's solo home run in the top of the eighth accounted for the Mets' fourth and final run.

Pitcher vs. Manager

"My major problem was with the way Gene used me," disclosed Belinsky. "He got me because I was supposed to be his fourth starting pitcher. Then he used me starting, in long relief, and in short relief. My arm just couldn't take it. I never really was a very good pitcher after the 1965 season. I would have to say Gene Mauch had an awful lot to do with that."[47]

Belinsky had a concern in addition to Mauch's decisions regarding the pitching roster. More like an annoyance, really. His old boss stayed on a path to collect a hotel bill dating back two years. Angels owner Gene Autry claimed that Belinsky never paid for a stay at the Continental Hotel; Belinsky said he got a rate at the Los Angeles facility at more than one-third off the price. According to the entertainment mogul, Belinsky owed $210.

The parties did not disagree on whether Belinsky owed money, he just didn't accede to the amount because he believed his rate to be $30 per day, not $44. "It must be something personal," Belinsky opined. "My attorney says Autry's attorney told him Autry is willing to spend $1,000 just to collect. They wanted to garnishee [sic] my wages, but they set the hearing for a travel day and nobody appeared."

Whether bad blood enhanced the dispute belonged in the category of speculation. Belinsky thought so, explaining that the Angels gave him a raise of $3,000 and paid off his Cadillac after his no-hitter in 1962. But when he went to collect the money, he heard a different story. "At the end of the year I went in for my check and got the $3,000. Then I asked about the car payment. They said that was included in the $3,000, that they couldn't give me gifts."[48]

Reputational Baggage

The Phillies ended 1965 with an 85–76–1 record. As the holiday season cloaked Philadelphia in good cheer a couple of months later, thoughts about baseball had given way to the Eagles and 76ers. But Belinsky appeared in a tongue-in-cheek reference by the *Inquirer*'s Frank Dolson concerning the basketball team and its schedule, including a game in State Line [*sic*], Nevada, abutting Lake Tahoe's shoreline, without informing or seeking the permission of the NBA. It happened because the team voted on a venue after being promised a visit to Las Vegas if they won three of four road games.

> The 76ers instead decided on Lake Tahoe, a quieter place. Dolson pointed out that Philly's basketball team had wanted Playboy Bunnies to be mascots, an idea that the NBA squashed because fans would be ogling the women instead of absorbing themselves in the game. What the 76ers need is a general manager with the right qualifications—a motel on Lake Tahoe and a lifetime membership in the Playboy Club.
> Bo Belinsky might be an ideal choice. Or Dean Martin, if he's available. This team needs a social director, not a general manager.[49]

Indeed, reporters used Belinsky as a barometer for socializing. A profile of *The Man from U.N.C.L.E* star Robert Vaughn began, "If he put his mind to it, Robert Vaughn could be right up there with the top-ranked American playboys ... swingers like Hugh Hefner, Paul Hornung and Bo Belinsky."[50]

Reporters used him as a baseline for being a social bee buzzing from flower to flower, a metaphor applicable to bars or women. Belinsky simply could not shake the label, nor could he avoid a nasty reputation from the clash with Dyer. In early December 1965, a syndicated article from Copley News Service compared the fight to a recent dustup between singer Tommy Sands—who had begun an acting career—and a movie critic. Sands gained the nickname Sluggo when he went to the guy's office in an LA newspaper and belted him in the hall. Using the pitcher as a barometer for violence, the article read in part, "Fortunately, few performers in either sport or entertainment react to criticism with the belligerence of a Bo Belinsky or Sluggo Sands."[51]

1966 Spring Training

By mid–February of the Phillies' 1966 spring training, a group of 11 players—including Belinsky—had not signed a contract[52]; he signed on February 15.[53] However, "the colorful and often controversial hurler" refused to show up to the first practice. It worsened an already tense situation between Belinsky and his skipper, whom he blamed for his 4–9 record in 1965. Plus, the left-hander disapproved of working as a relief pitcher and theorized that Mauch would keep him on the roster rather than place him on the trading block, allowing a demotion to a team in the Phillies' farm system.

No explanation surfaced, at least not an apparent one. But Phillies GM John Quinn emphasized that contract terms did not yet require players to report. Invitations before the report date can be refused without a penalty, financial or otherwise.[54]

Belinsky ended his disappearing act on February 27, arriving in Clearwater, Florida, with an explanation about snow and car trouble in Texas delaying his journey from southern California. His tale included needing to get his Lincoln Continental towed 40 miles to Austin, where it took a day for repairs on top of him suffering from the flu. Besides this journey that Neil Simon could have used as comedy fodder for a screenplay, Belinsky addressed his off-season comments underscoring the friction between him and Mauch. "I just felt I had to answer Gene, and then put a stop to it," explained the pitcher. "Words weren't going to help anyone win any ball games."[55]

Mauch tapped Belinsky to be in his starting trio of hurlers along with Jim Bunning and Chris Short for the first exhibition game against the Reds,[56] which the Phillies lost, 4–2; Leo Cardenas banged a game-winning, two-run homer off Belinsky.[57] In his next game, Belinsky gave up one run and four hits during his four-inning stay on the mound against the Mets; it ended in a 3–3 tie after 15 innings. Mauch praised the pitcher, an occasion that hadn't been too evident in 1965. "If he takes that kind of stuff out there every time, he'll come back a winner," declared the Phillies' manager.[58]

Optimism lasted a few days. On March 22, an injury in his right leg forced Belinsky from the game in the fifth inning, sourced by "either a pulled muscle or a pinched nerve." It marred an otherwise exciting game, won by Bobby Wine breaking a 2–2 tie in the 12th inning with a leadoff round-tripper.[59] The following day, doctors diagnosed Belinsky with a pulled muscle to be treated by ice and heat plus trips to the whirlpool.[60] A week later, Belinsky contributed by pitching in batting practice for a bit but admitted that the leg was not 100 percent[61]. Another week went by and he did the same duty, with the leg described as "much improved."[62]

The *Inquirer* labeled him a "temperamental southpaw"[63] in a layout consisting of players' head shots and brief descriptions, accompanied by an equally unkind profile that could be viewed, perhaps justified, as payback because it referenced a Belinsky statement from the previous summer. "Philadelphia social life is for the birds," he had said. "As soon as the season ends, it will take me just two minutes to leave Philly."

Baseball can be a fickle game. The idea of a permanent exit from the game led Belinsky to posit, "I might just go to Hawaii and spend the rest of my life on a surfboard."

The *Inquirer*'s response: "A genuine flake, that Bo."[64]

8

Play Me or Trade Me

"Baseball is how I make my living"

As spring training wound down, Phillies fans had reason to believe that the 1966 team would be competitive, if not dominant, given their 85–76 record in 1965. But the National League had three teams that won at least 90 games and two more with better records, which left Philadelphia in sixth place for a ten-team league.

All eyes focused on the Dodgers now that the joint salary holdout by Sandy Koufax and Don Drysdale, lasting from late February to late March, had ended. Delighting not only Dodgers fans but also the front offices of NL teams relying on the duo to fill their stands when the Dodgers visited, the star pitchers and Dodgers general manager Buzzie Bavasi came to terms.

A key weapon in the arsenal of a team with two World Series titles in the last three seasons, Koufax led the majors with 382 strikeouts in 1965, exceeding the next-highest number by more than 100. Belinsky could compete with Koufax for fame, but it was sourced to his social life rather than his ballplaying. The man labeled "controversial" and "colorful" for his off-the-field actions had healed his leg injury enough to throw two innings in a game against the Pirates at the end of spring training. Belinsky gave up a hit and a walk in the 11–5 victory.

On April 20, Gene Mauch put him on the mound to start the top of the eighth inning with the Phillies trailing the Braves, 7–0, at Connie Mack Stadium. The sixth pitcher for the home team on this dismal night, he got a touch of immortality—the kind that pitchers likely didn't want—when Hank Aaron hit his second homer of the night and the 400th of his career, a solo dinger that rocketed more than 500 feet to lead off the top of the ninth inning. Philadelphia managed one run in their half of the inning.

Belinsky got the sign wrong. Clay Dalrymple wanted the lefty to throw a screwball, a prominent pitch in Belinsky's repertoire. But the slumping Aaron, who had one homer so far in 1966, bashed a fastball. The Braves won 8–1.[1]

Mauch showed his confidence in Belinsky two nights later when the Phillies had an 8–5 lead and the Reds scored two runs in the bottom of the eighth inning, closing the cushion to one run. With two outs and men on second and third, Belinsky came in and walked Pete Rose to load the bases, but he got the third out with Vada Pinson's ground ball to second baseman Tony Taylor, who flipped it to Dick Groat for a force out at second base. The Phillies scored in the top of the ninth for a 9–7 victory.

On May 14, Mauch used four pitchers in a home game against the Astros. Bob Buhl started and left in the top of the fifth inning with the score 3–1. Facing Joe Morgan on second base after a two-run double with one out, Darold Knowles retired Sonny Jackson on a grounder to Tony Taylor at third base. An intentional walk to Jimmy Wynn was followed by a walk to Jim Gentile. He escaped damage with the bases loaded by striking out Rusty Staub. Belinsky started the top of the sixth; Philadelphia tied the game thanks to Taylor's two-run triple in the bottom of the inning.

Houston nicked Belinsky for two walks and four hits, but no runs in four innings. Mauch sent in Harvey Kuenn to pinch-hit for the southpaw after Taylor hit a one-out single in the bottom of the ninth. Philly failed to score. Houston notched three runs in the top of the 11th, and the Phillies responded with two runs, giving the visitors a 6–5 win.

Belinsky's first start in 1966 took place at the Astrodome on May 20. The Astros scored two runs in the bottom of the second inning on Felix Mantilla's solo home run and Larry Dierker's RBI single. Belinsky contributed a run in the top of the third by knocking a leadoff single, going to second base on Taylor's single, sprinting to third on Groat's double-play grounder, and scoring on Bill White's single. Mauch pulled him in the bottom of the third after Jackson struck out and Wynn got on base with an infield single. Cookie Rojas won the game for the Phillies in the top of the tenth inning with a sacrifice fly that scored Kuenn, who had reached third base on a double and Bob Uecker's sacrifice bunt; Uecker got on first anyway with a fielder's choice.

On May 29, Belinsky performed the duties of a closer and started the bottom of the 10th inning at Candlestick Park with Philadelphia and San Francisco tied, 5–5. He hit Jim Ray Hart, who went to third base on Jim Davenport's single and scored the game-winning run on Ollie Brown's single.

The southpaw made one thing clear at the beginning of June. He wanted to pitch. Period. If Mauch didn't have opportunities for him, then perhaps the team's minor league system did. But the press continuing to use words like "colorful" added to a carefree image that Belinsky tried to discourage regarding his job. "I make $17,000 [a] year and I spend every cent of it," he revealed. "Some people have the idea that baseball is just a sideline with me, but that's not so. Baseball is how I make my living, and I just don't want to get buried. I have too good an arm."

There was no friction with his manager or the front office, at least not publicly. Belinsky needed spots; whatever Mauch offered did not suffice. Praising the ball club, which he predicted would win the NL flag, Belinsky shared, "I want to be a part of it, but being used the way I am is just eating me up inside."[2]

He got another chance on June 5 against the Giants at Connie Mack Stadium. It began on a positive note but didn't end well. Ray Herbert relieved Bob Buhl with a 6–5 lead in the top of the ninth, but San Francisco played some fundamental baseball to tie the score. Tito Fuentes singled and advanced on Len Gabrielson's sacrifice bunt, then scored when Willie Mays singled. Belinsky relieved Herbert with one out, striking out Willie McCovey and fielding Hart's grounder for the third out.

In the top of the 10th, Belinsky had nobody on base and two outs when Hal Lanier, San Francisco's #8 hitter, came to the plate. Phillies catcher Clay Dalrymple decided that a fastball would be appropriate. Belinsky disagreed and tossed "a high, hanging curve ball" that Lanier—who sported a .191 batting average before the game—crushed off the Philadelphia ballpark's façade in the upper deck, left field to be precise, and broke the 6–6 tie.

Mauch's comments reflected the frustration felt by Phillies fans, though his reported words were likely more moderate than the actual verbiage. "It disturbs you a little bit when your catcher and pitcher let a No. 8 hitter hit a home run with the pitcher coming up next."[3]

San Diego

Eight days later, the Phillies sent Belinsky to their Triple-A farm team—the San Diego Padres in the Pacific Coast League. He couldn't escape his reputation, even upon his egress. The caption for his photo in the *Inquirer* read: "Controversial lefthander Bo Belinsky, who was farmed out to San Diego by the Phillies on Monday."[4]

The Padres had a rich history dating back to 1903, when the Sacramento Solons became one of six charter members of the Pacific Coast League. The team continued through a brief mid-season change of location and name in 1914 to the San Francisco Missions; a three-year stint as the Salt Lake Bees; 11 years as the Hollywood Stars; and the San Diego Padres since 1936. Ted Williams, Bobby Doerr, Minnie Miñoso, Tommy

Helms, and Tony Pérez had all worn the Padres' uniform, so Belinsky would be joining a roster with royalty in its lineage.

You can't beat the weather in southern California, a great bonus for the New Jersey native. Practicality also intervened. San Diego offered a sunny retreat where he could hone his skills. If Belinsky either delayed his exodus or didn't go, another club would likely not touch him. "I still thought I could pitch," he said. "I was fooling myself because I didn't want to face up to any alternatives. I was twenty-nine, had no dough, a bad arm, and no future. It looked pretty sour for a while. But I figured I could get myself together in a place like San Diego. There would be no pressure, and maybe I would do well enough to get another job with another club."[5]

Belinsky had experienced the heights of success with the no-hitter complemented by the perquisites of fame in Los Angeles. His life may have seemed desirable as he dated actresses and played in the major leagues, but few understood the cost demanded of a ballplayer with his notoriety. Anonymity proved impossible. Workouts could be grueling. Plus, he endured the mental toll of being shipped to the minor leagues and trying to prove himself worthy of joining a major league club again.

The weather plus San Diego's laid-back lifestyle made a good combination for the fun-loving, loose-living ballplayer who had accepted his fate while believing it was unwarranted. "But sometimes a demotion is the best thing, so you can get started again," Belinsky opined. "I have too many splinters in my tail here."[6]

Moreover, he had the idea to play for the Padres because the Phillies presented a lack of sufficient opportunities under Gene Mauch's leadership. Or so he claimed. "Let's face it; I'm not going to get anywhere on the Phils as long as he's there. So I want out."[7] Whoever had the idea, it surprised Padres manager Frank Lucchesi. "I knew there was a possibility we might get Belinsky, but I knew nothing about his optioning when I left San Diego," he revealed.[8]

Belinsky delighted San Diegans in his debut with the Padres on June 18 for the first six innings, blanking the Seattle Angels before faltering in the seventh. Seattle scored a run in the seventh on a walk, a stolen base, another walk, a wild throw by the third baseman that sent the runner on second to third, a pinch-hit RBI single, and another RBI single. Belinsky managed to retire two Angels along the way, but he went to the clubhouse after the second Angels run. San Diego lost, 6–1, after winning a makeup game, 5–1, in Tacoma earlier that day against the Giants.

Belinsky faced his old team, the Islanders, in his next start on June 24. Again, control became a factor for the lanky southpaw; two wild pitches led to Hawaii's first run. Jerry Kushner drew a walk to lead off the bottom of the third inning, took second on a wild pitch, reached third on an infield out, and scored on the second wild pitch. Belinsky gave up a second run in the sixth inning, which prompted Lucchesi to call on his bullpen. Hawaii won, 4–3.[9]

The journey to Belinsky's first victory with San Diego was anything but smooth. After losing his first two games, the Padres' new import delivered a 4–3 win against the Portland Beavers on June 29 with 10 strikeouts, three walks, five hits, and one hit by pitch. Portland's offense worked him to a full count 10 times; Belinsky registered five strikeouts in these situations. Owning a 4–1 lead into the ninth inning, he stumbled when the Beavers drew a leadoff walk followed by a two-run clout. Two relief pitchers combined to stem the bleeding and protect the 4–3 lead. Belinsky threw 129 pitches.[10]

Finding His Place

Moving to San Diego had a therapeutic significance that he likely would not have gotten in a more rural and less cosmopolitan city. Knowing that he did not belong in the upper echelon of pitchers neither diminished nor depressed Belinsky but distinguished him as a fellow who knew his station and just wanted to play baseball. His name would not be associated with Koufax, Drysdale, Kaat, Marichal, Grant, or Gibson. But he believed in his value like a Wall Street analyst believes in an undervalued stock. "Coming here is the best thing that could happen to me physically, even if it may not be the best thing for my career," said the left-hander. "But then, sometimes you have to change direction a few times to get where you're going."[11]

After he retired from baseball, Belinsky clarified that the experience in San Diego and other stops in his minor league career provided perspective on a see-saw journey back and forth to the majors. "If I had to live my life over, I wouldn't mind pitching in the minor leagues for twenty years," said Belinsky. "There are a hell of a lot worse ways to make a living. There are some swinging towns in this country, and you can pretty much call your own shot down there. There's no pressure in the minor leagues, not much competition, and nobody is trying to use you to get ahead with somebody or something."[12]

Padres games aired on KOGO-AM, which could be picked up in the Los Angeles area.

Los Angeles Times writer Don Page encouraged baseball fans to tune in and declared, "Belinsky is the hottest attraction San Diego's had since the zoo."[13] Heading toward his second win on July 3, which would have extended San Diego's winning streak to five, Belinsky had a 5–3 lead against the Phoenix Giants in the eighth inning and left the Westgate Park mound after walking the leadoff batter; a three-run bashing gave Phoenix a 6–5 victory.[14]

The Padres inaugurated a 15-game homestand on July 8 with Belinsky pitching against the Islanders, dominating his former team with a 10–1 victory marked by nine strikeouts; three home runs highlighted the offense. But control issues emerged during his seven innings on the mound. Although the southpaw allowed three hits, he went to a full count eight times.[15]

For women interested in Belinsky's eligibility, an item in the column of *San Diego Union* scribe Frank Rhoades squashed their notions; a fashion model from Los Angeles had been visiting the pitcher, who next took on the Seattle club.[16] He had the July 12 home game in his hands. Literally. A passed ball on a third strike led to an unearned run, marring an otherwise unblemished performance by the model-dating pitcher until the sixth inning. Jay Johnstone got on base when Belinsky "was slow to cover" on a ground ball hit to Cal Emery, San Diego's first baseman. Felix Torres—his former teammate—smacked the ball back to the mound. Belinsky "bobbled" it and then "threw wildly," and Johnstone scored. Bubba Morton notched one of his three singles, which accounted for another score when Torres crossed the plate.

In the seventh inning, Seattle scored three more times to secure a 6–0 shutout. Belinsky left with two outs, and even though the score might be disappointing, Padres fans could be comforted by the southpaw having great control at times—two walks and seven strikeouts. Angels pitcher Andy Messersmith did not allow a Padres hit; Bill Kelso limited them to one hit for the rest of the game.[17]

Belinsky had pitched in six games with 44 strikeouts in 41 innings and a 3.29 ERA. But the Seattle game was the last for a while as Belinsky nursed "a sore foot," plus he received a $50 fine for coming late to a game.[18] Lucchesi called on him for some light relief work against the Denver Bears on July 29—one batter resulting in a strikeout. Denver won, 4–3.[19]

In the summer of 1966, the espionage genre dominated popular culture. There had been three additional James Bond movies since *Dr. No* premiered in 1962; TV audiences watched reruns of *The Man from U.N.C.L.E.*, *I Spy*, and *Get Smart*. This last show, a parody, starred Don Adams as Maxwell Smart, a spy with the code name Agent 86 working for the agency CONTROL. It featured many hallmarks—shoe phone, Cone of Silence, and the phrase "Would you believe_____?" when Smart tried to convince the other person of something. Harrington's, an appliance store with two locations in the North Park neighborhood of San Diego and the city of El Cajon, utilized this popular culture iconography in a newspaper advertisement that *San Diego Union* readers absorbed on their way to find out the latest information on Belinsky and their beloved Padres. The caption at the top of the ad read: "Would You Believe? Appliance prices are lower now at Harrington's than they were in 1949—make us prove it!!"[20]

Belinsky started against the Tulsa Oilers on August 6, taking a 4–0 lead into the seventh inning. Tulsa put two men on base with back-to-back singles; Belinsky left the game. A wild pitch by relief pitcher Ed Roebuck sent the first Oiler across the plate; a two-run single closed the Padres' lead to 4–3. Tulsa rebounded with two more runs in the eighth inning for a 5–4 comeback victory.[21]

The Padres gave Belinsky terrific run support to start his next outing on August 11, scoring four times against the Phoenix Giants in the top of the first inning. Phoenix responded with a triple and a single for a run. Three successive walks began the bottom of the second inning. Lucchesi went to the mound; Belinsky went to the clubhouse. San Diego scored five more times. Thankfully, Bill Wilson handled the opposition; Steve Ridzik secured a 9–3 win for the Padres.[22]

If his performance in Arizona disappointed, then his next one in Tulsa depressed. The *San Diego Union* described it as "disastrous." That's putting it mildly. San Diego drew first blood with two runs in the top of the first inning. The Oilers pounded Belinsky for six runs in their half before they registered an out. Wilson relieved him and struck out 10 in the Padres' 15–9 victory.[23]

Belinsky's subpar displays didn't seem to affect the assessment by the Phillies' front office, which recalled the southpaw to the parent club in late August, along with fellow Padres hurlers Gary Wagner and Grant Jackson, in addition to buying Padres backstop Jim Schaffer and recalling shortstop Gary Sutherland. But it wasn't yet clear whether Belinsky and the pitchers would need to report after the Padres' season ended or to spring training with Philadelphia. In early October, Belinsky and three other pitchers plus another shortstop got released to San Diego.[24]

An appearance in mid-October had already been scheduled for the Dodgers' two-game exhibition in Hawaii against an amalgamation of players called the All-Stars. "I've been working pretty hard to get my pitching arm in shape," said Belinsky. "I am not anticipating a long tenure on the mound but I'll go as long as I can. And I'll give it all I have."[25]

He threw four innings in the first game. Result: two hits, two runs, one walk, and one strikeout. The Dodgers won, 6–2. He kept them in goose eggs for two innings in the second game.[26]

It had been quite a year. Belinsky got his name in the newspaper aside from his personal life or professional achievements when the September

9 edition of the *Shreveport Journal* used his first name as the "6 Down" answer to the clue "Belinsky" in a crossword puzzle.[27]

Houston in '67

Belinsky's 2–4 record with the Padres encompassed a 4.83 ERA across 54 innings pitched in 13 games. But when he had control, it was as obvious as a sunset over Coronado Island, averaging one strikeout per inning. *Honolulu Advertiser* sports editor Red McQueen used Belinsky's exhibition performance as a foundation for a scenario that undoubtedly whetted the appetites of sportswriters, particularly those in southern California— Bo Belinsky in a Dodgers uniform. Describing the pitcher as being in "rare form," McQueen acknowledged Belinsky's clash with Braven Dyer but pointed out that no incidents had occurred since then. "It is our guess that he still has some years to go as a Major League pitcher," wrote the scribe. "If nothing else, he could work four or five effective innings as either a starter or a reliever."[28]

Jim Hackleman's game account for the same day's edition of the *Honolulu Star-Bulletin* complemented McQueen's idea: "Dodgers were impressed by Bo Belinsky's showing in the Sunday night game, and more than one indicated they wouldn't mind having the carefree southpaw on their side."[29]

Alas, it was not to be. During an off-season stint in the Venezuelan League, Belinsky learned of his next team change; Houston selected him in baseball's winter meetings draft with a $25,000 price tag. It partially fulfilled a prediction that Belinsky had offered in mid-September: the Astros would obtain him in a trade with the Phillies.[30]

Pittsburgh took another 29-year-old left-hander in the draft—Juan Pizarro. Astros skipper Grady Hatton dismissed the controversies about Belinsky leaving the Angels after slugging Dyer and being southern California's answer to Casanova. "So what if he likes girls. Who doesn't? He attracts attention wherever he goes, and he gets publicity. I'm sure the Mamie Van Doren thing helped give him the image he has, and the incident with the baseball writer did too. But he keeps himself in shape; that's what counts."

Hatton pointed out that a southpaw filled the team's needs and revealed his strategy on assigning Belinsky to the bullpen, with a chance to become a starter if one of the starting pitchers didn't perform up to expectations. "I just talked to him, and he was very happy," said the Astros' manager. "His exact words were, 'I can win. I can help your ball club.' He's very happy to come with us."[31]

Belinsky had traveled around baseball like a nomad but remained optimistic about playing for the Astros. From his standpoint, neither attitude nor ability prevented him from contributing to a major league team. If he got the ball, he could add value. That's what he believed, anyway. The Astros, too. Houston presented a clean slate, which Belinsky honored with eagerness, confidence, and flexibility. "I'd like a chance to start, but I'll pitch anywhere Hatton wants me to," said the hurler. "If he wants me to pitch relief, I'll be glad to do it. I know I can still win up there. [Gene] Mauch never gave me much of an opportunity at Philadelphia."[32]

Humility emerged. But his reputation, whether earned or embellished, had chipped away at the passion that one presumes is a prerequisite to be a professional athlete at the highest level. Baseball remained a focus, though not a primary one. "I want to play baseball, but I don't have the true desire for a great champion," disclosed Belinsky. Even for a member of an eighth-place team, those are not the words that fans want to hear from any player. Belinsky mentioned that the Dyer incident and the Angels' suspension caused him to take the game in a less serious manner.[33]

During spring training in Cocoa, Florida, he got the structure that he needed in the way that a fish needs water. Bunking with 60 players in the team's dormitory may have been bland and boring, as Belinsky pointed out the 180-degree difference from the Riviera Hotel in Palm Springs, where the Angels stayed during spring training. "But this is all right for me," observed the southpaw. "It's a novelty, and it keeps me in tow. I'll get regular sleep and maintain my weight. I never felt healthier than I do now. At any age you sort of welcome a situation like this. It's sort of a second breath."[34]

Belinsky's assessment of the Astros lasted through spring training. In late March, he emphasized again that he wanted to work but added praise for pitching coach Gordon Jones deciphering mistakes and tailoring solutions that were not generic. "Gordon has encouraged me," said the lefty. "He tries to treat you as an individual pitcher. In a lot of camps, like Philadelphia, they say Chris Short and Jim Bunning are successful this way, so you do it that way, too."[35]

But the pitcher's reputation for late-night escapades overshadowed his ballplaying once again when he broke curfew, even after he got an extension past the midnight deadline. It was reported that six players had previously been fined during spring training. Hatton assessed him a $100 fine. Belinsky confessed, "I've kept the curfew since I've been here, but a guy's got to break it sometime if he is human. So I joined the other fellows."[36]

Spring training gave Belinsky a bonding opportunity beyond collaboration with coaches and socializing with the opposite sex, though. He took a liking to a black and white sheep terrier that began to hang around the Astros' facility. And vice versa. *Alfie* had been a popular film recently, inspiring him to use the name for the dog. A bit mangy at first, Alfie benefited from Belinsky's largesse—a visit to the veterinarian for a thorough grooming and to get rid of ticks. Alfie complemented Belinsky, who maintained a new maturity while putting his reputation in context. "Everybody makes mistakes," he said. "I made a few but not as many as they said. And never real big ones. I mean where I was in serious trouble."[37]

A man came to the Astros' spring training clubhouse, claiming to be the dog's owner. After some haggling, Belinsky agreed to buy the dog—"a black and grey cocker spaniel and poodle" whose original name was Brownie—for a team photo, two baseballs autographed by the team, signed photos of every player, and $30.[38]

Another surprise visitor for Belinsky did not get as welcoming a treatment as Alfie did, when a woman pounded on the door of his hotel room in Oklahoma City. Though he wasn't known for rebuffing members of the fairer sex often, Belinsky kept his door closed to the woman, who remained "unidentified" in press reports. Her insistence mattered nothing to Belinsky, who said that he was on the phone with his parents in Trenton and "had a hard time explaining to them about the pounding on the door." After 45 minutes, Belinsky had enough. A "house detective" took the woman away.[39]

In the first few weeks of the season, Hatton used Belinsky three times, all in Astros losses against the Reds. He pitched one and one-third innings on April 15. Houston's manager used six pitchers including Belinsky—who pitched two-thirds of an inning—on April 22. The following day, Belinsky replaced Don Wilson with no outs in the first inning after Cincinnati's batsmen smacked five consecutive singles and scored four runs.

Houston rebounded in the bottom of the second. John Bateman and Bob Aspromonte singled, and Ron Davis's homer put the Astros within a run. Belinsky handled the Reds through five innings, allowing one base hit when Tommy Helms doubled to lead off the fourth. Helms doubled again in the sixth, off Carroll Sembera. It scored Tony Pérez, who had also doubled, for the game's final run and a 5–3 loss for Houston.[40]

Hatton dubbed Belinsky the starting pitcher against the Cubs at the Astrodome on April 30. He left the game with a 4–0 deficit after six innings, but a positive note could not be overlooked. Seven strikeouts displayed his control. Belinsky went back to the bullpen and got called twice for fireman's work in May, against the Giants on May 14 and against the Dodgers on May 16.

Three weeks later, he made his second start. It was a glorious night for the Astros. They took on the Cardinals and exploded for a 17–1 victory at Busch Stadium on June 7; St. Louis used six pitchers. Belinsky had been working a shutout with a 3–0 lead in the sixth inning when the home team scored its only run courtesy of Orlando Cepeda drawing a walk, moving to second base on Mike Shannon's groundout, and scoring on Tim McCarver's double. It was the fifth hit for St. Louis.

Alex Johnson had led off the inning with a strikeout, Belinsky's only "K" in his five and two-thirds innings. Claude Raymond came in from the bullpen and rode an amazing offensive display. Three runs in the top of the seventh. Six runs in the top of the eighth. Five runs in the top of the ninth.

Houston's pummeling did not include a home run among the 23 hits. Aspromonte, Rusty Staub, Jim Landis, and Ron Brand anchored the batsmen by knocking in three runs each. Landis scored once, and the rest of the quartet scored twice. Belinsky showed gratitude in getting the opportunity to be a starter but kept an eye on the past for context, not bitterness. "I'm glad that Mr. Hatton had the confidence to start me," said the hurler. "I felt bad because I hadn't been in many games after coming from the Gene Mauch regime [at Philadelphia] for two years."[41]

Hatton gave him another chance on June 11. Belinsky showed some endurance in the second game of a doubleheader against the Reds at Crosley Field, lasting seven and one-third innings in which he scattered five hits, allowed three runs, walked two, and struck out two. Belinsky departed with a 4–3 lead, but Cincinnati's five-run rally in the bottom of the ninth gave the Astros an 8–4 loss and a no-decision for him.

A story about Belinsky's social life reminded Houston's fans about the baggage that came with the lefty. While amusing, the alleged antics might also trigger questions about dedication to ballplaying, especially considering the nonchalant response to a fine for breaking the team's curfew. The date of the incident was uncertain, but an item in the *Cincinnati Enquirer* mentioned that it happened "recently" and caused Hatton to declare the $100 penalty. According to Hatton, Belinsky replied, "That's okay, Skip. This night was worth it."[42]

Belinsky's behavior couldn't have been far from the minds of Astros fans, players, and management when the Braves tagged him for three runs—two unearned—in the top of the first inning on June 16 at the Astrodome. A walk, a hit by pitch, and two wild pitches highlighted a lack of control. Belinsky left the game with two outs in the second inning; Atlanta had runners on first and second thanks to two walks. Later, Houston whittled down the visitors' 8–3 lead to tie the game, but the Braves scored a run in the top of the 10th inning to win.

Rebounding with a respectable showing by tossing seven innings in his next start against the St. Louis Cardinals on June 20, Belinsky showed better control—one walk and six hits. Hatton pulled him from the mound with Houston trailing, 3–2. St. Louis piled on three more runs in the eighth for a 6–2 victory.

He had a similar outing on June 25, lasting six and one-third innings against the Cubs in the second game of a Wrigley Field doubleheader. The teams battled in a scoreless tie through five innings; Ernie Banks's two-run homer in the sixth broke it; and Belinsky ended his stay in the Friendly Confines with the Cubs leading, 4–0. More runs followed, giving Chicago's NL ball club an 8–0 victory.

While music during the "Summer of Love" filled the hearts of America's youth with "Happy Together," "All You Need Is Love," "Somebody to Love," and other songs emblemizing peace, togetherness, and amity, baseball filled the hearts of its followers with another outstanding season. Jim Lonborg, Earl Wilson, and Mike McCormick each won 22 games, tying them for the most wins in the majors.

Tom Seaver showcased his repertoire, stamina, and dedication, leading to Rookie of the Year honors and a tie for second place in complete games in the majors with Dean Chance, Juan Marichal, and Gaylord Perry. Chance threw a no-hitter; Eddie Mathews hit his 500th home run; and Carl Yastrzemski clobbered American League pitchers on his way to winning the Triple Crown.

Belinsky plodded along against this backdrop with a display of dominance against the Mets on July 31. But the game didn't start on a positive note. The New Yorkers tallied two runs in the top of the first during a sequence that began with Bud Harrelson walking and Bob Aspromonte's error allowing Cleon Jones to get to first base. Tommy Davis—imported from the Dodgers in a trade the day after the Astros selected Belinsky—banged a base hit, scoring Harrelson from second base and advancing Jones to third. Belinsky loaded the bases with a walk to Ron Swoboda and sent Jones across the plate for the second Met run on a wild pitch while facing Ed Charles. Settling down, he struck out Charles and Greg Goossen.

Ron Davis hit a leadoff home run in the bottom of the first. Joe Morgan followed with a double, a steal, and the second Houston run when Jimmy Wynn grounded out to Harrelson at shortstop. Bob Lillis put the home team up, 3–2, with an RBI single in the bottom of the fourth.

Belinsky gave a bravura performance after walking Harrelson with two outs in the second inning. Ending 19 consecutive at-bats by the Mets with a return to the bench, Belinsky displayed the composure that Houston's front office craved. Pitching a one-hitter looked like a highly significant possibility as Belinsky took the Astrodome's mound in the ninth inning with a one-run lead, but Davis banged a single for his second hit of the night. Mets skipper Wes Westrum replaced him with pinch-runner Dick Selma. Swoboda walked, inspiring Hatton to spell Belinsky with Larry Sherry. Charles grounded out to Astros shortstop Lillis, resulting in a force out of Swoboda at second base, while Selma took third. Larry Stahl pinch-hit for Goossen and popped up to Lillis, followed by Ed Kranepool whiffing to end the game and give Belinsky the win for a 3–6 record.

Hatton provided insight on Houston's ace of the moment, who revived negatives instead of focusing on positives. "Sure, Bo likes the limelight," said the skipper. "I tell him to go out and win 20 games, there's the limelight. But he always goes back to the past. To some manager. To somebody he punched in the nose 10 years ago. I don't give a corn dog about the past."[43]

Echoing his comments when the Astros selected Belinsky and affirming that the recent curfew breaking was not an isolated instance, Hatton favored potential instead of postgame activities: "He's got a fantastic arm. The other stuff, that playboy stuff, I don't give a damn about. I didn't get the SOB to raise. I got him to pitch. I got three children of my own to raise. I got enough trouble raising them. He knows the rules. If he breaks them, he pays. Sometimes he comes to me with money and says 'Here, it was worth it.'"[44]

Belinsky lost his next two starts, bringing his record to 3–8. On August 9, Hatton removed him after he gave up five runs to the Reds in two and two-thirds innings, underscored by hitting a batter and Tony Pérez's two-run blast. Houston lost the game, 7–3. He didn't last even that long against the Braves on August 13: one and two-thirds innings. Hatton yanked Belinsky after Atlanta scored four times in the first inning courtesy of two homers—Mack Jones's solo shot and Rico Carty's blast with Joe Torre and Clete Boyer on base—and once in the second inning. With two outs, Dave Eilers replaced him. Astros relievers Carroll Sembera and Sherry also pitched in the 8–4 loss.

The next two starts resulted in no-decisions. Belinsky had a 4–2 lead against the Braves on August 24 with six strikeouts going into the seventh inning, but Charlie Lau's pinch-hit, leadoff walk caused Hatton to replace him with Sherry. Atlanta later tied the game, but Houston scored in the bottom of the tenth for a 5–4 victory credited to Eilers. A week later, Belinsky had an uneven showing with seven strikeouts and five walks in seven innings at the second facility named Busch Stadium, which debuted in 1966. St. Louis led, 3–1, when Belinsky left the game and added a couple of insurance runs for a final score of 5–1.

Belinsky finished his 1967 season at Dodger Stadium with a splendid performance in terms of stamina, but control issues surfaced again. Through nine innings, he struck out six and walked six in the second game of a doubleheader; Belinsky hadn't gone that far for Houston until this game. LA notched three hits, and both teams failed to score until Jimmy Wynn led off the top of the 11th inning with a home run. Handling the Dodgers in the 10th and 11th innings gave Eilers credit for the 1–0 victory. Los Angeles won the first game, 4–1.

Off the field, Belinsky enjoyed the good life. During road trips, the Astros paired him with catcher Ron Brand. They were about as different as Felix and Oscar in *The Odd Couple*, a recent play authored by comedy genius Neil Simon. "Brand was a nondrinking, nonsmoking Mormon whose most foul word was 'shoot,'" wrote Maury Allen. Belinsky's roommate recalled one night in New York, where they had dinner at Voisin, a high-end restaurant. "I think of those days with Bo and I can only think how insecure he was, how much he did for show, how much he had to live up to what people expected of him. He would always say, 'I never did half of what guys write about me, but it doesn't hurt so I let it go on.' In a way, it was sad, very sad."[45]

Hatton praised Belinsky for his efforts throughout the season. "He has pitched some real good ball games for us," said the manager. "He pitched well twice against the Cards and twice against the Reds." Further insight came from Dodgers outfielder Al Ferrara, who said, "People look at his record (3–9) and think Bo can't pitch, but he sure looks good every time I see him. He has great stuff."[46]

It wasn't great enough. In mid–November, the Astros' front office identified Belinsky, Eilers, Dan Schneider, and Howie Reed from the pitching staff, along with infielder Lee Bales and outfielder Duke Sims, for assignment with the Oklahoma City 89ers in the Pacific Coast League. Belinsky did not adhere to the orders right away. It would take a sizable salary, though he kept his desired range to himself. "If they want me to play for Oklahoma City, it will have to be for a considerable amount of money," declared the newly designated hurler.[47]

9

Aloha, Again!

The Playboy and the Playmate

As the Astros prepared for the 1968 season in February at their facility in Cocoa, Florida, Bo Belinsky hadn't yet put his John Hancock on a contract. It prompted a palpable despondency for one admirer—Alfie, the dog who had gained his affection during the previous year's spring training and lived with one of Belinsky's friends during the winter. "Alfie ran from player to player apparently searching for his old friend, but finally gave up and sat forlornly waiting for him," reported a local newspaper.[1]

Through late February, Belinsky remained the only unsigned member of the pitching staff.[2] Technically, he belonged to the Astros' Oklahoma City squad, though the preseason offered an opportunity to make the major leagues again.[3] But his problem during spring training of 1968 did not concern signing his contract, honing his curveball, or remembering a batter's tendencies. It involved a woman. Naturally.

Jo Collins was *Playboy*'s Playmate of the Year in 1965 and the Playmate of the Month in December 1964. Beyond tantalizing thousands of men with her beauty, Collins served her country by fulfilling the request of soldiers stationed in Vietnam. It began with a letter. On behalf of his fellow soldiers in Company B, 2nd Battalion, 503rd Infantry, 173rd Airborne Brigade, 2nd Lt. John Price wrote to *Playboy* founder and editor Hugh Hefner in November 1965, about the challenges of being thousands of miles from home.

Roses are the order of the day as two members of Company B welcome Jo to Vietnam on behalf of their wounded Project Playmate officer, Lietutenant John Price, hospitalized at battalion headquarters in Bien Hoa.

> The loneliness here is a terrible thing—and we long to see a real, living, breathing American girl. Therefore, we have enclosed with this letter a money order for a lifetime subscription to PLAYBOY magazine for B Company. It is our understanding that, with the purchase of a lifetime subscription in the U.S.,

> the first issue is personally delivered by a Playmate. It is our most fervent hope that this policy can be extended to include us. ... Any one of the current Playmates of the Month would be welcomed with open arms, but if we have any choice in the matter, we have unanimously decided that we would prefer the 1965 Playmate of the Year—Miss Jo Collins.
>
> If we are not important enough ... to send a Playmate for, please just forget about us and we will quietly fade back into the jungle.

Hefner took action because, in his words, the words were "too moving to just put aside and forget."

Navigating around the bureaucracy for what Hefner labeled Project Playmate, he worked with the Defense Department to speed up the operation because Price got wounded on January 3, 1966. Six days later, Collins, along with her chaperone and photographer, left San Francisco for South Vietnam, where she met Price as he recovered from his "severely wounded arm" at a combat hospital.

On January 13, Collins and her troupe left the war-torn region with an abundance of pride and emotion. Later recalling her hospital visits, she emphasized a poignant moment that would have shaken a five-star general to his core.

> A couple of times I was sure I would break down and bawl like a baby, but I managed to control myself until they brought in a badly wounded buddy who asked if he could see me before going into surgery. When I got to his side, he was bleeding heavily from both legs and I didn't know what to do or say to comfort him. Then he looked up at me with his best tough-guy grin and simply said, "Hi, gorgeous." After that, I lost all control and the old tears really flowed.

She had begun her entertainment career as a model presenting products on the game show *Queen for a Day*.[4] At an art show displaying Liberace's work, a *Playboy* photographer asked her to pose. Initially declining, she took his card and later reached out when money got tight.[5] Film producers cast her in minor film roles, beginning with an uncredited role in *Ski Party* followed by *How to Stuff a Wild Bikini*, *Sergeant Dead Head*, *Lord Love a Duck*, and *Fireball 500*. It seemed like Collins had a platform for a solid acting career, but she saw that show business in the 1960s had requirements that she refused to endure. "To make it as a big star you have to pay a terrible price," observed the *Playboy* model. "I didn't want to sleep around with producers and agents. I didn't want to go out with guys just to get my name in the papers. I thought I could become a good actress just by hard work. But there's a hell of a lot more to Hollywood success than that."[6]

Collins captured the imagination of thousands of *Playboy* readers and the gratitude of those soldiers, but she had Belinsky's heart. The couple met in Hawaii. Belinsky ambled to a cabana where "several of his friends had gathered for an afternoon drink." Among them was the woman whom Belinsky had stood up the previous night. She sulked and chastised Belinsky, who began to talk with a beach boy named Fat, whom Collins knew as well. Fat suggested that a group go to a different place, and Belinsky tagged along when he saw that Collins was leaving. He kissed her at the bar, and a romance began.

Although she kept a date that night with another guy, Belinsky occupied her thoughts. The next morning, he sent her roses with a card asking her out to dinner. Contrary to what people might have intuited regarding Belinsky's idea of a good date based on press accounts of him frequenting bars and nightclubs, they enjoyed a rather mellow evening. "We went out, had a very pleasant, very quiet, very romantic dinner that night," said Collins. "He was so kind, so considerate, so gentle and amusing. When he took me home, I knew that I had fallen in love with Bo Belinsky."[7]

The feeling was mutual. Belinsky said, "For the first time in my life I just wanted to be with a girl I love every minute of every day."[8]

That included spring training. Belinsky wanted to stay with Collins, but she wasn't legally divorced from her first husband. The Astros required a marriage certificate.[9] Wanting an exception to the team's midnight curfew for at least one night, the southpaw stayed with Collins at a motel in Cocoa Beach anyway until 3:00 a.m. despite not getting a green light from general manager Spec Richardson. "When Bo did come in, he didn't bother to hang around or leave a forwarding address," wrote John Wilson in an article on the front page of the *Houston Chronicle*. "He packed his gear and departed."[10]

Belinsky hadn't taken the mound yet for spring training; Houston limited him to batting practice. In his view, management had been unresponsive to his needs. *Houston Post* reporter Joe Heiling reached out to the pitcher and got an explanation, though not a detailed one. "I'm ready to take off," said Belinsky. "I just have problems—definitely a few problems. I talked to them about the problems, but they weren't understanding enough to recognize them. So I left."

But he still wanted to play. There was a potential path if the friction with the Astros' front office could be lessened. "I'd like to get one or two more years in," he revealed. "They've got expansion coming up and there might be something there for me."[11]

Suspended immediately, Belinsky bolted training camp later that day.[12]

Belinsky's escapade provided a curiosity, certainly a controversy, but not a terribly concerning one to Houstonians, who probably had low expectations anyway given his 3–9 record in 1967. The evident discord with Astros management might lead to tension in the clubhouse and on the field. Belinsky showed a nonchalant attitude about the team's rules and his career when he described his relationship with Collins as "true love" and said that he might be ready to say goodbye to baseball—again—and welcome a new chapter in his life. "If something can't be worked out, I'll go to Hawaii where I invested money in a dude ranch this past winter," explained Belinsky. "I guess it's time I settled down, but I'm not going to lead a dull, blah life."[13]

Tamping down any talk of illicitness or impropriety, the left-hander claimed that he and Collins spent the night in question discussing their relationship, though it's hard to imagine anyone needing to do that until three in the morning. "When I asked for permission to stay out late Saturday night, it wasn't to gallavant [sic] around," Belinsky stated. "Miss Collins and I had some personal problems to work out."[14]

Moreover, the celebrity pairing seemed to have substance. Since Belinsky's relationship with Mamie Van Doren, no woman had captured his heart to the extent of being on the path to happily ever after. While marriage did not manifest with Van Doren, Belinsky said that the coupling with Collins was headed toward the altar. "We plan to marry as soon as her divorce becomes final. She's been separated a year now. I guess you'd call it a definite verbal engagement."[15]

But the press still liked the image of Belinsky being on the prowl in bars, nightclubs, and any place where women gathered to meet men and vice versa. If the nuptials happened—and there was no reason to think they wouldn't—baseball's scribes would lose a fantastic source for their stories and columns. Ed Levitt of the *Oakland Tribune* mourned the loss of a prized social life rather than advocating for the "true love" that Belinsky declared. Gossip, whether it got into print or quietly remained the subject of conversation in baseball circles, would be in jeopardy. "Such talk may soon end," wrote Levitt. "Too bad. Bo and bachelorhood deserve each other."[16]

Lest anyone need clarification about Belinsky's attitude toward women, an interview in Frank Luksa's column for the *Fort Worth Star-Telegram* underscored the lothario's preference for them being attractive and silent. "My advice to women would be to keep your mouth shut until you know what you're talking about," counseled Belinsky. "You're just as sexy with your mouth closed. Most men with good taste like women on the quiet side. Take pride in personal appearance. Men don't like to wait while they're making up, but the man does want his woman as pretty as possible. If it takes an extra hour to do it, go ahead. That little extra going for you that night may keep his eyes from roaming around the room."[17]

Belinsky being off the market surely upset attractive women who desired the famous ballplayer for courtship and other activities; Houston enjoyed a steady pipeline of business, ranching, and oil heiresses who had looks, poise, and personality. But Belinsky and Collins had a female fan regarding the relationship—his mother.

According to Belinsky, she kept herself apprised of his actions by reading newspapers from other cities, but articles about her son's social life created trouble because you're still a kid to your parents no matter how much success you might achieve. Reporters could spice up a story taking place at a nightclub or bar just by mentioning Belinsky's presence when it happened, which fostered agita. "But people know I love pretty girls and go for night clubbing and the impression is left that I'm a drunk," he said. "Mom knows I'm not like that. Yet, she reads those stories, and it confuses her."[18]

Hawaii sportswriter Red McQueen posited a scenario for Belinsky to come to the 50th state and rejoin the Islanders, now part of the Chicago White Sox organization. Belinsky would be a marquee attraction given his previous stint in Hawaii; McQueen reminded readers that he drew 15,000 fans in his first game as an Islander. Additionally, Belinsky had declared his affinity for the land of luaus, hula dancing, and great surfing. Houston could arrange for Belinsky to be in a holding pattern for major league play until expansion took place, when his marketability would likely increase. "The Chisox could work a lend-lease arrangement with Oklahoma for Belinsky and then assign him to the Islanders," wrote McQueen.[19]

McQueen's idea came pretty close to the bullseye. Islanders general manager Jack Quinn confirmed, "[I am] definitely interested in getting Belinsky, but there are several things that have to be worked out."[20] Indeed, Belinsky's familiarity with Hawaii's baseball fans factored into the acquisition as well as his potential value on the mound. "But I think we'll have our best team ever this year, and I think we'll draw with or without Bo," said Quinn.[21]

While Quinn examined the pros and cons of signing Belinsky, the rift between the headline-making pitcher and the Astros' front office closed. He signed his contract. In a two-inning effort for the Dallas-Fort Worth Spurs—Houston's Texas League team—against the Charlotte Hornets of the Southern League, Belinsky had a solid performance to close the 7–4 victory with three strikeouts, one walk, and no hits. Plus he knocked in a run with a single.[22]

After signing with the Astros' organization and assessing the competition, he intuited that Houston's major league squad would not be his home in 1968. A trade seemed likely. "Atlanta, for instance, could use some left-handed pitching," observed Belinsky. "So could some others. This is how things stand." He also mentioned possibilities created by expansion, which hadn't been certified yet but ultimately happened when the majors amplified their roster of teams in 1969 with the San Diego Padres, Montreal Expos, Kansas City Royals, and Seattle Pilots.[23]

Collins played a role in Belinsky's next baseball job. She asked to see Richardson, and he met her in her car outside the ballpark. Asked if her boyfriend could be sent to the Hawaii Islanders, Richardson hemmed and hawed, but Collins knew how to employ her feminine wiles. A whiff of perfume and a toss of her hair complemented by a moment where she "tugged on her sweater a little," combined to persuade Richardson.[24] "That's where Jo and I wanted to go," said the pitcher. "I've got nothing against Oklahoma City. But it's not for me. If I'm going to fade into the sunset, I want it to be in Hawaii."[25]

Houston to Hawaii

Belinsky and McQueen saw their respective prophecies come true. Richardson sold the pitcher's contract to the Hawaii club, which followed a mandatory rule for Chicago's minor league system in spring training: no wives, no girlfriends. The Islanders had the same public stance as the Phillies when Belinsky signed with them—his personal life mattered little, if any, to the team's need for a southpaw if it didn't interfere with his duties. "He can pitch, and can help our ballclub," stated Islanders skipper Bill Adair. "That's all we're interested in."[26]

Actually, they set the bar high. Quinn declared, "We're not looking to Belinsky for only a 12–11 record. We're thinking more in terms of 15 to 17 wins."[27] Reinforcing his projection of value a week later, albeit in general terms, Quinn described Belinsky and Don Nottebart of Hawaii's pitching staff. "Bo is a definite asset to the club, and I'm sure Nottebart will be of tremendous help," said the general manager. "Both are major league pitchers, and I am convinced they will perform like major leaguers."[28]

Nottebart broke in with the Milwaukee Braves in 1960 and stayed there through 1962; he played with the Astros from 1963 to 1965 and the Reds from 1966 to 1967. In 1963, he threw the first no-hitter in Houston's major league history.

Belinsky's carefree approach to life seemed like a good fit for a place identified by leisure. Visitors, natives, and transplants to Hawaii are attracted, sustained, and inspired by its beaches, sunsets, history, lore, and a welcoming atmosphere furthered through an undeniable place in American culture. A U.S. territory since 1900, Hawaii had been the site of America's entry into World War II's Pacific Theater, prompted by the Japanese bombing Pearl Harbor on December 7, 1941. It became the 50th state in 1959, eight months after Alaska achieved statehood. Coinciding with the beginning of statehood, James Michener's epic novel *Hawaii* documented the evolution of Hawaii from volcanos forming the islands to ascendance as a commercial giant in the 1950s. Hollywood came calling, too. Malibu's favorite teenaged surfer girl left the beautiful beaches of southern California in the 1961 movie *Gidget Goes Hawaiian*, starring Deborah Walley in the title role. Elvis Presley filmed three movies in Hawaii: *Blue Hawaii*, *Girls! Girls! Girls!*, and *Paradise, Hawaiian Style*.

Warner Brothers produced *Hawaiian Eye* for ABC, which debuted in 1959 and aired until 1963. The show's title reflected the characters' fictional company that provided investigation and security services for the Hawaiian Village Hotel in Honolulu while tending to additional clientele.

CBS debuted *Hawaii Five O* in the fall of 1968. Revolving around a fictional police task force led by gubernatorial appointee and former navy intelligence officer Steve McGarrett, *Hawaii Five O* aired for 12 seasons on CBS. It became a prime time juggernaut with an iconic theme song that ran over visuals akin to a video travelogue in the introductory credits.

By the late 1960s, Hawaii's allure had increased through cultural and commercial influences. Belinsky sought to stay in this paradise when his career ended, describing his ranch investment as a guy's hangout: "It'll be a home away from home thing. A place for the 'swingers' to get together."[29]

But if people thought that he would favor fun and frivolity over discipline and dedication with the Islanders, they were mistaken. During practice, Belinsky stayed the longest on the field and admitted that he had to make up for lost time, plus the relationship with Collins appeared to give him a sense of comportment and a purpose of stability. "You know Jo (Collins) and I are going to get married as soon as we can," affirmed the southpaw.[30]

He intrigued but didn't overwhelm Islanders fans in his season debut on April 20. Technically, Belinsky had a no-hitter against the Vancouver Mounties in the seventh inning at Honolulu Stadium, but a bases-loaded balk in addition to errors and walks led to a 5–1 victory for the visitors. His second game added confidence. Against the Portland Beavers at home on April 25, Belinsky hurled a complete game, struck out seven, walked four, allowed six hits, and neutralized the batsmen for a 5–1 entry in Hawaii's win column. Lou Piniella led off Portland's ninth inning with a strikeout; Lou Klimchock followed with a single and scored on Alan Diamond's double for the visitors' sole run. Belinsky struck out the next two batters to finish strong.[31]

Belinsky had a 3–1 count when Diamond smacked his RBI double, but the hurler thought the umpire erred by calling two pitches balls instead of strikes. Acknowledging Diamond's ability, he revealed, "I didn't want to walk the kid. Still, he hit it good. More power to him." Regarding his personal appraisal of himself, Belinsky showed modesty: "I still don't feel I'm at my best yet."[32]

The *Honolulu Star-Bulletin* emphasized Belinsky's output—through nearly 16 innings in his first two starts, he allowed three earned runs. "By now Bo Belinsky has erased all doubts that he's come here to pitch." It wasn't just a result of ability, though. Where Belinsky once made headlines for activities other than ballplaying, there appeared to be a change in demeanor, attitude, and dedication. Noting the impact of Quinn, Belinsky reminded Hawaii's baseball community: "I owe Jack a lot, especially for his confidence in me. I know I can still pitch in the major leagues—and as a starting pitcher, I'm just grateful for this chance."[33]

Belinsky proved Quinn right in his next game, even though the April 29 rematch against the Mounties in Vancouver's Nat Bailey Stadium resulted in a 1–0 loss for the Islanders. Through eight innings, he struck out eight, allowed five hits, and walked three batters. Vancouver scored on Stan Wojcik's single that sent Joe Rudi across the plate from second base in the second inning.[34]

Through his first three games, Belinsky had a 1–2 record, 24 innings pitched and an outstanding 1.50 ERA.[35] His next start was a 6–0 loss to the Spokane Indians on May 4, giving the Islanders their eighth defeat in the last nine games. Spokane, the home team, jumped ahead early—six hits and four earned runs in the first four innings.[36]

A winning streak of five games during a road trip offset by one loss raised spirits as the team returned to Honolulu for a 19-game homestand. Belinsky took the hill against Spokane for the first game and lasted seven innings in the 4–0 loss; he gave up three runs—one unearned—and Nottebart got tagged for the other run, which happened in the ninth inning.[37]

A blister might have caused some frustration, if not anguish. Belinsky disclosed, "It opened up again in the second inning and I couldn't throw my screwball or sinking fastball."[38]

The *Honolulu Advertiser*'s Hal Wood mentioned the lack of offensive support for the southpaw now owning a 1–4 record, with the losses being three shutouts and a game where the Islanders scored one run. Meanwhile, Belinsky had an ERA of 2.57.[39]

On May 18, the Islanders failed again to give run support for Belinsky. Trailing the Indians, 3–1, Belinsky left the game in the eighth inning and did not get credit for the comeback culminating in a 4–3 victory. The Islanders got some help from opposing backstop Ted Sizemore's two errors.[40]

Whether Belinsky could tackle major league hitters again may have provoked concerns among baseball insiders, but not his manager. Once linked with a social life more entertaining to read about than most of his time on the mound—excluding the no-hitter in 1962 and a few outstanding games—Belinsky received an endorsement from the Islanders' manager that instilled confidence. "First of all, let me say that Bo is no problem to a club," stated Bill Adair. "He doesn't drink. Maybe he's a bit lazy when it comes to running. But he has pitched well. He has had trouble with that blister on his finger, but I think that is just about over. I would say that Bo still is capable of pitching in the majors."[41]

Belinsky's next outing on May 22 pitted him against the Phoenix Giants, a "hapless, injury-hexed" club. Still, it gave him a reason to rejoice. Belinsky threw a two-hitter, tallied eight strikeouts, and brought his ERA to 2.08 for the season. Bob Burda marked the lefty for a pair of singles; Hawaii's offense pounded 10 hits in the 5–0 victory. The adage about patience being a virtue proved correct because the Islanders didn't score in the first five innings. Further, they suffered the burden of Adair getting kicked out of the game after questioning an umpire's call on one of Belinsky's pitches.[42]

A few days after the Phoenix game, the *Honolulu Star-Bulletin* ran a feature highlighting the wives of the Islanders and included Collins, who revealed her childhood connection to the national pastime. "I belonged to a girls team called 'The Lumber Jills.' We played softball and we thought we were pretty good. Until I met Bo, I was a football fan, but now baseball's my game."[43]

No-Hitter, Part Deux

An Islanders game two months hence excited Hawaii's baseball fans as much as a 30-foot wave at Waimea Bay excites surfers. Belinsky fired the second no-hitter of his professional career—and the first for an Islander—with a 1–0 victory against the Tacoma Cubs on August 19. Adjusting his approach in the ninth inning almost detoured him from the achievement, though. After the game, he explained, "I only threw fastballs. I didn't want to throw anything into the dirt with runners on base."[44]

Aaron Pointer pinch-hit for Cubs pitcher Joe Decker and drew a walk—Belinsky's third of the game—followed by Islanders shortstop Rich Morales committing an error on Jim Qualls's ground ball, which put runners on first and second. "Really, though, I just tried to throw the ball before I had it," explained Morales. Belinsky got Vic La Rose out on a fly ball, but he walked Clarence Jones with a full count to load the bases. Then, John Boccabella crushed a ball "that backed rightfielder Joe Gaines to the fence." It was not a moment for the faint of heart when Gaines snared the sphere for the final out.[45]

Belinsky credited his battery mate, Buddy Booker, who had already caught three no-hitters. "Buddy was my best pitch," lauded Belinsky. "He called a great game. He was right with me all the way." According to Booker, two of Belinsky's four walks happened after Belinsky disagreed with the catcher's signs.[46] Hawaii's defense added tremendous value to Belinsky's pitching, well needed because of the one-run margin of victory. Left fielder Ernie Fazio, for example, "made a fine, over-the-shoulder running catch just like a football end."[47]

Decker had a stellar performance for Tacoma, limiting Hawaii to four hits. Qualls fulfilled the role of a spoiler a year later when, as a rookie with the Chicago Cubs, he banged a single with one out in the top of the ninth inning to prevent New York Mets ace Tom Seaver from adding a perfect game to his curriculum vitae.

With the no-hitter came accolades, optimism, and expectations. Belinsky cautioned against them. "That was the worst mistake I made," he said. "That got all the scouts looking at me again. I would have to go back to the big leagues. I didn't want to go. I was too happy in Hawaii."[48]

There was another reason for Belinsky's composure, and it didn't have to do with baseball. Al Michaels, an Islanders announcer before he found fame and success on the national level with NFL, MLB, and Olympics broadcasts, acknowledged Collins's impact on Belinsky's state of mind. "Bo was really happy in Hawaii," explained Michaels, who spontaneously shouted "Do you believe in miracles? Yes!" when the U.S. hockey team defeated the USSR in the 1980 Winter Olympics. "He seemed very much in love with Jo. Nobody had any trouble with him. Nobody ever heard about Bo staying out late except with Jo. He was a model husband."[49]

Belinsky and Collins weren't married yet. But the sentiment was true. Collins attended the no-hitter and shared her insights on her paramour: "I knew how much he wanted it. He wanted to prove to everybody he could still pitch. It gave him a tremendous lift. It really restored his confidence, not only in his pitching ability but in himself. He was a hell of a lot easier to live with after that."[50]

Faring not nearly as well in his next outing—a 3–0 loss on August 22, also against Tacoma and the last home game before an 18-game road trip wrapped up the 1968 season—Belinsky threw more than 70 pitches and gave up all three runs in two and two-thirds innings. Hawaii's no-hit hurler had retired two Tacomans before loading the bases on three walks in the third inning; Daniel Murphy took over and shut down the Cubs, who managed four hits the rest of the game.

Clarence Jones's first-inning homer gave Tacoma its first two runs. Vic La Rose, Jim Qualls, and Jim Campbell singled an inning later, resulting in La Rose crossing the plate and Belinsky leaving the mound.

"I'm sorry I wasn't at my best," said the left-hander. There was a bright spot, however. The *Star-Bulletin* pointed out that the Islanders' attendance—11,185—was the second-largest so far at Honolulu Stadium in 1968. It symbolized the team's record season attendance, which exceeded 255,000 and far surpassed the previous record: 236,848 in 1963.[51]

Belinsky's 9–14 record in 1968 obscures a solid contribution to the team. He led the Islanders in games started (25), shutouts (3), strikeouts (181), and ERA (2.97). His ERA was the fourteenth-lowest in the Pacific Coast League; teammates Jerry Nyman, Bill Fischer, and Billy Wynne were also in the top 20 in this category.

His three shutouts tied with eight other pitchers for fourth place, and he was fifth in strikeouts. In the off-season, Belinsky pitched in the Venezuelan League and said aloha to the Islanders when the team sold him to the Astros, who put him on the Oklahoma City 89ers' roster. But it didn't last long. On December 1, the St. Louis Cardinals selected him during the baseball meetings. Price tag: $25,000.[52]

Slinging with St. Louis

Belinsky welcomed the move to St. Louis, which not only would place him with an outstanding group of pitchers—Bob Gibson, Nelson Briles, Steve Carlton, Ray Washburn, Joe Hoerner—but also lacked the friction between a team's front office and the manager that he had experienced elsewhere in the majors. According to Belinsky, Cardinals skipper Red Schoendienst and general manager Bing Devine were on the same page. "Picking me up was no fluke. Both think I can help them."[53]

Again, Belinsky couldn't escape the labels of his past even though he had been publicly complimented on his stability and relationship with Collins. UPI began its recounting of the Cardinals' new hurler by calling him "playboy pitcher Bo Belinsky, baseball's foremost exponent of the good life and bright life."[54] An article about Nelson Briles by the syndicator Newspaper Enterprise Association used Belinsky and his former running buddy as barometers for bachelorhood and bacchanalia: "Not everybody in baseball lives like Bo Belinsky or Dean Chance but then not everybody wants to."[55]

But Belinsky had been settling into a groove with Collins. If he concerned Devine and Schoendienst, they kept it quiet if not silent. Schoendienst said, "We consider him a big protection for us. He could be a spot starter or reliever."[56] Echoing Gene Mauch's appraisal when Belinsky wore a Phillies uniform, Devine said, "His reputation has nothing to do with his pitching. We know he has a good arm."[57]

With St. Louis, Belinsky would have a chance to play with a stellar team that had gone to the World Series three of the last five years and won two titles. In 1968, Gibson and Briles placed in the top 10 in wins in the majors. Gibson topped all pitchers in ERA and shutouts, landing in the top 10 in winning percentage and innings pitched in addition to tying for second in complete games.

Belinsky signed his 1969 contract in mid-February.[58] If Devine and Schoendienst needed the southpaw to add value to an already strong pitching staff, Belinsky needed their approval not only for his pride but also for financial reasons. "I'm broke and if I don't make it with the Cardinals, a good ball club, I'll be hurting," revealed the pitcher, who seemed to be the antithesis to the athlete full of charm and swagger who could once go into any bar on the Sunset Strip and get served drinks on the house while men praised and women adored him. Belinsky now embodied introspection, humility, and acceptance. "I had a helluva good time, but I burned the candle at both ends," he said.[59]

Though earnest, Belinsky would not be destined to play with Gibson et al. Collins believed that the publicity rubbed the Cardinals' front office and the players' wives the wrong way. "We didn't make the team because we weren't the typical baseball family," she said. "We didn't have the right image. We said the wrong things. If Bo was a star he could get away with it. If he wasn't he had to kiss the right asses and say the right things to hang around. Bo isn't like that. It just wasn't worth it to him."[60]

At the end of March, St. Louis put him on waivers, with Houston having the first opportunity to sign him. Press reports indicated that Astros management had no interest in reclaiming the southpaw, who performed well though without sufficient opportunities in his opinion—a 1.95 ERA over 12 and two-thirds innings. Belinsky called the situation "a joke" and wondered, "Why would they pick someone up if they don't use him?"[61]

The Islanders stepped in. Price tag: $12,500.[62]

Happy in Hawaii

Jack Quinn had initially declined to bring the left-hander back into the fold but declared him "too good a bargain to pass up," while the team's new manager, Chuck Tanner, believed that Belinsky got dismissed because St. Louis already had tremendous pitching. "I think Bo has one of the best arms in baseball," stated Tanner, starting his first of two seasons piloting the Islanders.[63]

Excelling in 1969 with a 12–5 record, Belinsky justified Quinn's outlook. On May 20, the Islanders owned a six-game winning streak as they took the field at Honolulu Stadium for a night game against the Phoenix Giants. Belinsky and his brethren delivered number seven thanks to a combination of skillful pitching, offensive power, and solid defense in a 6–0 shutout. The Islanders managed six hits, including two homers by Winston Llenas, each with a man on base, while Belinsky limited the Giants to four hits and got them to hit into three double plays.[64] Their winning streak ended the following night when Phoenix defeated them, 6–2.

During a road trip, Belinsky notched an 8–1 victory against the Portland Beavers on June 4. Portland's sole tally happened in the first inning because of two mistakes by the southpaw, who pitched eight and one-third innings. Gary Sprague banged a leadoff single, scampered to second base on a wild pitch, and scored on a pickoff attempt when Belinsky made an off-target throw that also went wild. The Beavers only notched three other hits. Hawaii's first baseman, Charlie Vinson, went four-for-four with two RBI; Tomas Silverio, a power-hitting center fielder, smacked a double for two RBI; and Marty Perez had a two-run single. Belinsky's 1969 ERA to date: 2.82.[65]

On June 17, a more important event than a baseball game caused celebration throughout the summer of 1969 for the pitcher and the model in Apartment A-1204 at 4300 Waiaiae Avenue in Honolulu. Stephanie Lehua Belinsky. Stevie.[66] Mother and daughter came to the Islanders games to cheer on the patriarch. Michaels remembered the contradiction between these scenes and the public image of the ballplayer known as the "playboy pitcher." "It certainly wasn't the picture of Bo Belinsky we all knew. I can't remember a baby having a greater impact on a man's life than that baby did on Bo's. He used to bore everybody silly talking about the baby."[67]

When Belinsky won his eighth consecutive game—a 5–3 victory against the Eugene Emeralds in which he knocked in two runs with a single—*Star-Bulletin* sportswriter Bill Kwon pointed out his present record of 11–5, a stark difference from going 9–14 in 1968. "That's the new Bo Belinsky that the fans like and will get to see in the final homestand, even if the Islanders may be mathematically out of the pennant race by then."[68]

He extended his streak to nine straight wins for the Islanders on July 28. Lasting seven innings, Belinsky left with a 6–1 lead against the Giants; John Werhas tacked on two more runs with a single in the top of the eighth. Belinsky's fifth-inning single also accounted for two RBI.[69]

The Southpaw and Steel City

Kwon's prediction did not get realized, however. The Islanders sold their ace to Pittsburgh in late July, forcing a bittersweet acknowledgment that Belinsky deserved his escalation. "We hate to lose Belinsky, but there is no place like the big leagues," said Quinn. "We would be remiss not to give the fellow an opportunity to pitch once again in the majors."

For Belinsky, saying aloha to the Islanders meant saying goodbye to a place of familiarity, contentment, and belonging. "It's like my home there," he said. "But I hope I can get the job done for [the Pirates], but if things don't work out I sure hope I can pitch for Hawaii again."[70]

At the time of the exchange, the Cubs owned first place with a formidable lead of eight games over the Mets and 11½ games over the third-place Pirates. A solid left-hander could help close the gap. In his column, *Pittsburgh Press* sports editor Roy McHugh gave the usual summary of Belinsky's career: minor leagues, no-hitter for the Angels, dating actresses, marrying Collins. McHugh and his brethren used the southpaw's notorious past like a house painter used primer—as a foundation for whatever topic would follow. It was a reflex, arguably. Not mentioning Belinsky's past socializing with Hollywood's sex symbols would be like talking about the early days of rock and roll without mentioning Elvis Presley.

But they also emphasized Belinsky's turnaround, making the 12–5 record and 2.82 ERA for Hawaii even more dramatic. McHugh noted Belinsky's comportment, an important factor for Pirates fans to consider, especially if they hadn't known the details of Belinsky's tenure with the Islanders. Besides highlighting accolades from the Islanders' manager about ability, McHugh conveyed, "Tanner also described Belinsky's general conduct to terms that would do justice to an Eagle Scout."[71]

Charley Feeney of the *Pittsburgh Post-Gazette* defended Belinsky. "Ask anybody who ever shared a clubhouse locker with Bo and they will tell you that he is a good guy," wrote Feeney. "A fun guy, sure, but a good guy, too." Of Belinsky's past dalliances and relationships with "the cream of Hollywood society," Feeney reminded his readers, "He was a lucky guy, and often lucky guys are envied by others."[72]

The Pirates' announcement appeared in the July 30 newspapers, eight games into a 13-game homestand against the Cardinals, Padres, Dodgers, and Giants scheduled to finish on August 3. They started off well, going 6–2 against the Forbes Field visitors and ending at 9–4.

August 4 was a travel day to the West Coast for a road trip where they would take on the National League's California teams, beginning on the night of August 5 at Dodger Stadium. It would have been easy, not to mention practical, for Belinsky to catch a plane for Los Angeles and settle in for a couple of days before the arrival of his new teammates. Not a chance. He underlined his fierce determination to be part of a squad by going to Pittsburgh and traveling with his new baseball brothers to LA. Feeney observed, "The old Bo Belinsky would have waited for them there. The New Bo Belinsky couldn't wait."[73]

10

The End of a Long and Winding Road

Pittsburgh's Baseball Legacy

If Chicago represents the big shoulders of America, as Carl Sandburg once described it, then Pittsburgh signifies a backbone. Home of the nation's steel industry, this metropolis in western Pennsylvania boasts a working-class aura enveloping its laborers, whose muscles constantly ache from making the alloy found in products ranging from scalpels that fit in a surgeon's hand to girders that support skyscrapers.

Tensile strength measures steel's power. If passion for sports had a similar indicator, then Pittsburghers would rival Samson. They did not have an entry in the original octet that began the National League in 1876, but the city's first professional baseball team—then called the Alleghenys—belonged to the initial roster of clubs in the American Association, which birthed in 1882. Joining the NL five years later, Pittsburgh's ball club played at Recreation Park and Exposition Park before Forbes Field's unveiling in 1909, succeeded by the debuts of Ebbets Field, Fenway Park, the Polo Grounds, and Weeghman Park—later renamed Wrigley Field—all before 1915.

About six weeks before Bo Belinsky joined the Pirates, Three Rivers Stadium replaced Forbes Field. On July 16, 1970, the home team lost to the Reds, 3–2, inaugurating the latest example of a multi-purpose, circular stadium overtaking a ballpark that had served fans with charm, uniqueness, and legacies stretching back decades. Shea Stadium, DC Stadium, the Astrodome, San Diego Stadium, Atlanta-Fulton County Stadium, and the Oakland Coliseum predated Three Rivers Stadium in the 1960s. Riverfront Stadium, Veterans Stadium, and the Kingdome debuted in the 1970s.

Belinsky latched onto an organization with a new home, a prideful fan base, and a rich legacy. Honus Wagner won the NL batting title eight times and topped the major leagues thrice. Like Wagner, the fraternal duo of Paul Waner and Lloyd Waner—nicknamed Big Poison and Little Poison—are in the Baseball Hall of Fame, as is power hitter Ralph Kiner, who led the majors in home runs six consecutive seasons with Pittsburgh, and the NL, seven.

Bill Mazeroski neared the end of his 17-year, Hall of Fame career in 1970, crowned by seven All-Star teams, eight Gold Glove Awards for his stellar fielding as the Pirates' second baseman, and the bottom-of-the-ninth home run that gave the Pirates a 10–9 win over the Yankees in Game Seven of the 1960 World Series and sealed the championship. Roberto Clemente was also in the sunset years of his career. On a humanitarian mission to help victims of an earthquake in Nicaragua, he died in a plane crash on New Year's Eve, 1972, which also claimed the lives of the other four people aboard. A five-tool player, Clemente left behind one of baseball's richest opuses: lifetime average of .317, a Gold Glove Award 12 straight seasons, 12 All-Star teams, three-time major league batting champion, four-time NL batting champion, and 3,000 hits.

Waiving the requirement of a five-year waiting period after a player ends his career, the Hall of Fame inducted Clemente in 1973.

Family Man

If there were a Hall of Fame for nightlife, then Belinsky's membership would be certain. But he went to Pittsburgh a calmer, centered man because of his marriage to Collins. Drinking and carousing were in the past. "I stay at home almost all the time these days," said the 32-year-old, who had traveled an arc from epic indulgence to quiet appreciation, confusing those who had chronicled his exploits either verbally or in the press. Marriage and fatherhood became his lodestars. No longer would his lifestyle lead to provocative stories. No longer would he be an avatar for men who dreamed about the perquisites of money, fame, and women that came with being a major leaguer, amplified by the no-hitter immersing oneself in sports immortality.

Pittsburgh scribe Phil Musick voiced his dismay with a hint of disapproval: "Will the real Bo Belinsky please stand up? What happened to the satin-slick, pool-shooting, let-'er-rip-you-can't-get-out-of-this-world-alive-anyhow dazzler who launched a hundred romances and a thousand tales?"[1]

To the consternation of Musick and his brethren, Belinsky became the living, breathing embodiment of Saint Paul's words in his famed letter to the Corinthians: "When I was a child, I spoke like a child, I thought like a child, I reasoned like a child. When I became a man, I gave up childish ways."[2]

Collins had been married but was long estranged from her husband. She went with Belinsky to Mexico so she could get a quick divorce followed by a marriage ceremony, which took 34 seconds for the couple to be legally wed. It became a tidy legal issue when a private detective found her first husband—Robert Anderson—who did not argue against the divorce, allowing the pitcher and the *Playboy* model to repeat a wedding ceremony in the United States.[3]

Bud Furillo enjoyed a vantage point better than most. Witnessing the zenith of Belinsky's fame and its consequences during the Angels tenure gave the *Los Angeles Herald Examiner* reporter a full-blown trajectory with an insider's view. In a profile, Furillo confirmed that the ballplayer known for whom he dated as much as whom he struck out—if not more so—had turned toward a quieter, stabler life anchored by marriage, even though women still attempted to be with him. "I'm through going out on the town," said Belinsky. "I feel in love, and I try to never be separated from my wife. She's with me on this trip. When Cupid shot that dart, he must have hit the right spot." Buck Rodgers, his former battery mate with the Angels, addressed the metamorphosis. "You wouldn't believe him now. You ask him out for a beer after the game, and he says I have to go home to the wife."[4]

With a player of Belinsky's celebrity, it would be natural to question the reason for adding him to Pittsburgh's roster. Was it simply a ploy to sell tickets and get more press coverage? Doubtful. Pirates general manager Joe Brown confirmed that Belinsky enhanced the team's pitching.[5] Noting that his ethnicity matched a significant demographic in Pittsburgh, Belinsky promised his best because "after all I'm Polish, and I don't want those Polish fans to cuss me out in Polish."[6]

Pitching for the Pirates

His opportunities were somewhat sporadic and hardly dominant. Trailing the Giants, 3–1, Pirates skipper Larry Shepard put him in a game to replace Jim Bunning in the top of the eighth inning. Belinsky gave up a single to Dave Marshall and began the ninth inning by plunking Willie McCovey, who left the game for pinch-runner Bob Burda. Dick Dietz's sacrifice bunt moved Burda to second. Ken Henderson drew a walk, and Jim Davenport's two-run double scored both runners in a 5–1 victory for San Francisco.

At his former home, Belinsky faced the Dodgers at Dodger Stadium in another relief effort on August 6. The Pirates had used four pitchers before he took the mound for the bottom of the seventh inning with a 7–3 deficit. He looked encouraging: Jeff Torborg grounded to Mazeroski, followed by the rhyming Dodgers tandem of Tom Hutton and Don Sutton striking out looking and whiffing, respectively.

The Pirates notched a run in the top of the eighth thanks to Al Oliver's solo shot; Belinsky and his fellow Bucs prevented LA from scoring in the bottom half of the inning. After Sutton began the top of the ninth by retiring Mazeroski on a grounder to third baseman Bill Sudakis, José Pagán pinch-hit for Belinsky and homered. Jim Brewer replaced Sutton, and the score stayed 7–5 until the end.

On August 12, Belinsky pitched the bottom of the eighth inning against the Giants at Candlestick Park. The home team led, 6–1. He walked Dietz but got Burda to ground into a double play. Hal Lanier and Gaylord Perry hit back-to-back singles, and Clemente nailed Lanier at third base with a right arm that could throw a baseball toward its target as true as a bullet fired from a sniper's rifle.

Dormant for two weeks, Belinsky pitched three innings against the Braves at Forbes Field on August 26. Atlanta led, 6–0, when he began the top of the sixth. Belinsky kept the score static and struck out Hank Aaron in the eighth inning; Pittsburgh scored twice in the bottom of the eighth and twice again in the bottom of the ninth. Final score: 6–4.

Making his first start for the Pirates on August 30, Belinsky lasted four innings against the Astros at the Astrodome in a good news—bad news type of outing that ended in a 2–1 defeat for the visitors. Five strikeouts proved he could handle himself, but four walks proved inconsistency. Belinsky limited Houston to three hits and allowed two runs in rather dreary sequences for the Pirates. He hit Denis Menke to start the bottom of the second, followed by walking Marty Martinez and Leon McFadden to load the bases. After Larry Dierker struck out, Menke scored on a passed ball.

In the bottom of the third, Jesus Alou knocked a leadoff double. Belinsky struck out Jimmy Wynn, but Alou went to third base on Gary Kolb's second passed ball. Doug Rader struck out, Menke drew a walk, and Martinez singled home Alou. Shepard replaced Belinsky with Bruce Dal Canton in the fifth inning, and Joe Gibbon succeeded him in the seventh. Pittsburgh nicked Larry Dierker for its only run when Gene Alley's solo homer led off the top of the sixth.

Belinsky pitched an inning in an 8–1 loss to the Braves on September 3, giving up a leadoff walk to Sonny Jackson in the bottom of the eighth and retiring the next three batters. Atlanta's offense had exploded for all their runs in the sixth inning.

After the first week of September, the third-place Pirates had a 75–61 record. It seemed like a year of destiny for Cubs manager Leo Durocher, helming his third team after the Brooklyn Dodgers and New York Giants; Chicago stood tall with leads of two-and-a-half games over the Mets and seven-and-a-half games over the Pirates in the newly formed Eastern Division of the National League. Belinsky saw Durocher's ball club as admirable but not unbeatable. "You have to think pennant," said the hurler. "You wanna know how we're gonna do it? The Mets'll be in first place by the time we play them [for four games] in Pittsburgh this weekend; then we'll knock 'em off and take over."[7]

His words were uplifting. His pitching, not so much. Belinsky didn't even endure a full inning in his next start, the second game of a twin bill against St. Louis on September 10. Shepard sent Belinsky to the Forbes Field clubhouse after the Cardinals scored a pair of runs on a double, a single, and three walks. The southpaw blamed his failing fastball for his lack of control. Pittsburgh lost both games, 11–2 and 2–1.[8]

He faced the Phillies on September 15 in another uneven performance, resulting in a loss and an 0–3 record in his three starts. Five strikeouts, two walks, five hits, and four runs scored in four innings before his exodus; Philadelphia led, 4–2. Pittsburgh managed another run after Belinsky left and kept their rivals scoreless, entering a 4–3 loss on their ledger for the Bucs' eighth defeat in the last 10 games.

Baseball fans in Steel City endured volatility in the home stretch of the 1969 season. Celebrations flourished when Bob Moose threw a no-hitter against the Mets on September 20 at Shea Stadium, the third such blanking in Pirates history. Less than a week later, questions arose when Joe Brown gave Larry Shepard a pink slip even though the team had risen from sixth place in 1968 to an almost certain third-place finish in 1969. Brown remained as tight-lipped as Marcel Marceau on his reason. "It's enough that I fired him," stated the general manager. "To indict him would only hurt him more."[9]

Third-base coach Alex Grammas fulfilled the leadership slot as interim manager, guiding the Pirates to a 4–1 record in their last five games. Indeed, they remained in third place with 12 games separating them from the first-place Mets, who obliterated the NL competition with winning streaks of ten and nine games in September. New York captured the NL East flag with a cushion of eight games distancing them from the Cubs.

A couple of weeks after Tom Seaver et al. surprised experts and beat Baltimore in five games to win the World Series, Belinsky got notified of a change in employers when the Pirates sold him, along with Ron Davis and Gary Kolb, to the organization's triple-A team—the Columbus Jets—in the International League.[10]

Considering the Future

The world changed in 1969. It began with Richard Nixon getting inaugurated as the 37th U.S. president. Apollo 11 made the first manned moon landing, followed by Apollo 12 four months later; there had been two other Apollo missions earlier in the year. Woodstock epitomized the peace movement with three days of rock and roll complemented by rainy, muddy weather.

ABC premiered family-friendly comedies that became popular culture touchstones: *The Brady Bunch, Room 222, Nanny and the Professor, The Courtship of Eddie's Father,* and *Love, American Style.* The James Bond brand got a makeover as George Lazenby made his only portrayal of 007 in *On Her Majesty's Secret Service. Medium Cool* showcased the innovative filmmaking technique of cinéma verité, which served as a template for aspiring cinematographers and directors. Belinsky spent the winter in Venezuela, where he played baseball, enjoyed time with Collins, and got "treated marvelously" because the baseball fans remembered his last tenure there.[11]

When 1970 began, Hollywood's creative expansion continued with the premiere of 20th Century–Fox's *M*A*S*H*, based on the novel by Richard Hooker, né Hornberger, who used his experience as a surgeon in Mobile Army Surgical Hospital #8055 during the Korean War as the foundation. *M*A*S*H* did not have an underlying plot, but the scenes and vignettes were dramatic, comedic, and powerful. CBS's TV version premiered in 1972 and aired for 11 seasons.

Fox also released *Patton*. With a running time of nearly three hours, this film about legendary general George Patton got nominated for 10 Oscars and won seven, including Best Actor for George C. Scott in the title role. On February 5, 1970, Fox hosted the film's New York City premiere, the same day that newspapers reported Bo Belinsky's latest change—the Pirates shuttled Belinsky to the Reds, though technically it came under the auspices of the Columbus Jets and the Indianapolis Indians, Cincinnati's Triple–A team in the American Association. In exchange, Pittsburgh got Dennis Ribant, a right-hander.

Again, Belinsky packed his bags and emphasized his willingness to contribute to a ball club. No longer complacent, he craved the opportunity to compete and dominate. "I'll relieve if they want," said the pitcher about to join his 16th team since starting his professional baseball career in 1956. "The only thing is that I have to be used. When I sit around, I become a wild man. I feel I have to be a world-beater when I go in there, and you just can't do it when you don't pitch often."[12]

Accepting a domesticated Belinsky still had not become a certainty in some quarters. Musick had called him "one of baseball's all-time great swingers, bonniest of the game's bon vivants" in his column welcoming the hurler to Pittsburgh.[13] Upon the move to the Reds organization, *Cincinnati Enquirer* sportswriter Bob Hertzel also used the phrase "bon vivant" and relayed a telephone interview where he said to the pitcher: "We must have a bad connection. I could have sworn I heard you say your wife's just a regular housewife now and that you're nothing but a family man."[14]

Indeed. Belinsky not only enjoyed being at their home in Whitaker, Pennsylvania, but also contributed to running the house with culinary skills. "I make Cornish hen and crepes suzette and pate de fois gras and things like that," explained Belinsky about his cooking repertoire. "We stay home most of the time and play house. There are some real good guys in this town. It is a shot-and-a-beer town just outside of Pittsburgh. We have some guys over and they kid me about my cooking, but they eat every drop."[15]

It seemed that baseball's model patriarch would have a lot more family time in 1970 when he didn't show up for the Reds' training camp despite an invitation and declared retirement after shunning a salary offer of $12,000 from Indianapolis—the minimum for the major leagues. Belinsky and the Indians squared away their differences a week later, but the 33-year-old ballplayer had another opportunity to pitch in the majors if he proved his worth in Cincinnati's spring training before March 20, when the Triple-A squad started its preseason regimen.[16]

Belinsky began that journey on March 10. The Reds made an impression on him, igniting optimism for the future. "They seem like a great bunch of guys," said the pitcher. "I'd sure like to stay here. Maybe I'll do well at Indianapolis, and they'll call me back."[17]

There was some support in the press for Belinsky to get a spot on the parent club. Veteran scribe and *Tampa Times* sports editor Frank Klein observed him to be "stronger and healthier than he was this time last year, at least."[18] But robustness did not pertain only to his physical ability. Belinsky seemed to be in a better state of mind. More centered. Less distracted. He wanted to play in the majors again but acknowledged that his delay in signing a contract might be a factor for his future because it took three weeks away from working out with the Reds.

If he went to the Indianapolis club, so be it. Remaining positive, he pointed out his allure for attendance with Hawaii as an example. Commitment remained steadfast. "I will bust my gut so I can help the big leaguers when they want me," stated Belinsky.[19]

Reds manager Sparky Anderson gave the striving southpaw an opportunity in an exhibition game against the Mets; Belinsky threw two innings and blanked the World Series champs. Larry Shepard, now a pitching coach with Cincinnati, homed in on a perpetual challenge. "Bo has always had good stuff," observed his former skipper. "His pitching problem has always been the same ... control. He's just got to realize he doesn't have to nibble at the plate. With his stuff he shouldn't be afraid to throw strikes. And if he does, there's no reason why he can't relieve instead of start."[20]

Anderson needed to see him in a game situation for assessment. Even though he wouldn't make the Reds for Opening Day, there was always the possibility of getting a call during the season. Plus, the Reds' skipper praised Belinsky's attitude as "great."[21] An aura of humility surrounded Belinsky, which could disappoint or confuse people who wanted the man about town rather than a domesticated ballplayer. "I know I've made my mistakes the way I acted," revealed the Trenton native. "If I'd started with another ball club, not the Angels, it would have been different. The Angels were a social club ... when I got over to the National League [with the Phillies] it was too competitive."[22]

The Volatile Side

Collins got pregnant, a result of an argument over birth control pills. Belinsky wanted her to stop using them. But insecurity intervened, and he got rid of them. "Bo decided the only way he could hold me, the only way he would be sure of me was by having a baby. I didn't want to have a baby just then. I wanted to live a little, have fun, continue working, doing the things I wanted to do. Bo wouldn't hear of it. He wanted me to have a baby right away, right now." When he found the birth control pills, he "went into a rage."[23]

As far as the press knew, everything was copacetic in the Belinsky home. They could not let go of the past. In his column, Frank Dolson of the *Philadelphia Inquirer* mourned Belinsky's extinguishing the infernal nightlife for a staid home, notwithstanding being married to a *Playboy* playmate and having an infant daughter. "The wonderful world of Bo Belinsky is not what it used to be. The big league swinger has become a minor league pitcher. The playboy has become a family man. The no-hit hero who once made headlines on and off the field is trying to make a living."[24]

It was good copy but lousy humanity. Belinsky hardly entered the priesthood. For red-blooded American males who envied athletic talent and didn't read *Playboy* for the interviews and articles, Belinsky had a terrific life. He should have been lauded, not lamented, for settling down, refocusing attention, and trying to get on a major league roster.

It looked like Belinsky might reach his goal. On April 5, a special report in the *Cincinnati Enquirer* boasted the headline "Belinsky Is Likely

10. The End of a Long and Winding Road

to Stick Around." Anderson had to cut two players before the team flew to Cincinnati later that day; Opening Day was April 6. Belinsky's spring training stats satisfied Anderson: six innings in four games, five strikeouts, four walks, three hits, and two runs.[25]

Reflecting on his journey, Belinsky offered context regarding the previous year with Pittsburgh. An impressive group of starting pitchers didn't leave a slot for Belinsky, which affected his performance. "I pitched 11 innings for the first six weeks I was there and, to tell you the truth, I was terrible. I think I was just trying too hard. I felt I had to be another Koufax or Drysdale every time I came in."[26]

Getting Another Shot

Anderson used the lefty in three relief appearances before optioning him to Indianapolis. With the score 10–8 in the top of the seventh inning at Crosley Field on April 18, Clay Carroll walked Willie McCovey and Ken Henderson, struck out Al Gallagher, and gave up a two-run double to Russ Gibson. Enter Belinsky—the Reds' fifth pitcher of the night—who gave up two more runs to make the score 14–8 and another two runs in the eighth inning. Lee May's solo homer led off the bottom of the ninth, but the score stayed 16–9.

Chicago led, 10–5, at Wrigley Field on May 8 when Belinsky started the bottom of the sixth inning. He stifled the opposition as Cincinnati scored twice for a 10–7 loss that broke an eight-game winning streak. Belinsky's next opportunity happened at Crosley Field on May 18, also against Chicago. Reds right-hander Ray Washburn had been pummeled for six runs when Anderson called on the lefty with two outs in the top of the second inning. The Cubs scored three times against Belinsky, who lasted through the top of the fifth. Behind 9–0, the Reds clawed for four runs in the bottom of the fifth and another run an inning later. Chicago tacked on three more runs in the top of the ninth for a 12–5 final score.

It stopped a three-game winning streak for the Reds, who won 15 of the next 20 games. The next day, Cincinnati sent Belinsky to the Indianapolis Indians and promoted Pedro Borbón. True to form, obstinacy emerged. Belinsky wanted a deal, preferably a trade to the Islanders if he could no longer be a major leaguer because he and Jo lived in Hawaii. There would be a psychological value to working there in addition to the good will that he had earned with his two stints playing for the Islanders. Regarding his production, or lack thereof, Belinsky pointed to a lack of playing time as the culprit and argued that "they were just waiting for my earned run average to go above 3.00 so they could make the move."

Further, he projected that outstanding performances in Indianapolis would not return him to Ohio's NL ball club later in the year. "I don't think I'd come back to the Reds in September if I went down there and went 10–0. If they're not pitching me now, I can't see how they will in September."[27]

After being dismissed from the Pirates, Belinsky believed that Shepard played a major role because of a personality conflict. "I think I lost out because the pitching coach didn't like me," said the hurler.[28]

A Violent Incident

Drinking accelerated to numb the pain of a major league career likely being over for good. Fueled by vodka, Belinsky turned violent, bordering on deadly, one night when he pulled a gun on his wife during an argument. Grabbing her hair, shouting at her, and threatening to kill her terrified Collins, who said that Belinsky pulled the trigger when he had the gun to her head. "I don't really know to this day whether or not he knew the gun was not loaded," she revealed. But Collins refused to sign a complaint with the police after Belinsky apologized and "blamed it all on the booze, convinced Jo he didn't mean it, admitted he was overly depressed and promised her it wouldn't happen again."

Collins and their infant daughter spent the night with Pete Rose and his wife. Life went back to normal, or as normal as they could be. "The next day we got back together again," she explained. "Bo had sobered up and he was calmed down. What could I do? I loved the guy. He needed me."[29]

The Last Season

Belinsky's inauguration to the Indianapolis squad happened in an epic contest that took two nights to complete. After 17 innings, the Indians were tied with the 89ers, 5–5, in a game that began at 8:00 p.m. and approached the five-hour mark at Oklahoma City's All Sports Stadium, where an American Association rule forbade an inning to begin after 12:50 a.m. The deadlock had existed since the eighth inning. Belinsky gave up Oklahoma City's quintet of scores, though he showcased strength in the beginning with three strikeouts among the first six 89er batters.[30]

In his four and one-third innings, he tacked on another strikeout. The teams squared off a night later; Indianapolis won, 10–7, in 23 innings. Another game began afterward, which also ran into the 12:50 a.m. curfew block; it delayed the game's completion until the following night—the Indians won, 5–4, in 12 innings.³¹

In his next start, a home game against the 89ers on June 5, Belinsky looked promising again at the beginning. He lasted six and one-third innings; Oklahoma City tagged him for five runs on five hits and five walks. But only one hit was "a solid poke." The visitors got on base twice with bunts and twice with "pop fly singles."

Belinsky walked three 89ers before getting removed in the seventh inning, and César Cedeño crushed a grand slam off relief pitcher Ronald Welsch. Indianapolis's defense made five errors in the 9–6 loss charged to Belinsky, who hit a double and a single in his offensive opportunities and said, "I was hoping that I could give five or six good innings. I had thrown 96 pitches at the end of six innings, and I just tired out in the seventh."³²

After blanking the Tulsa Oilers, 3–0, on June 9, he credited his screwball and the fielders. "But let's say it was a team game," stated the left-hander, who pitched a complete game and tallied nine strikeouts. "Those guys really played great ball behind me. No errors, no mental mistakes and some really find plays. They played a great game." A lion's share of the praise went to his battery mate. "That [Bill] Plummer did a heck of a job catching me tonight. He blocked several pitches in the dirt that would have advanced runners had they got away. What a prospect he is."³³

A 4–1 victory against the Omaha Royals followed for the lefty, who struck out four, allowed five hits, and threw a complete game on June 13. In his next outing, Belinsky relied on an array of slower pitches against the Evansville Triplets to prevent tiring. It worked. He won the first game of a double-header on June 17, going the full nine in a 5–2 victory. Evansville managed five hits and four walks, and Belinsky struck out four. The Indians lost the second game, 6–5, in 14 innings.³⁴

As the spring of 1970 turned to summer, Belinsky had his best production for the Indians when he added his fourth consecutive victory with a two-hitter on June 21—another complete game—against the Royals. He retired 19 batters in a row during one stretch. Besides the pair of singles, he allowed two walks and struck out seven.³⁵ His streak of complete-game victories ended there. On June 25, Indianapolis trailed the Denver Bears, 3–2, in the eighth inning when Belinsky walked a batter on a full count with one out to load the bases. The southpaw felt that the batter struck out looking. Denver enhanced their lead, ending the game with a 5–2 victory and Belinsky's second defeat with the Indians.³⁶

Taking on the Wichita Aeros, Belinsky enjoyed a 5–1 lead when the Indians took the field for the bottom of the sixth inning at Lawrence Stadium. But home runs by Richie Scheinblum and John Lowenstein tied the game, forcing him from the mound; Scheinblum went yard again in the bottom of the ninth with his second solo blast to win the game for the Aeros.[37]

On July 3, Belinsky got his fifth win when Indianapolis beat Evansville, 5–4, at home in Owen J. Bush Stadium. He went six and two-thirds innings, leaving after three straight walks and a "pinch bloop single" by Charlie Manuel whittled a 5–2 lead to 5–4 in the top of the seventh. Pat House relieved him, but Mother Nature intervened with rain and stopped the game early. Belinsky pointed to a lack of rest as the cause for his recent slide. "I guess I just don't have enough 'gas' to pitch every four days," surmised the hurler. "I need that extra day's rest, but with [Bill] Harrelson gone and double-headers coming up, we're short of starters."[38]

An outstanding effort on July 7 yielded 14 strikeouts for the pitcher trying to claw his way back to the majors. "I've quit trying to throw a slider and I'm concentrating more on the curve ball," revealed Belinsky, who left the game in the bottom of the seventh inning for a pinch-hitter. Dooley Womack threw two innings in relief and struck out three. "I threw quite a few curves tonight, but mostly it was the screwball and some fastballs." Belinsky's impressiveness and the Indianapolis offense combined for a 6–2 win.[39]

The Aeros combatted him in his next game, scoring three times in two innings and sending him to the clubhouse. Indianapolis trailed, 5–2, going to the bottom of the ninth inning but mounted a terrific rally to win, 6–5. It was the second game of a doubleheader on July 11; Indianapolis won the first game, 2–1.[40]

Pitching on two days' rest, Belinsky got pummeled again by the Aeros in the second game of a twin bill and registered his third loss. Wichita also won the first game, 9–4. The kids from Kansas scored in the top of the first inning when Belinsky hit a batter with the bases loaded and knocked him for a pair of tallies an inning later. His fellow hurlers got a similar pounding—Wichita finished with a decisive 11–2 victory.[41]

The southpaw had a good though uneven performance against the Iowa Oaks on July 17, allowing one hit and striking out eight through five innings. But he also threw three wild pitches and walked five batters. In the sixth inning, he gave up two homers. Welsch relieved him, and Indianapolis lost, 3–1.[42]

A 3–2 victory against Evansville on July 22 gave Belinsky a 7–4 record. He left in the seventh inning, striking out 10 and walking five.[43] His fifth loss occurred at the hands of the Oaks, who pounded the lefty for six runs in the fourth inning on July 26 before he got pulled with one out. Indianapolis tacked three runs on to the scoreboard; Joe Hamende and his fellow Indians limited Iowa to the half-dozen tallies in the 6–3 loss.[44]

Another disaster took place in Belinsky's next start, the second game of a July 31 double-header against the Tulsa Oilers. Indians skipper

Vern Rapp replaced him after one and one-third innings that resulted in four runs. Tulsa's batsmen had compiled three hits, two walks, and a hit-by-pitch; Belinsky also threw a pair of wild pitches. The Indians lost both games, 6–2 and 5–4.[45]

A pulled back muscle caused a hiatus for Belinsky and a controversy. Indians executives displaced him from the squad and requested that their counterparts in Cincinnati send him to another club. Belinsky claimed that the injury happened on July 21, exacerbated a day later in the game against Evansville. He also said that Rapp overworked him despite the back injury.[46] "Bo now has informed us that he is ready to begin working out after a period of 10 days of complete rest," said Indians president Max Schumacher. Further, Belinsky disclosed that he tried to reach out to the Reds' front office but got no response.[47]

There may have been an intangible factor in eliminating his status as an Indian. The *Indianapolis News* reported that Belinsky "hadn't been overly popular with other Tribe players and frequently complained, some players said, of not getting enough runs and pitching too often."[48] A week after the request to the Reds, Belinsky found a new home with the Asheville Tourists in the Double-A Southern League.[49] His first opportunity came on August 23 in relief of Charles Higgins, who had given up three runs to the Birmingham A's; Belinsky threw three innings and allowed two runs. Birmingham won, 6–2.[50]

On August 28, Belinsky faced the A's again in his first start for Asheville. There were seven strikeouts and no walks on his watch, which lasted seven innings; Birmingham notched seven hits and two runs off the southpaw. Asheville scored once. Birmingham tacked on an insurance run against reliever Doug Dreier in the eighth for a 3–1 final score.[51]

Belinsky started Asheville's last game of the season, a 4–3 win against the Columbus Astros on August 31. He put on quite a show. In addition to striking out nine—and walking six—Belinsky banged a one-out single in the bottom of the seventh inning with the Tourists behind, 2–1. He followed it by stealing second, taking third on Otis Thornton's errant throw, and crossing the plate on Gregg Slape's base hit to tie the score at 2–2. In the eighth, Belinsky gave up a leadoff double and a single, which put runners at the corners. He got relieved; Columbus went ahead by a run, but the Tourists rallied in the bottom of the ninth to win, 4–3.[52]

It was the last professional baseball game for Bo Belinsky. In late October, the Reds awarded all players, no matter how long they'd been with the team during the season, a share of their 1970 bounty for reaching the World Series. Belinsky got $1,000.[53] A little more than two months later, he declared the end of his baseball career.[54]

His statistics were hardly notable: 28–51 in the majors, 77–77 in the minors. He had a 4.10 ERA against major leaguers. Whether by intent or circumstance, he played with 17 teams starting in 1956, never finding traction with a club for more than three seasons. Though inconsistent, he had moments when he soared. Making headlines for glorious achievements like no-hitters for the Angels and the Islanders plus a social life with an array of beautiful, famous women synonymized Belinsky's name with celebrity.

His moniker became prominent in another sport during his last season; a greyhound dubbed Bo Belinsky competed in racing at the track in Black Hills, South Dakota, and racked up 11 victories.[55]

Anna Belinsky blamed the institution of baseball for her son's failings.

> You know, I think the people in baseball tried to break his spirit. They never really wanted to see him happy. But they couldn't do it. Bo isn't like that. He just goes along and gets ready for the next day. He never looks back. He'll never say a bad thing about anybody. He'll never blame anybody. He's a happy boy but a lot of that is all on the outside. Inside, he's burning up and he has a right to it, the way they treated him in ball. Sometimes he would come home and his stomach would be all upset and he would have to take those pills to settle his stomach.
>
> Nobody ever tells you about that in baseball, nobody ever tells you how they take a boy and pay him nothing and ship him away from home and expect him to be able to do everything on his own. The ball clubs just don't watch out enough for the boys.[56]

Both parents mourned the end of their son's career and targeted baseball's overseers who didn't pay attention to his talent. "He would have made more of himself if they only had let him alone," said Anna. "They didn't really give him a chance, they moved him around, they told lies about him, they were always against him. He was outspoken. Baseball doesn't like people like that." Ed Belinsky inquired about his son's status in the bullpen rather than the starting rotation. "Why, if they left him alone as a starter, he might have been a really great pitcher. He had the arm, I know he did, he really did."[57]

They had a point. But management expects ballplayers to have desire and discipline. Belinsky didn't have either. "Bo just wouldn't work," said Bill Rigney. "He thought all there was to pitching was showing up at the park five minutes before the game, grabbing the ball, and shutting somebody out. The worst thing that ever happened to him was that damn no-hitter. He got to thinking he was so good he didn't have to anything else except go right to the Hall of Fame."[58]

Gene Mauch concurred. "He had a great arm, great stuff, and he knew how to pitch. He just didn't really understand what baseball was all about, the dedication, the work, the wanting to succeed, the sweating and the discomforts of playing the game. He wanted the fun and the glory. None of that comes without the pain."[59]

But Belinsky had no problem with those intangibles when he played with the Hawaii Islanders, probably the best fit for him. Or maybe being married gave him a foundation that carried over to his job. "He worked hard, he did his running, he did everything a manager could want," said former Islanders manager Chuck Tanner. "He did the most important thing, he won."[60]

Too little, too late? Perhaps. Probably.

Belinsky's marriage headed toward an end, too. "Jo is a beautiful girl, and I really tried to make a go of married life, but I just have to be myself and go my own way," said the ballplayer.[61] Hence, a separation; divorce followed. Where some see marriage as a vehicle for stability, he ultimately saw it as a restriction on freedom.

But freedom can be deceptive. Without discipline, what felt like the wind at his back thrust him toward rock bottom.

11

Say It Ain't So, Bo

After a ballplayer doffs his cap, tosses his uniform in the laundry bin, and hangs up his spikes for the last time, he may be forgotten by the baseball community, only to resurface for Old Timers games, retrospective interviews, and documentaries. If Bo Belinsky had his way, he would not have to wait very long to be back in the public eye.

Just a few months after he threw his last pitch in professional baseball, Belinsky revealed that he wanted to star in a film based on his life. "That's the biggest thing I'm working on," said the now-retired pitcher. "I've got a few old friends from the good days [around] LA who are willing to put up, say, $100,000, but we're not going to expose all my escapades unless we do it right."[1]

It didn't happen.

In 1972, *Sports Illustrated* profiled Belinsky's downward trajectory in a cautionary tale underlined by the precept that choices have consequences. Since debuting in 1954, the magazine's mantra had been honesty. No pandering. No soft soap. By the early 1970s, *Sports Illustrated*—or *SI* as the magazine's readers often called it—had well earned its status as a magazine respecting its readers by delivering candid, insightful, and enlightening journalism. Pat Jordan's piece, "Once He Was an Angel," ran six pages, slicing the spectrum of Belinsky's life into shades, nuances, and hues that had become duller because of his situation even if the subject didn't see it that way. But that's what happens when people mistake lust for love, superficiality for substance, and adrenaline for contentment. Whatever stability he enjoyed with Collins had evaporated.

Belinsky acknowledged that he had mismanaged his baseball career, perhaps seduced by the attention and adoration of the public as much as by women. "It was no big thing," said the 35-year-old, now living in a Hollywood Hills house owned by a guy named Lennie—no last name given in the article—and populated with "seven or eight people in various states of sprawl," including an 18-year-old named Bonnie, whom the ex–major leaguer met on the Sunset Strip the night before the writer visited him.

She "wants to stay," according to Belinsky. It was not quite Xanadu. Jordan's opus depicted a sad man craving companionship. If substantive relationships were five-course meals, Belinsky settled for crumbs out of the breadbasket.

His personality overpowered the fact that inconsistency combined with flashes of greatness defined his career rather than sustainability. The ballplayer who dated actresses and got feted by the press for his quotes lived to enjoy, not to endure. "My philosophy of life?" pondered Belinsky. "That's easy. If music be the food of love, by all means let the band play on."[2] There's no question that he provoked interest, whether being sent to the minors or bouncing from squad to squad in the majors trying to convince coaches, managers, teammates, opposing teams, and perhaps himself, that he had the goods to succeed. But a palpable loneliness orbited Belinsky; liquor and sex helped mollify it but could never replace the sustenance of a solid marriage.

If he had some pennants and World Series titles like Mickey Mantle had, that might have helped counter the isolation, but walking off the field with no baseball in his future except for Old Timers games left Belinsky in the precarious position of wondering what to do next with his life. He faced a dim situation. A devil-may-care attitude plus a sports media hungry for his latest escapade put Belinsky in a position that no matter what he did, the public would likely look at him askance. Or worse, with pity.

Moreover, he had the advantage of being handsome, personable, and quotable reinforced by the abundance of stories featuring his social life. Publicity can be heady. But what's enjoyable and permissible to a man in his 20s becomes tiresome in his 30s, particularly when the evidence shows that his skills will no longer allow him the chance to compete at the highest level in his craft.

Jordan observed that a milestone birthday a few years before the interview created a turning point in Belinsky's persona from bon vivant to boorish. "At 30, there were no more peaks in sight. He knew that the public, which once had found him an entertaining young man, had grown increasingly weary and annoyed with what it felt was his unstable and self-destructive behavior. As an aging and unsuccessful playboy, Belinsky had become a parody of himself."[3]

He also contended that the southpaw "had dissipated a promising career," but there's no way to know for certain. There are plenty of pitchers who have mediocre careers but a moment of glory. Don Larsen owns the only perfect game in World Series history. He played for the Browns/Orioles, Yankees, Athletics, White Sox, Giants, Astros, Orioles, and Cubs from 1953 to 1967. In 1954, he led the majors with 21 losses. Lifetime record: 81–91.

Don Nottebart threw the first no-hitter for the Houston Colt .45s in 1963; he played in the majors for nine seasons with a 36–51 record. Tom Phoebus's no-hitter for Baltimore in 1968 belied a 56–52 record in his journeys with the Orioles, Padres, and Cubs from 1966 to 1972. Len Barker pitched a perfect game for the Cleveland Indians in 1981 but retired after 11 seasons with a 74–76 record.

Belinsky debated the impact of his actions on his career but tossed aside any doubts. "Besides, there's no way I could have lived my life differently," he said. "Can a leopard change his spots? You can shave all the fur off the poor beast, and he's still got his spots, right? Who can explain it? Why does a mad dog howl at the moon? Why did I do the things I did?"[4]

Recounting his time with the Amarillo Gold Sox in 1959, it became clear that wanderlust solidified as Belinsky went bar-hopping, attracted by jazz musicians in front of the establishments. "What I didn't know was that all these bars hired jazz bands to lure customers inside. Man, after that bar, it seemed like every step I took there were these buglers waiting for me. I woke up six days later in a hotel room in Acapulco."[5]

But Belinsky's present behavior exceeded indulgence. When another houseguest complained about calls from friends of the former ballplayer occurring in the middle of the night, Belinsky tore the phones off the walls and tossed them in the swimming pool. This egregious act didn't happen in a vacuum. Still a bar-hopper, he had gone with a quartet of guys to nightclubs on the famed Sunset Strip and ran into *Playboy* chieftain Hugh Hefner, who invited them to the Playboy Mansion in Holmby Hills. According to Jordan's retelling, Hefner remained nonchalant and quiet as he observed his guests' "ardent strivings" regarding the mansion's accoutrements. Deference disappeared. "The guests began talking loudly about 'deals' and 'scores' they could make with proper backing," wrote the *SI* scribe. But when the sun rose over southern California, the night owls in one of the most famous homes in America got ushered out, though politely, by their host.

Belinsky—who had a link to his host because of Collins—revealed that he believed Hefner and *Playboy* "use women," though the ballplayer seemed more disturbed by his companions. "But still, Hef's a gracious host. I wanted my friends to enjoy themselves. It was a score for them, something they could talk about for a week. Instead, they tried to hock his silverware."[6]

There were other revelations regarding his baseball career. Prominent among them: Belinsky loved the game. Those times that he quit? "But that was just a bluff on my part. There was no way I could quit. I had learned to love the game by then."[7] He also claimed that Len Shecter had offered to collaborate with him on a tell-all book before the sportswriter connected with Jim Bouton for *Ball Four*. "I told him I wasn't interested. I couldn't rat on guys I'd played with."[8]

Alcohol stayed a constant companion for Belinsky. Liquor bottles and beer taps hold lubricants to help diminish the stress created by any ailment of everyday life for millions of people.

An unreasonable boss changes a deadline from a month to two weeks. Gin and tonic, please.

The mother-in-law is about to visit for a holiday weekend. Scotch on the rocks, thanks.

Another argument with the wife. Budweiser on draft, if you have it.

But booze can have an enhancing effect, leading to its use as a symbol of celebration—making a toast at a wedding, getting a promotion, or closing a business deal. Belinsky didn't need a special occasion. He drank because it felt good. When he walked into bars, nightclubs, or restaurants in the Los Angeles area during his time with the Angels, they became social playgrounds where he could cash in the currency of fame for attention, whether from men who wanted to hear his baseball stories or women who wanted to take him home.

Belinsky's demons had gotten the better of him. Melancholy bordered on depression as he pursued a high that could never be achieved with any permanence. A no-hitter? You're only as good as your last game. Another team challenged a starting pitcher every four or five days. Partying with beautiful women deep into the night and perhaps the dawn? Sexual pleasures are temporary. A typical pattern provides the height of ecstasy, the afterglow, and then sleep followed the next morning by the everyday minutiae of life. Cleaning the kitchen. Taking the car to the mechanic. Dropping off suits at the dry cleaners. But that's assuming a baseline of being a responsible adult, which did not seem to be the case, as depicted in the *SI* article.

Belinsky had friends. Or acquaintances at the very least. Jordan's words oppose this theorem, giving the sense that loneliness pervaded the life of this man in his mid-30s hanging out with an 18-year-old in a house full of people. The physical energy spent on socializing shielded Belinsky from any emotional energy for inquiring about the needs within one's soul and self. It's an exhausting way to live. Belinsky didn't seem to know any other way but fast and straight ahead. Detours with sustainable relationships fell victim to his volatility and capriciousness.

Al Ferrara played against Belinsky in the minors and the majors and saw the downfall in the mid–1970s.

> After baseball, I ran a restaurant. I was the host and Maître d at the Martoni Marquis on the Sunset Strip. Bo was pretty down and out. Strung out. I took care of him. Guys in the restaurant would be interested in talking with him.

They'd pick up his tab. One night, I had a party after work and told Bo. He came up and he was having a hard time. He said, "I gotta get out of here. I gotta go to Hawaii." I had $700 and gave him $500. This was about 1973–1974. Years later, a mutual friend handed me $1,000 and said, "Bo sent it to you and said thank you." It was double payment for what I did for him.

He was one of the nicest guys I ever met. He'd never say anything bad about anybody.[9]

When Belinsky met Jane Weyerhauser in 1974, he tried to conquer alcohol addiction with valium "and other drugs." Their encounter took place in the water when he rescued the timber heiress from dangerous waves in Sandy Beach in Honolulu. "I didn't even know it was her, she was sort of floating there. I grabbed her and pushed her out of the way and got caught myself, it almost broke my neck. I got out with a popped neck and all scraped up, and she nursed me back. Hawaii's always been a lucky place for me."[10]

They married in 1975. To say they had a tempestuous relationship is like saying John D. Rockefeller did okay financially.

Belinsky had more than love on his mind. With Weyerhauser's access to money, he could easily obtain cocaine. Drug use compounded his entrenched narcissism, preventing joy when Weyerhauser got pregnant with twin girls and went into labor only seven-and-a-half months into the pregnancy. "I was so dead that when I finally came to the hospital and saw those two little girls, I had no feeling for them whatsoever, and I had no feeling for Jane. All I could think about was me."[11]

It didn't end there. The hospital kept the babies under observation, but Weyerhauser went home. She would have been better off just about anywhere else. High on drugs, Belinsky waved around his .38 revolver and "started shooting all over the place," including at his wife. "The bullet went through her hip. Maybe a quarter of an inch up and she's dead. Simple as that." When Belinsky pointed the gun at his head and cocked it, Weyerhauser pleaded, "What are you doing? What are you doing?"[12]

He relinquished the gun. Weyerhauser did not file a police report. "I was very lucky," she said. "The bullet didn't hit any bone. I should have called the police, but I didn't. I loved him." Belinsky abandoned her and got smashed in LA, finally going to rehab. It wasn't the first time, though this stay at Saint John's Hospital in Santa Monica begat Belinsky's first journey to Alcoholics Anonymous. It seemed like he was on a path to sobriety. He wasn't. Despite Weyerhauser's generosity, financial and otherwise—reflected by living in the Doheny Estates section of Beverly Hills, driving a Maserati, and golfing at Riviera Country Club—Belinsky could not control his urges. "He grabbed me by the throat and pushed me in front of our children," declared Weyerhauser, who divorced him in 1981.

Belinsky had a minimal relationship with his twin daughters until it became nonexistent in the mid-1980s.[13]

Though he claimed it was an undeserved description, Belinsky ranked as a notorious drinker. In 1975, a feature article by the Associated Press quoted him as saying that the boozing happened after he retired. "It's a sneaky drug, I'm glad I got it over with quickly," said Belinsky. "It's a sociable type drug, and you don't realize you're becoming a lush until you get to the point where you become sickening to yourself."[14]

One could explain—but in no way excuse—his behavior with Weyerhauser being a result of addiction complemented by the increasing permissiveness regarding drugs and alcohol that began in the mid-1960s with the Rolling Stones describing the use of tranquilizers in "Mother's Little Helper," followed by The Association's anthem for marijuana, "Along Comes Mary." It escalated in the 1970s, thanks to popular culture playing a major role. The Eagles emblemized drug use with the song "Life in the Fast Lane," referring to Don Henley's drug dealer talking about driving at 90 miles an hour in a Corvette heading to a poker game.[15]

Saturday Night Live reflected drug use with humor aimed to its target audience of teenagers and young adults. NBC premiered the show, then called *Saturday Night*, on October 11, 1975; George Carlin hosted. In the 1977 sketch, "Ask President Carter," Dan Aykroyd plays the nation's chief executive answering questions from citizens calling the White House. One caller says that he's taken some acid. The president asks for details about the pills, shows his knowledge of drug slang, and talks him down from a severe high.[16]

Network insiders were aware that marijuana and cocaine were popular among the cast and behind-the-scenes personnel. "It would have been hard not to have known it," observed Doug Hill and Jeff Weingrad, co-authors of *Saturday Night*, a masterful account of the show's first ten years. "The odor of grass was commonplace not only on the 17th floor [of 30 Rockefeller Center] but also in the hallways and offices around studio 8H. The dressing room on the ninth floor for the *Saturday Night* band was widely referred to, by NBC's Guest Relations staff as well as those on the show, as 'the Departure Lounge.' The Guest Relations staff also knew that an individual who attended the show almost every week as a guest was, in fact, one of *Saturday Night*'s drug connections."[17]

Woody Allen used the popularity of cocaine in the late 1970s for laughs in the film *Annie Hall*. Prodded by his girlfriend, the title character, Alvy Singer, attempts to snort cocaine for the first time at a small get-together in a Hollywood apartment. Holding the small container of powder—which his host informs him costs $2,000 an ounce—Alvy sneezes and ruins the anticipated, costly high. Though Allen has been lauded as a gifted filmmaker, this iconic moment was an accident. But it fit with his character, who already seemed out of place at the party, and became a hallmark scene of the 1977 movie.[18]

Drug use didn't just affect elite Manhattanites. A report from the Department of Defense in 1971 regarding soldiers assigned to the Vietnam War summarized, "Results showed 45% to have used narcotics, amphetamines, or barbiturates at least once in Vietnam. Narcotics were used by 43%; amphetamines by 25%; and barbiturates by 23%."[19]

Though set in 1962, *Animal House* had a late 1970s sensibility of humor and carefreeness regarding drugs and alcohol. The blockbuster 1978 film about a fraternity at the fictional Faber College featured a scene involving students smoking marijuana with one of their professors and several scenes highlighting the consumption of alcohol at fraternity parties. Bluto, played by John Belushi, chugs a bottle of whiskey when the dean shuts down the fraternity house.

Another 1978 film showcased marijuana. *FM* starred Michael Brandon as Jeff Dugan, the program director of LA rock station QSKY, battling his corporate overseers, who want more commercials even if it risks diluting the quality of the programming and causes listeners to bolt. The Army wants a package of commercials to correspond with QSKY's audience, explained by a lieutenant who tokes up while giving his explanation.

In the first episode of *Eight Is Enough*, which aired on ABC on March 15, 1977, one of the eight Bradford children—15-year-old Elizabeth—is arrested for obstructing justice. Her friend Stanley drives through a Stop sign and gets pulled over, but he has contraband in the car, unbeknownst to Elizabeth until that moment. "Mom, I didn't even know he had the junk in the car," she explains. "I mean, I knew he smokes pot. Everybody smokes pot. But I didn't think he was doing pills. And when he started shoving the stuff under the seat, what was I supposed to do? Make a citizens arrest?"

The Bradfords hire a lawyer who gets her charges reduced. Lamenting his brood growing up—including the eldest son, David, a construction worker, moving into his own apartment—patriarch Tom Bradford says to his wife, Joan, "One day they're on the potty, the next day they're smoking pot."[20]

Thank God It's Friday leveraged disco's popularity in a storyline that took place seemingly in real time over 90 minutes at the Zoo, a fictional discotheque in Los Angeles. Jeff Goldblum starred as the owner, a lecherous ladies' man looking for his next prey; Donna Summer sang her signature song, *Last Dance*. At the beginning of this 1978 movie, two young men smoked marijuana in the car on the way to the disco.

In the pilot episode for *The Mary Tyler Moore Show* airing on CBS on September 19, 1970, Lou Grant represented the looseness of boundaries in the workplace when he poured himself liquor while interviewing Moore's character, Mary Richards, for a job as associate producer of the WJM-TV six o'clock news show in Minneapolis. Grant's drinking in the office indicated a pervading attitude in corporate America, which neither condoned nor condemned alcohol consumption among middle-class and upper-middle-class workers. It simply existed, like smoking cigarettes.[21]

Occasionally, Hollywood tackled the subject of alcoholism head-on but without preaching. In 1973, CBS aired a two-episode story on *Maude* revolving around the excessive drinking of Maude Findlay's husband, Walter, which he emphatically denies; a loud, passionate discussion about his behavior culminates in Walter slapping her. It causes him to break down and seek help.[22]

The Bad News Bears starred Walter Matthau as Morris Buttermaker, a former minor league pitcher who guzzles beer and makes a living by cleaning pools. Buttermaker also likes whiskey. Los Angeles City Councilman Bob Whitewood corrals him into coaching the Bears in the North Valley League after suing it to allow subpar players—including his son, Toby—to play. Although the Bears lose the climactic game against the Yankees, they celebrate the end of the season by shaking up beer cans provided by Buttermaker and showering each other with the suds.

Permissiveness toward alcohol and drugs in 1970s America matched something in the air that could be defined as a loosening of standards by some and an expansion of compassion by others. *The Partridge Family* aired on ABC from 1970 to 1974, featuring a quintet of kids ranging from elementary school to high school and their widowed mom, Shirley Partridge—played by Academy Award winner Shirley Jones—based in northern California, performing as a soft rock group in front of live audiences and recording songs.

A first-season episode in 1970 showed the Partridge Family singing for prisoners. The matriarch praises the crowd, "Thank you. Thank you very much. I can honestly say you're the best audience we've ever had. But then we've never appeared before a captive audience before. I can't imagine what it's like to be a convict. But I think in some real way, we're all prisoners."[23]

Save the Tiger starred Jack Lemmon as a financially burdened fashion executive living beyond his means in Beverly Hills and contemplating arson of his factory to get insurance money. On the brink of a breakdown throughout the story, Lemmon's character, Harry Stoner, a World War II veteran, picks up a pretty hitchhiker half his age and has sex with her. Hitchhiking was common in the era. The dialogue emphasizes the generation gap between the characters but makes no moral judgment on Harry, who has an attractive, supportive wife at home.

Lemmon won an Oscar for his performance in this 1973 film.

Hollywood expanded its use of language as well. An episode of M*A*S*H from 1975 provides an example of sarcasm that would never get an okay from TV network censors in subsequent decades. "House Arrest" featured Mary Wickes as a colonel making a pass at Major Frank Burns, then screaming "rape" when he denies her advances. Hawkeye Pierce emerges from his tent, nicknamed the Swamp, where he and his friends are watching a movie from a projector, and says, "Rape? What a night. A movie and vaudeville." Trapper John says, "I never been to a rape before." Hawkeye responds, "Maybe for your next birthday."

Music factored into the liberal aura of the 1970s as well. *Running on Empty* and *Me and You and a Dog Named Boo* offered stories about freedom while traveling on the open roads of America. *Afternoon Delight*, *That's the Way I Like It*, and *Do That to Me One More Time* escalated the depiction of sex in songwriting with lyrics that were not quite graphic, but pretty close. Donna Summer's rendition of *Love to Love You Baby* got closer with orgasmic moans.

Helen Reddy's *I Am Woman* reflected the increasing potency of feminism in America, complemented by characters in television like Margaret Houlihan in M*A*S*H, Charley Drake in *All's Fair*, Maude Findlay in *Maude*, and Mary Richards in *The Mary Tyler Moore Show*.

The culture had certainly loosened by the time Belinsky lived in that crowded house. But there's a difference between using booze and drugs as a casual indulgence rather than a daily routine. When former First Lady Betty Ford revealed in 1978 that she had been addicted to alcohol and drugs, it inspired millions of people and let them know that they were not alone in their battles. Four years later, the Betty Ford Center opened in Rancho Mirage, California.

Either Belinsky did not have the internal wherewithal to figure out his addiction or didn't care. He had too much fun to worry about self-destructive behavior. Or so it seemed. His marriage with Jo Collins weakened and moved toward divorce. A disturbing event happened in 1970 after the couple went out to dinner. They drank. An argument in the car on Pacific Coast Highway in Malibu caused Bo to "[lose] control of the car, smashing it head-on into a steel utility pole. Jo's right arm was so badly crushed that emergency room doctors initially considered amputating it."[24]

In May 1971, Collins went to Denver, where she worked for the Playboy Club; Belinsky lived in Malibu and visited his wife and daughter "periodically," but reconciliation was not in the cards.[25] *Playboy* offered the former Playmate an opportunity to work in Chicago. Collins accepted. A single mom, she balanced her work with her maternal obligations in raising Stevie. But another maternal figure intervened—Anna Belinsky advocated for her son, acknowledging the blame for their deteriorating marriage on his behalf and asking to avoid a permanent solution of divorce. "He is begging you to wait. He says he thinks he can change and be a good husband."[26]

It didn't work. Collins found peace and fulfillment. But an event in Los Angeles required her attendance, which Belinsky discovered and consequently pestered Collins's mother for information. Being a kindhearted, forgiving woman, Collins agreed that he could meet her and Stevie at the airport. "He could drive me to my hotel, we could talk for a few minutes, and that would be it."

That wasn't it. Roses and perfume for her plus "a stuffed animal" for Stevie broke the ice. Belinsky melted it when he asked her out to dinner. "I looked at him, he smiled at me, and I knew then, dammit, that I was still in love with him."[27] But any détente did not result in a reconciliation, no matter how strong the attraction.

In southern California, Belinsky commanded attention even if those entering his orbit did so for selfish reasons. It had been several years since the no-hitter and his presence in gossip columns, but he had enough celebrity to be recognized, adored, and even targeted. "There were always guys, fat middle-aged men, losers, hangers-on, who would carry him for a free meal, a free bed, a sweater, a couple of gallons of gas, anything he needed for survival," wrote Maury Allen in *Bo: Pitching and Wooing*. "His dependency on them was what they craved. They used him to promote themselves. It was no longer Autry and Ann-Margret and Walter Winchell, but in Malibu, in some late-night parties, Bo Belinsky still had some drawing power. The leeches would hang on to him, steal his pride, suck his blood, use him cruelly, rape him until he was dry. Then they would sail off. In a flash, another animal would appear from the jungle and the cycle would start again."[28]

Among these parasitic types were folks who could have had the LAPD coming to put Belinsky in bracelets, and not the kind from Van Cleef & Arpels. "The pimps and gangsters in Los Angeles were the only ones who'd accept me," he later recalled. "As a matter of fact, they gave me a couple of draws and were going to put me in the business, but I was too drunk. They introduced me to cocaine. I had to stop drinking, because it was bad for me, so I did cocaine."[29]

Maybe he liked the attention, though fleeting, even if it came from people with self-serving interests who could send him to the LA penal system. They validated the ex-ballplayer who would never hold a baseball except for Old Timers games and memorabilia shows, revered in Los Angeles for the no-hitter in 1962 and the roster of actresses whom he dated. There are worse things to be remembered for.

But the impact of drugs and liquor had Belinsky in a mental tailspin. Stability was his kryptonite. Van Doren couldn't tame him. Same went for Collins and Weyerhauser. Belinsky found solutions for whatever bothered him through whatever substances were available. "It was unreal," described the ex-pitcher. "I never killed anybody, and I'm fortunate. The things that happened to me, the physical damage that happened to me—I just didn't care. I wanted to die. I didn't want to die. I had no idea. All I knew is that I was in pain."[30]

Dean Chance became his pal's rescuer by placing him in Akron's St. Thomas Hospital. His stay lasted 28 days. But finding traction for sobriety there was about as effective for Belinsky as climbing a block of ice with your hands covered by Vaseline. He ignored whatever strategies the hospital staff and visiting members of Alcoholics Anonymous imparted, then compounded his problem by choosing companions who were questionable at best and dangerous at worst.

In the Allen book, Belinsky described the genesis of his relationship with a prostitute. Yes, a relationship. Their coupling began at a beach party where they hit it off. "We go home and soon we are setting up housekeeping together," said Belinsky. "Helen's a hooker by trade and works at night. She is home for coffee and service by day. It is what I need. We dig each other. She has been divorced, has kids someplace, can understand the complications and complexities of a man in trouble with his head. It is nice."

Allen further described the arrangement as an exchange of work for companionship. "She asked nothing in return but a little love, a little affection, a little attention. Belinsky could always manage that. He could turn his head at a girl, focus those eyes, throw out that smile, and wipe away all doubts."[31]

The sportswriter also culled a recollection from Belinsky's playing days that showed compassion for a fellow ballplayer. In a game against the Twins, his pitch hit Jimmie Hall in the face. "He never was the same again," said the southpaw. "A thing like that stays with you. I almost cost a guy his life."[32]

When the book was published, Allen and Belinsky had a gold star opportunity for publicity—but Belinsky couldn't manage a simple responsibility even for his benefit. Allen found that out when they were supposed to appear on NBC's *Today* to promote the book. It seemed like a foolproof plan. The publisher's publicists escort him to the gate for his red-eye flight from LAX to JFK; a limousine driver takes him from the airport to 30 Rockefeller Center, where he joins Allen to answer questions for a national audience. Belinsky got sidetracked in Los Angeles by a woman waiting for the same flight. The publicists had already left. Their obligation ended with getting him to the gate, not waiting until he got on the plane.

Belinsky and his new friend departed the airport; he never got to New

York for the interview. Allen did it solo. Like so many others, Allen felt betrayed by Belinsky's lack of consideration. Like so many others, he succumbed to forgiveness. "I was so angry," said Allen. "I told myself I'd never talk to that cocksucker again. But I couldn't stay mad at Bo. He called and apologized, and I said, 'All right.'"[33]

His appearances included an Old Timers game at Yankee Stadium in 1974 and another one at Angel Stadium in 1985, where Mamie Van Doren posed with him, Gene Autry, and Dean Chance. He hadn't been forgotten. Syndicated columnist Anna Quindlen mentioned him in a 1988 column about relationships. "The central dating advice of my youth was to mime interest in the things boys were interested in, which is how I know who Paul Hornung and Bo Belinsky were."[34]

Belinsky had relocated to Hawaii in 1982. His "lucky place." By this time, he claimed that he had seven years of sobriety to give him perspective, but the evidence doesn't bear it out. "I was doing things that I thought were sane," said Belinsky. "I was living like I was going to die tomorrow. I was in different parts of the world and country. I was self-destructing and it came to a bitter end."[35]

Van Doren also had some time to consider the tiresome approach to life that her former fiancé endorsed and the negative impact it had on their relationship. With candor and grace, she outlined the toll of being with a guy who sought pleasure like a bee seeks flowers. "Funny about Bo," she began in a quoted excerpt in the same article. "He had this way of ruining a beautiful day. He was always looking for something better and he wasn't [satisfied] until he found it. It was the same with women. He was never satisfied and wanted to run around and have fun. And for me, this was a very romantic time in my life, and I thought this might be it."[36]

Belinsky and Van Doren had last seen each other when he asked for her assistance in promoting the book. "That last time I met Bo, he was like a lost soul," disclosed Van Doren. "He was very unhappy."[37]

Lost, indeed. In the late 1970s, Belinsky's whereabouts were a question mark for his family. "The last I heard, he was somewhere in the Marina del Rey area in Los Angeles," said his mother, Anna. "Maybe somebody out there knows his number."[38]

Belinsky's sister, Lorraine Riley, revealed the fear that her family endured through his shenanigans. "He had my parents in a frenzy because we didn't know where he was," she said in 1982. "He had no friends, no money, he was living house-to-house. I don't know why he didn't come home. It got bad after he was divorced from Jo [in 1973]. Maybe he couldn't keep up with the lifestyle. I didn't know about his problem until he called me one day and said, 'Do you know I almost died? I was in an alcoholic ward and had complications from drinking?'"[39]

In 1985, a feature article in the *Honolulu Star-Bulletin* emphasized his sobriety. It provided an opportunity for nostalgia regarding his baseball career because playing for the Hawaii Islanders gave him great joy. "I remember the fans huddling in the Manoa Mist, their friendliness and that certain quality of old Honolulu Stadium that we'll never see in Hawaii again," described Belinsky. "It was relaxing to play and watch games there."[40]

Battling addiction is an ongoing concern. One day at a time. A restless sort ever since growing up in Trenton, Belinsky had been on a self-destructive path resulting in severed relationships. The most important one was with himself. But his unease dated back to his 1950s childhood, inspiring him always to be on the move as a defense mechanism. "Even as a 16-year-old pool shark, Bo had often been consumed by dread," stated Steve Oney in a lengthy profile of Belinsky for *Los Angeles* magazine in 2005. "He had developed his hustle as a tactic to, in his words, 'down those people' who might hurt him."[41]

His no-hitter in 1962 exacerbated the difficulty because it gave him countless idolaters, which seemed like a boon at the time. After bouncing around the minor leagues, he got his break with the Angels when television shows and movies depicted southern California as a land of excitement, opportunity, and year-round sunshine. An attractive place whose identity had once been primarily linked to show business, the LA region developed into a lucrative site for the sports world by the time Belinsky first donned an Angels uniform in 1962. In five years, Los Angeles had welcomed the Dodgers and Lakers as transplanted teams while establishing the Angels for expansion in the major leagues. The Hollywood Stars and Los Angeles Angels were stalwarts of the Pacific Coast League, but the new Angels ball club further reinforced the city's major league status.

Bo Belinsky in the mid-1980s (Los Angeles Public Library, *Los Angeles Herald Examiner* Photo Collection).

LA had everything that the son of a TV repairman growing up with New Jersey winters could want in 1962. The opulence of Beverly Hills. The exuberance of beachgoers. The expansion of the suburbs. The enthusiasm of fans for the Angels' sophomore year. Belinsky's openness, charm, and fame led to adoration, praise, and sex, but the couplings that made the newspapers were the ones with actresses about whom men fantasized. Leggy females with perfectly coiffed hair and terrific figures made for great copy and further kindled men's hero worship for the pitcher.

The paradigm begs a question. What man could have withstood this temptation? It seemed to be a never-ending parade of hand shakers, back slappers, and female companions while the alcohol flowed, and the energy of LA nightlife pulsated with the Sunset Strip at the heart of Belinsky's antics. But there's a great difference between indulgence once in a while and indulgence as a habit. His sobriety in the 1980s was positive news, though maybe not so meaningful for those who got wounded by the emotional shrapnel caused from his actions, words, and ignorance. "I was an egotistical bastard," explained Belinsky in 1985. "I was so cool that I was freezing myself to death."[42]

To the public and the press, his life seemed glorious. But when the demons overtook Belinsky, who admitted that sobriety took a back seat during the waning years of his career, they sent him plummeting toward despair. He once held the hands of gorgeous women for companionship. Addiction found him new items for succor. "I went from a major league ballplayer to hanging on to a brown bag under the bridge," he revealed in the same interview. "I look at a player throwing away $600,000 today and think he has to be insane, but that's what I was, too. Sick and insane. I wasn't playing with a full deck. I was destined to die a horrible death."[43]

But the hard work to get and remain sober inspired Belinsky to help others. He spoke to "business organizations, the Betty Ford Center, and several major league baseball teams" about his journey, as a caveat to not let self-destructive urges override common sense. He also reached out to an old teammate suffering from alcoholism. "Bo and I had never been that close," admitted Eli Grba. "He was too Hollywood. But he came and got me and took me to an AA meeting. I was nervous," but Bo said, "Don't worry, Eli, they're all drunks just like you and me." It got Grba started on a path of sobriety.[44]

A woman named Bobbi captured his focus in Hawaii, and Belinsky married for a third time in the mid–1980s; they divorced by the end of the decade.

Belinsky accepted the impact of his decisions. If reconciliations happened with his ex-wives and children, that would be wonderful. But for now, he had to focus on staying sober. His life at the end of the 1980s was reminiscent of Al Pacino's locker room speech in the 1999 football movie

Any Given Sunday: "I made every wrong choice a middle-aged man can make. I, uh, I pissed away all my money, believe it or not. I chased off anyone who's ever loved me. And lately, I can't even stand the face I see in the mirror."[45]

Most of all, Belinsky craved to be part of a team again. He found one thanks to a former athlete in a city known to attract people escaping their problems, not confronting them.

Las Vegas.

12

Las Vegas

When Bo Belinsky settled in Las Vegas in 1990, he was a different person from the one that fans remembered. If people met him during the 1990s, they would find an ex-ballplayer who still kept in shape, with hair beginning to turn gray and a manner more courtly than clamorous. "A lot of people are surprised to see me now," said the pitcher in a 1992 profile for the *Los Angeles Times*. "They come looking for one thing, and they sort of find another. I don't have to take the responsibility of being the Great Bo Belinsky any more. The world functions just fine without him."[1]

When Belinsky gallivanted around the hot spots of major league cities with women wanting to bed one of the most famous players in baseball, one would think that he had everything a man in his 20s could want. Despite the idolatry from men who wanted to hear stories of the diamond and women who wanted time alone with him, Belinsky suffered an emotional void. Life in the fast lane can be exhilarating. For someone who never lacked companionship, it provided a necessary salve for wounds that nobody could forecast, identify, or bind. "I was very inconsiderate in those days," he admitted in the same 1992 piece. "I was very confused and had a lot of fear. Basically, I was lonely, and I wasn't going to slow down long enough to see just how lonely I was."[2]

A child resulted from one liaison. Born in 1963, Don Carroll first met Belinsky in the late 1980s and forged a connection filled with stories about the high life and realizations that genetics linked the two men. "He got to tell me all his stories and his philosophy on life with the live fast, die young and all that," said Carroll. "One of the best stories was that I heard how nobody could beat him at pool, and I had been playing pool my whole life. And when I met him in Vegas, my girlfriend at the time took a picture of us from behind and we walked the same way. It was a trip."[3]

Belinsky had calmed in the 1990s after living in Hawaii and avoiding notice if possible. Or at least trying to. The ballplayer who used to be the social barometer for ball clubs became a recluse. His third marriage went down the same avenue as the previous two, leaving him alone. Hanging out in Las Vegas and playing golf led to a day that changed his life. His partners were car dealers who encouraged him to work in the car business. The man who once had to sell managers on his excuses for misbehavior and breaking curfews now sold cars for a company named Findlay.

Though Belinsky later left the company, he returned to use his gift of personality as a community relations director. He assisted when Findlay built batting cages and hosted events for kids, offering advice not only about baseball fundamentals but also about life's pitfalls. There was a certain amount of gladhanding to the position. It might have tired others, but Belinsky needed this outlet where he could get attention, have a place to go every day, and continue on his path of stability. The *Times* piece described his duties. "He scours the community, promoting the dealership. He plays host when VIPs come to town, playing golf, showing the sights and arranging hotel accommodations."[4]

Rich Abajian was Belinsky's North Star in Las Vegas. An alumnus of the University of Nevada—Reno, Abajian had played fullback on the football team and later coached at the university's Las Vegas campus. His leadership, charisma, and ability to connect with customers boosted him to lead Findlay Automotive, a Goliath in the car dealership industry of southern Nevada. Abajian's confidence could make a salesperson believe that selling sand at the beach was not only possible but lucrative.

Belinsky looked up to him even though Abajian was about 20 years younger. He used to dress up in a baseball uniform and get insights from his manager on how to approach pitching situations. With Findlay, he dressed up in sport jackets, dress shirts, and slacks and got insights from Abajian on how to approach customers.

Tyler Corder, Findlay's CFO, was Abajian's right-hand man and best friend until Abajian passed away suddenly in 2016 at the age of 62.

> Rich was an ex-football coach and treated business just like sports. He recruited competitive people to join the team. He wanted people that hated to lose. His manager and sales meetings were often like pregame speeches. He was a very motivational leader and focused on every individual reaching their maximum potential. Employees became very loyal to Rich and worked hard to achieve success.
>
> Rich met Bo in the early nineties and asked him to come aboard at Saturn. Bo served as a customer liaison and marketing representative. Essentially, his job was to make customers feel welcomed at the dealership and to represent Saturn at community events. I think that Bo as an ex-athlete was drawn to Rich as a coach. Rich saw that Bo had skills and talents that he wasn't using and saw it as a challenge to get the most out of Bo. The combination clicked well and Bo felt productive and successful during his time working for Rich.
>
> I think working at Findlay gave Bo a purpose in life. He liked the team atmosphere and he liked to listen to Rich Abajian's motivational talks. Many

people didn't know who Bo was. However, those who were baseball fans were definitely impressed to meet him. I once introduced him to one of our bankers who was just thrilled to meet Bo and ask him about his baseball career.

Bo used to go across the street to a café and bring back breakfast for me and Rich. I remember thinking how odd it was that this famous professional baseball star was bringing me breakfast. Bo was so humble about it. I think he just wanted to do it to express how happy he was to be part of the team. The Bo I remember was just a genuinely nice man. He didn't seem to have an ego. He was just happy to be part of the Findlay team and really enjoyed developing personal relationships with other employees.[5]

During the 1990s, Findlay's business expanded largely because of Abajian. Corder notes the evolution of Findlay into a powerhouse.

> Pete Findlay founded Findlay Automotive in 1961 when he opened Findlay Oldsmobile in Las Vegas. Pete retired in the 1980's and his son Cliff took the reins. The organization has since grown to 35 dealerships. Now Cliff's three sons are active in management of the organization. The Findlay group now employs more than 2,600 people in 5 states. The growth of the organization can be attributed to an intense focus on community involvement combined with customer satisfaction and loyalty.
>
> Findlay's Saturn of West Sahara was one of the 13 original Saturn facilities that opened in October 1990. Under the leadership of Rich Abajian, Saturn of West Sahara quickly became the nation's leading Saturn retailer and was dominant in car sales in Las Vegas. The tremendous success of Saturn of West Sahara led to additional opportunities and fueled the rapid growth of Findlay Automotive.[6]

Scott Keene knew Bo Belinsky for decades longer than the folks at Findlay, but his assessment matches theirs. Working as a batboy for the Angels since their debut season of 1961, when he was 14 years old, he had an insider's view of baseball's playboy pitcher.

> Bo was jubilant after the no-hitter.
> It wasn't about "how great am I?" He was real cordial and congenial. He was cocky in a way, especially coming into spring training in 1962 and demanding a raise. During his playing days, he was a character like Joe Charboneau and Mark Fidrych. They come along once in a while.
> It was like Elvis. He could have any woman. He was the big man on campus. Anybody around who was a teenager on up could remember those first five starts, and then it kind of leveled off after that. Bo was probably in the fast lane since he was in his teens. By the 1990s, he was a more humble person. I read about him selling cars in Waikiki, and my wife and two daughters went over to see him. He was real cordial and congenial. I didn't call him often because I didn't want to overextend myself.
> As a guy who accepted Jesus Christ at a Billy Graham crusade at the LA Coliseum in 1963, I believe you'll see people in heaven you expect to see and

people you don't expect to see. I expect to see Mickey Mantle and Bo Belinsky. That's a happy ending.⁷

Belinsky worked with Dean Chance during the latter's travails in carnivals and boxing. Bruce Trampler, a promoter, met the duo when they were selling glow-in-the-dark posters at a county fair in Ohio. Trampler had left his job as Orlando Sports Stadium's director of boxing to become Madison Square Garden's assistant matchmaker when he recalled their initial meeting and a subsequent incident for the *New York Post* in 1978. Belinsky had provided the services of a ring announcer for a light-heavyweight managed by Chance; a snafu occurred because the opposing boxer didn't appear. Trampler said that Belinsky informed the audience of a cancellation, but an attendee at the festivities volunteered. "Bo says, 'Who are you?' and the guy answers, 'I'm the town bully.' He was drunk as a skunk but he went three [rounds]."⁸

Trampler further recalled:

> I met him through Dean Chance late in 1972 or early 1973. Bo was living with a woman in Wooster, Ohio, but also acting as Camp Director at the training facilities of heavyweight boxer Earnie Shavers in Canfield, Ohio, an hour away.
>
> A bunch of us went to a boxing show [Shavers vs Norton] at the-then Las Vegas Hilton in 1979, and then flew to Arizona the next day for another fight. We had a large suite at a resort hotel in Phoenix and later that night, we apparently were loud and rowdy, and Bo, who retired early to get his rest, emerged from his room in a silk smoking jacket with every hair in place and firmly and politely asked us all to pipe down. He didn't wait for us to agree, just turned and went back into his room and shut the door. We were stunned into silence but quickly lowered the TV and shut the hell up out of respect for Bo's wishes. Dean just sat there grinning, as usual. Then there was Bo as a boxing timekeeper and Bo snickering at Dean's failure to remember the name of a fighter he was introducing as ring announcer.
>
> Bo was introverted and introspective. He was quiet and observant. Not moody or sullen, just listened and learned. Had a twinkle in his eyes and a slight smile on his face. Seemed to know what was going on around him. Often seemed amused but didn't speak much unless asked a question or for a comment. Bo clearly didn't define his life from a baseball perspective, nor from a Hollywood perspective, either.⁹

Bob Case knew the notorious pitcher better than anyone.

> I met Bo when I was seventeen and working for the Angels as an equipment guy in 1962. He was the talk of the town with the sportswriters writing articles about him. Bo and Dean took me under their wing and took me out to dinner. In the 1980s, Bo had a ponytail and was living in an apartment on Pacific Coast Highway in Malibu with a guy who used a helicopter for the Brinks Robbery. We were going to Pasadena and driving on the freeway. Bo said, "Let's stop at a bar in the valley." There were lots of construction workers and a pool

table. Whoever played him thought they could beat him. One guy was up $400 because Bo misjudged him. All the guy has to do is sink the eight ball. All of a sudden, the guy miscues. Bo looks at me and says, "Let's get the fuck out of here." He spit in the guy's chalk.

But Bo could be tough. A guy robbed a sale from him at Findlay and talked shit about him. They went in the hallway and Bo slugged him. They shipped Bo to another dealership in Henderson like the Angels shipped him to Hawaii after knocking out Dyer. One word to describe Bo would be dignity. One time at a party in Vegas, a drunk guy asked him what it was like fucking Ursula Andress and Mamie Van Doren. Bo was getting pissed. I told the guy, "You better knock it off." He stopped.

At Findlay, everybody else treated him with respect. But others could be in awe of him. One day, he had to get medicine. We went to Rite Aid. The pharmacist asked if he was related to Bo Belinsky and almost passed out when Bo told him who he was. I saw things like that happen all the time. More people lined up for him at memorabilia shows than Steve Carlton or Gaylord Perry.

By the 1990s, he was closer to God. But he was home alone on a Friday night in Vegas. His marriages all ended in divorce. He said, "I'd rather be home and bore myself than have somebody bore me." But for an alcoholic, being alone is the worst thing in the world. There was a relapse and a suicide attempt. If I had to guess, I think it bothered him that he didn't talk to his daughters.[10]

Ray Dinardi is presently the general manager of Findlay's Jaguar Land Rover store. He was the sales manager of Saturn at West Sahara when Belinsky worked there, and he observed the impact of the boss on the former ballplayer feeling grounded in Las Vegas.

I think his relationship with Rich played a large part in that. Rich had a style of management that left room for everyone's uniqueness. Bo obviously was a man who danced to his own music and was not someone who had a high tolerance for people trying to "manage" him. Rich was a manager who could build a high performing team while allowing everyone that latitude. Bo's longtime friend Dean Chance was also in Las Vegas, and that I believe played a part.

Bo had tremendous latitude with his work at Findlay, he was above all else, an "ambassador" in the community. As you can imagine, being Bo Belinsky opened doors that would have not necessarily opened for most people. Rich and Bo had a lot in common with their sports background, and they hit it off like old friends. Bo was an amazing person, he had a heart that was bigger than his legend. Bo was our goodwill ambassador, he would meet with customers in the showroom, and often would represent the store at charitable events that we would sponsor. Everyone wanted to meet Bo Belinsky.

I first met Bo in the early 90s when he came from Hawaii to Las Vegas. I was working for Findlay Automotive Group at the Saturn of West Sahara dealership, when Bo went to work there. I have several really good memories of Bo. One in particular was when a very aggressive salesman at least 30 years younger than Bo started talking behind his back and doing the passive aggressive behavior that is not unusual with a team of aggressive young men.

Bo confronted him about it, and of course the young guy denied everything. This went on for several weeks, and finally Bo had reached his limit. Once again he confronted the young man, and once again the young man denied everything. Bo, a left-hander, offered his right hand to shake hands with the obvious liar, and when the young guy reached out and took Bo's hand, Bo smoothly pulled him into his still solid left! Problem solved. Bo was still a young man who just happened to be in an old man's body.

The guy went down but not out. He came up to me in my office with tears running down his swelling red face, telling me the story and expecting a reaction that was quite different from the one he got. I asked him if there were any witnesses, to which he said NO. I informed him that if there was no witness, as far as I was concerned, it didn't happen! I suspect that on some level Bo might have felt bad about it, but old habits about conflict resolution technique just die hard.

Another good memory of Bo was his response to some of our young staff when they would "fall in love." Their work performance would start to slip, and all they could think about was Miss Perfect. Bo, having experienced a little more than his fair share Miss Perfects in his life, would eventually wrap his arm around the young man's shoulder and say, "Just remember, kid, the fucking you're getting ain't going to be worth the fucking you'll get." What a classic Bo line.

If I would ask about something, he had great stories to tell, but he never struck me as someone who lived in the past. I remember one time Bo invited a friend of his who was a famous former Hollywood starlet to one of our company functions, there were several people who were old enough remember who she was, and they seemed to fall all over themselves, but Bo was never a name dropper, and certainly never seemed braggadocious about his past when we talked. If I asked about something, he was a great storyteller but was not one of those "let me tell you all about me" type. One of his lines he used often about his past was that he had a "million dollar arm and a five-cent brain."

At the time in his life when we met, Bo was not what you would call happy go lucky, but I would not describe him as mournful. He was sober by the time that we met, involved with AA, we often found ourselves at the same meeting, and he seemed to have made amends where needed and seemed to have accepted that the life he had is the life that he had made. With one possible exception being—and that I believe he had some sadness about—the lack of relationship with his daughters.

As you can imagine, when you are Bo Belinsky, the anonymous part of AA is not quite as it should be. But nonetheless, he was a regular attendee. To the best of my knowledge, Bo was not involved in sponsoring people, nor did he have a sponsor as far as I know, but I believe that he felt that in sobriety, he was given an opportunity however late in life it might have been, to make some amends where possible, and that seemed to give him some peace.

Bo was already sober when we met, so I really don't have any idea if there was a singular incident, or just a series of incidents that made him wake up one day and realize that maybe your life was not quite as you had imagined it would be, and with all the ex-wives and fractured relationships, one day to your total surprise, you just notice what the common denominator is and reach out for help. Or he may have had some health issues that made him evaluate his life, I really don't know.

Recovery is in and of itself a big challenge, but I suspect famous people have different challenges with sobriety by the lack of any real anonymity. When part of your fame is that of a "party animal" I suspect that is an extremely difficult thing to overcome. The no-hitter Bo pitched seemed to be a minor sideline story in his life to people who only wanted to hear about "the playboy pitcher." The anonymity that is vital in recovery is something that I am afraid famous people don't have the benefit of, and I think that would be a huge challenge.

I remember once in the late 90s, a European fashion magazine flew Bo to Europe for him to model a clothing line for their magazine shoot. I was amazed that many years after his baseball career was over Bo Belinsky was still a recognizable name that people wanted to associate themselves, and their products with.[11]

Still remembered fondly in Hawaii, Belinsky got the spotlight in a "Where Are They Now?" article for the *Honolulu Star-Bulletin* on March 21, 2001. It noted his health challenges—bladder cancer and hip issues—as well as his religious path. "Being a born-again Christian is no whimsical thing," said the ex-ballplayer once celebrated for carousing until dawn.

Bo Belinsky spent the last part of his life in Las Vegas, where he embraced religion. The once notorious pitcher asked, "Can you imagine [having] to come to Las Vegas to find Jesus Christ?" (Gary Friedman / *Los Angeles Times* via Getty Images).

"When it happens, it happens. Can you imagine [having] to come to Las Vegas to find Jesus Christ?"

Belinsky noted that his time with the Islanders began on a sour note but became an exalted period of his baseball career. "I went kicking and screaming, considering it a demotion, but I had the pleasure to pitch a no-hitter for the Islanders in '68," recalled Belinsky. "That was almost as exciting as pitching a no-hitter for a major league team."

Hawaii had been an elixir of sorts for the nomadic pitcher during his two stints with the Islanders. Maybe it was the laid-back quality of the 50th state. Maybe it was the tropical weather. Maybe it was the lack of media scrutiny for his playing on the field and his activities off it. More than 30 years had passed since Belinsky's baseball career ended, but Hawaii's allure never faded for the southpaw. "There will always be a place in my heart for that mystical, beautiful island," he said in the *Star-Bulletin* retrospective.[12]

Eight months later, Robert "Bo" Belinsky died on the day after Thanksgiving. Gordon Sakamoto, a retired AP Hawaii Bureau Chief, believed he'd soon see his friend again. "He called me just this past Wednesday, two days before he died," said Sakamoto. "Usually when he called that meant he was coming back."[13]

There were the usual highlights in his obituaries. The teenage years in pool halls. The no-hitter for the Angels during his rookie season. The drinking. The roster of beautiful actresses he dated—Connie Stevens, Juliet Prowse, Tina Louise, Ann-Margret. Mamie Van Doren recalled him with fondness; their bond may not have resulted in marriage, but it endured. "We've had a love affair that's continued a long time," said the actress, whose career had been sporadic since the late 1960s, highlighted by guest roles in Aaron Spelling's hit shows *Vega$* and *Fantasy Island* plus an appearance as herself on *L.A. Law*. "I lost someone that was a very special part of my life. This is very sad for me."[14]

Belinsky's life in Las Vegas had put him on a path of reality, if not redemption. He owned up to his sins of the past. Working at Findlay gave him a purpose. Going to church gave him a higher purpose. But the trail of devastation in his family life proved difficult, if not impossible, to repair. Ross Newhan's report in the *Los Angeles Times* revealed "several unsuccessful attempts to reunite with his three daughters." There's a sadness in realizing that Belinsky's life did not have a Hollywood ending, but a calmness in realizing that he attempted to reconcile; Abajian and another friend, Louis Rodophele, described him as being "at peace."

Belinsky had confessed an epiphany to Abajian, who revealed how he responded to the former ballplayer. "Bo would say to me, 'Rich, if I had led my life the way I'm leading it now, I'd have won a Cy Young Award.' And

I'd say, 'Bo, that may be true, but we all take different paths and we can't look back.'"[15]

On November 29, Dodger Stadium hosted a memorial service. Though Angel Stadium might have seemed like the logical place for this gathering, Belinsky threw his no-hitter at Dodger Stadium during the four-year period when the Angels shared it with the Dodgers. Albie Pearson reminded the crowd of about 100 people that he had roomed with Belinsky, who sought the excitement of a post-game nightlife rather than the quietude of a hotel room. "Actually, I mostly roomed with Bo's luggage, still packed," joked the outfielder, who won the Rookie of the Year Award for his 1958 season with the Washington Senators. If Belinsky committed any sins or infractions against teammates, former battery mate Buck Rodgers recalled, "Bo always had a twinkle in his eye. You couldn't stay mad at Bo for 15 minutes."[16]

The devil-may-care aspect of Belinsky's persona intrigued the public. As sports memorabilia shows increased in popularity, Belinsky found them to be good opportunities for bonding with fans after so many years of being a recluse. He recounted one show where the organizers put him next to Steve Carlton, a Hall of Famer who won 329 games, compiled 4,136 strikeouts, and had a 3.22 career ERA. When a kid asked for an autograph, Carlton naturally thought the request targeted him. "Steve reaches out, and one of the kids says, 'No, my dad said to get Mr. Belinsky's autograph.' I told Steve that he did it the easy way, by winning 300 games. You just try to get all this notoriety on 28 victories. Now that takes a lot of work."[17]

If Bo Belinsky cared about baseball as much as he cared about having fun, he'd be in the Hall of Fame. Ok, maybe he wouldn't have been Cooperstown-worthy, but it's hopeful to think that discipline against distractions would have boosted his record beyond 28–51 in the major leagues.

The no-hitter combined with playing for a team based in Los Angeles created a sense of awe complemented by fame, charisma, and geographical proximity to show business giving the left-hander access to delights that Casanova would have envied. Beautiful women wanted to bed him; bartenders from Playa del Rey to Pacoima poured him booze on the house. Happiness had no end. Or so he felt at the time.

Belinsky's relationship with Van Doren elevated his fame even further. Their celebrity coupling lasted through the 1963 baseball season. "Our life was a circus," said Van Doren when Belinsky died in 2001. "We were engaged on April Fool's Day and broke the engagement on Halloween. It was a wild ride, but a lot of fun."[18]

Had Belinsky played in the 1930s instead of the 1960s, Damon Runyon likely would have created a character based on him. For the guy who grew up hustling in the pool halls of Trenton, life presented itself as an amusement park with the goal of gorging on enjoyment, not a calendar segmented into professional responsibilities, familial obligations, and societal norms.

It is too facile to say that Belinsky's behavior resulted from the aura of the swinging Sixties because there always have been and always will be groupies who find their way into bars, nightclubs, and hotel lobbies, looking to seduce athletes after a game. His tale of addiction mirrors the chronology of America's attitudes. While Belinsky sought sobriety, ovations greeted celebrities on the talk show circuit when they confessed to going to rehab. Against this backdrop, he quietly tried to conquer the demons that had led him down a caustic path.

Bo Belinsky's story is captivating, exciting, and, most importantly, cautionary. What is his legacy? It depends on whom you ask. It's also complicated. He had a fantastic beginning to his rookie season, punctuated by the no-hitter, but he didn't buckle down regarding dedication to baseball with any consistency. He saved some people by advocating for AA, but he created emotional devastation in his marriages. He enjoyed the companionship of Hollywood's most famous actresses, including an engagement to a bombshell and a marriage to a *Playboy* model, but jealousy, insecurity, and restlessness prevented lasting relationships.

Belinsky's obituaries informed the public about the Las Vegas years being marked by the Findlay job and religious transformation. But his notoriety left an epic footprint. The back page of *The Trentonian* featured a photo of Belinsky flanked by photos of Louise, Van Doren, Stevens, and Ann-Margret with the caption "Area Baseball Legend Who Dated Hollywood's Top Vixens Dies of Heart Attack" and a headline—"Death of a Playboy."

During his heyday, Belinsky had no blinders. Actions have consequences, a fact that he knew but ignored like a businessman cheating on his taxes while realizing that the IRS may audit him. "I don't feel sorry for myself," he said in the 1972 *Sports Illustrated* piece. "I knew sooner or later I'd have to pay the piper. You can't beat the piper, Babe; I never thought I could. But I'll tell you who I do feel sorry for—all those guys who never heard music."[19]

Epilogue

>Davis Memorial Park
>Las Vegas
>2023

Now in my mid-50s, I'm the same age that Bo Belinsky was when he lived in Las Vegas. It's a period of your life when you begin to realize that sins of the past remain there unless you resurrect them through repetition or exorcise them through redemption. He tried the latter by going to AA meetings, embracing religion, and taking life one day at a time. If I could go back to his tenure in Las Vegas and interview him, I suppose that my first question would be: "Why wasn't it ever enough?"

The no-hitter and 5-0 start in his rookie season for the Angels gave Belinsky immediate respect, which he squandered in favor of postgame exploits instead of committing himself to his craft by getting sufficient rest. His social life included famous, beautiful women, but he moved from one to another like a pinball bouncing off the bumpers. I reached out to Jo Collins through *Playboy* and to Jane Weyerhauser through her family foundation for interviews but didn't receive a response from either woman. Attempts to track down his third wife resulted in a dead end.

A vacation in Las Vegas gave me an opportunity to meet with people who knew the ex-ballplayer and with whom I had spoken on the phone. Findlay Land Rover general manager Ray Dinardi treated me to an amazing chicken and rice lunch from a food truck that could rival the finest restaurants in Las Vegas, entertained me with stories about his former colleague, and answered my questions with the patience of a saint.

I also met with Tyler Corder, Chief Financial Officer of Findlay Automotive. Tyler has been a champion of this project from the beginning, answering my emails within a few hours and even within a few minutes on occasion. My phone conversations, email exchanges, and in-person meetings with Ray and Tyler yielded invaluable insights, especially regarding the relationship between Belinsky and Rich Abajian, Tyler's best friend and boss.

In addition, I visited the grave site of the person whom I neither met nor saw play but whose life I sought to chronicle. Geraldine Engel at Davis Memorial Park arranged my visit, escorted me to the site, and left me alone with my thoughts.

After reciting the *Kel Maleh Rachamim*—a Hebrew prayer for the soul of the departed in honor of Judaism from Belinsky's maternal side of the family—I wasn't sure what to say next. I stared at the tombstone, which included the name Robert "Bo" Belinsky along with the dates of his birth and death, an etching of a baseball, the date of his no-hitter for the Angels, and a cross signifying his religious pursuits during his final years.

Under the Las Vegas sunshine moderated by a cool breeze, I felt an unexpected serenity combined with an inspiration to continue my quest of researching the life of one of baseball's most controversial figures. It seemed appropriate to say something. The words came.

"Hi, Bo. My name is David Krell. I'm writing your biography. I hope you found the peace in the next life that you couldn't find in this one."

Chapter Notes

Chapter 1

1. Larry Merchant, "Bo Goes Pad, Sweet Pad," *Philadelphia Daily News*, June 23, 1965, 39.
2. Maury Allen, *Bo, Pitching and Wooing ... with the Uncensored Cooperation of Bo Belinsky* (New York: Dial Press, 1973), 5.
3. Ibid., 6.
4. Ibid., 16.
5. Allen Rich, "Gail a Hustler—at Pool, That Is," *Hollywood Citizen-News*, November 22, 1969, A-11.
6. Allen, 7.
7. Ibid., 29.
8. *Sunday Ledger-Enquirer* (Columbus, GA), "No-Hitter Over Brunswick, 3–0," June 3, 1956, D-3.
9. Allen, 30.
10. Ibid., 7.
11. Ibid., 31.
12. "Dons Seek Agreement with Baltimore—Davis," *Pensacola News-Journal*, March 10, 1957, 13; Earle Bowden, "Untried Dons, PJC Battle Today," *Pensacola News-Journal*, April 17, 1957, 13.
13. Earle Bowden, "Jays Throttle Dons, 5–4," *Pensacola News-Journal*, April 21, 1957, 14.
14. "Rebels Trip Dons, 7 to 5," *Pensacola News-Journal*, May 6, 1957, 6.
15. "Belinsky Foils Jet Nine, 3–1, With 7-Hitter," *Pensacola News-Journal*, May 9, 1957, 19.
16. Earle Bowden, "Oilers Throttle Pensacola, 9–4," *Pensacola News-Journal*, May 14, 1957, 8; "Dons Throttle Fliers, 6 to 4, With Six Hits," *Pensacola News-Journal*, May 15, 1957, 57.
17. "Dons' 19 Hits Waylay Fliers in 16–9 Spree," *Pensacola News-Journal*, May 23, 1957, 15.
18. Earle Bowden, "Jets Edge Dons in Ninth, 1 to 0," *Pensacola News-Journal*, June 1, 1957, 8.
19. "Belinsky Fans 17, Pensacola Tips Jets, 6–2," *Pensacola News-Journal*, June 5, 1957, 11; Earle Bowden, "Belinsky Allows 1 Hit, Whiffs 16," *Pensacola News-Journal*, June 9, 1957, 28.
20. Earle Bowden, "Belinsky, Dons Crush Rebs, 7–0," *Pensacola News-Journal* June 13, 1957, 17.
21. Earle Bowden, "Lambert, Dons Jar Jets, 13–7," *Pensacola News-Journal*, June 21, 1957, 18.
22. Al Padgett, "D's Halt Selma Rally, Win, 7–6," *Pensacola News-Journal*, July 11, 1957, 17.
23. Earle Bowden, "Belinsky Hurls Dons by Selma on Two-Hit Job," *Pensacola News-Journal*, July 19, 1957, 23; Earle Bowden, "Baseball Goes Nomadic," *Pensacola News-Journal*, July 21, 1957, 15.
24. Richard Daw, "Dons Chill Oilers, 6 to 1," *Pensacola News-Journal*, July 23, 1957, 8; Earle Bowden, "Earle of Sports," *Pensacola News-Journal*, August 11, 1957, 13.
25. Earle Bowden, "Dons, Lambert Celebrate, 4–0," *Pensacola News-Journal*, August 17, 1957, 6.
26. Allen, 31.
27. Ibid., 32.
28. Myron Cope, "Bo Belinsky's Dilemma, Baseball or Dames," *True*, October 1962, 48.
29. Earle Bowden, "Don-Baltimore Tieup Okayed; Belinsky Sold," *Pensacola News-Journal*, September 11, 1957, 11.
30. "Pheasants Home After Split with

Sox," *Aberdeen American-News*, July 11, 1958, 8.

31. "Belinsky Leads 'New' Pheasants Over Rox," *St. Cloud [MN] Daily Times*, July 15, 1958, 14.

32. "Minot Edges Rox, 1–0; Move to Fargo," *St. Cloud Daily Times*, July 23, 1958, 20.

33. "Goldeyes Top All-Stars," *Aberdeen American-News*, July 11, 1958, 8; Eugene Fitzgerald, "Winnipeg Host for 16th Game," Associated Press, *Bismarck Tribune*, July 26, 1958, 8.

34. "Jimenez, Terilli Named Polar All-Star Starters," *Daily Telegram* (Eau Claire, WI), July 26, 1958, 11; Don Blanchard, "Unser Figures Goldeyes Will Do Well Against Stars," *Winnipeg Free Press*, July 26, 1958, 41; "Belinsky Named Starter," *Winnipeg Tribune*, July 26, 1958, 18.

35. "All-Star Box," *St. Cloud Daily Times*), July 28, 1958, 16; "10th-Inning Homer Wins for 'Stars,'" *Winnipeg Free Press*, July 28, 1958, 19; John Robertson, "Good Game, Poor Crowd!," *Winnipeg Tribune*, July 28, 1958, 14; John Robertson, "Mike Connected But Pete's Still a Hero," *Winnipeg Tribune*, July 28, 1958, 14.

36. "Jim Schaffer Is Most Valuable in Northern Loop," *Bismarck Tribune*, September 5, 1958, 13; Cope, "Bo Belinsky's Dilemma, Baseball or Dames"; "Bonus Boy Nicholson Farmed to Wilson (NC)," *Knoxville Journal*, May 15, 1958, 13; Ted Riggs, "Smokies Hit Basement, Take to Road," *Knoxville News-Sentinel*, May 15, 1958, 45; "1958 Northern League Pitching Leaders, Baseball Reference, https://www.baseball-reference.com/register/leader.cgi?id=22281109&type=pitch (last accessed April 3, 2024).

37. Allen, 34.

38. "Lefthander Belinsky Bids for Mound Berth," *Amarillo Globe-Times*, March 30, 1959, 17.

39. Cope, "Bo Belinsky's Dilemma, Baseball or Dames"; "Lefthander Belinsky Bids for Mound Berth."

40. "Bo Belinsky Will Rejoin Pheasants," *Aberdeen American-News*, August 23, 1959, 14.

41. Al Goldfarb, "Strictly...for the Record," *Stockton Daily Evening Record*, May 25, 1959, 23.

42. "Stockton in 6-2 Victory Over Bears," *Stockton Daily Evening Record*, June 3, 1959, 33.

43. "Reno, Bakersfield Share Lead; Ports Win, Lose," Associated Press, *Stockton Daily Evening Record*, June 15, 1959, 25.

44. "Ports Give Release to Belinsky," *Stockton Daily Evening Record*, June 24, 1959, 36.

45. Charlie Somerby, "Dothan Pounds Pensacola, 5–1," *Pensacola News-Journal*, July 6, 1959, 11.

46. Doug Bradford, "Belinsky Returns; Cards First Victims," *Dothan Eagle*, July 9, 1959, 22; "Belinsky Spins 5-Hitter, Dons Trip Cards, 7–3," *Pensacola News-Journal*, July 9, 1959, 21.

47. "Belinsky Shoots Down Fliers On 5-Hitter, Dons Roll, 3–0," *Pensacola News-Journal*, July 13, 1959, 10.

48. Allen, 34–35.

49. *Ibid.*, 35.

50. *Ibid.*, 36.

51. *Ibid.*, 37.

52. *Ibid.*, 39.

53. Cope, "Bo Belinsky's Dilemma, Baseball or Dames."

54. Allen, 42–45.

55. *Ibid.*, 39.

56. Jim Bailey, "Geho, Bradey Finally Put Travs on Right Road, 9–6," *Arkansas Gazette*, April 11, 1961, 14.

57. "Testa Up to Old Tricks, Beats Travs in 10th, 3–2," *Arkansas Gazette*, April 15, 1961, 9; Charlie Adcock, "Sports Views," *Arkansas Democrat*, April 18, 1961, 15.

58. Jim Bailey, "Barons Overcome Deficit, Push Travelers Below .500," *Arkansas Gazette*, April 21, 1961, 20.

59. "Belinsky, Geho Spark Trav Win," *Arkansas Democrat*, April 25, 1961, 18.

60. Orville Henry, "Putting at Ease the Lefthanders," *Arkansas Gazette*, April 27, 1961, 14.

61. "Richardson's Blow Rescues Travs, 5–3," *Arkansas Gazette*, April 30, 1961, 21.

62. "Orville Henry, "Travs Win Series, 10–6, as Bo, Batters Produce," *Arkansas Gazette*, May 5, 1961, 22.

63. Jack Keady, "Travs, Belinsky Whip Crax, 10–6," *Arkansas Democrat*, May 5, 1961, 14; Henry, "Travs Win Series, 10–6, As Bo, Batters Produce."

64. "Sports' Big Innings Spell Double Loss for Travelers," *Arkansas Gazette*, May 10, 1961, 18; Orville Henry, "Vols Impress

In 3-0 Win," *Arkansas Gazette*, May 13, 1961, 9.

65. Charlie Adcock, "Sports Views," *Arkansas Democrat*, May 16, 1961, 25.

66. "Vols Beat Curfew, Take Second Game After Trav Victory," *Arkansas Gazette*, May 22, 1961, 11; "Travs Return Home to Face Sports," *Arkansas Democrat*, May 27, 1961, 8.

67. "Crax Batter Bo, 15-2," *Arkansas Gazette*, June 2, 1961, 22.

68. Charlie Roberts, "Crackers Rip Travs On Williams' 6 RBIs," *Atlanta Constitution*, June 2, 1961, 39; John Logue, "Rube's 'Slapsticks' Flatten Travelers," *Atlanta Journal*, June 2, 1961, 16.

69. Orville Henry, "Business for the Pencil," *Arkansas Gazette*, June 9, 1961, 22.

70. "Peaches Win by 7-4 as Travs Blow Lead," *Arkansas Democrat*, June 6, 1961, 19; "Travs Win, Then Fumble One," *Arkansas Gazette*, June 8, 1961, 14.

71. Robert Shaw, "Travs Strand 17, Go Down," *Arkansas Gazette*, June 12, 1961, 9; Jack Keady, "Losing Skid (7 of 9) Troubles Travs," *Arkansas Democrat*, June 12, 1961, 14.

72. "Travs Battle Back for Tie in Ninth But Lose in 10th," *Arkansas Gazette*, June 14, 1961, 14; Jack Keady, "Extra Inning Loss Adds to Trav Woes," *Arkansas Democrat*, June 14, 1961, 21.

73. "Koplitz Does It Again, Assures Barons Sweep," *Arkansas Gazette*, June 18, 1961, 19.

74. Jim Bailey, "Bo Rights Travelers, 3-2," *Arkansas Gazette*, June 24, 1961, 9.

75. Robert Shaw, "Bo Two-hits Bears," *Arkansas Gazette*, June 29, 1961, 19; Charlie Adcock, "Belinsky Spins 2-Hitter, Travs Win, 2-0," *Arkansas Democrat*, June 29, 1961, 18.

76. "Pitching Sours, Travs Succumb to Sports, 19-4," *Arkansas Gazette*, July 3, 1961, 7; "Sports Maul Trav Hurlers," *Arkansas Democrat*, July 3, 1961, 9.

77. Jack Keady, "Nashville Closes in on Travs, Wins Pair," *Arkansas Democrat*, July 5, 1961, 13; Orville Henry, "Vols Take Pair in Bid to Pass Charitable Travs," *Arkansas Gazette*, July 5, 1961, 15.

78. "Southern Leaders," *Arkansas Gazette*, July 6, 1961, 22; Orville Henry, "Rain Gives Travelers Timely Chance to Mend," *Arkansas Gazette*, July 7, 1961, 25; Fred Russell, "Sidelines," *Nashville Banner*, July 10, 1961, 18.

79. Orville Henry, "Travs Move Into Nashville on a Couple Hopeful Notes," *Arkansas Gazette*, July 12, 1961, 12; "Bo and Lehew Join to Blank Lookouts," *Arkansas Gazette*, July 17, 1961, 13; "Travs Prove Tough for Lookouts Milo," *Arkansas Democrat*, July 17, 1961, 9; "Crax Whip Travs Twice, on a Fly and Infield Hit," *Arkansas Gazette*, July 22, 1961, 9.

80. "Belinsky Fans 18, Travs Bow in 14th," *Arkansas Gazette*, July 27, 1961, 14; "Belinsky Fans 18, But Travs Lose," *Arkansas Democrat*, July 27, 1961, 23.

81. Jack Keady, "Belinsky Goes Home, Travs Get Fridley," *Arkansas Democrat*, August 1, 1961, 17; Jim Bailey, "Barons Catch Travs' Line Drives, Koplitz Escapes With 9-5 Win," *Arkansas Gazette*, August 1, 1961, 12; "Bo Returns; Fridley Gets Ump's Job," *Arkansas Gazette*, August 3, 1961, 18.

82. Jim Bailey, "Travs Win in 14th," *Arkansas Gazette*, August 4, 1961, 16; Jack Keady, "Travs End Giveaway in 14th, Top Macon," *Arkansas Democrat*, August 4, 1961, 13.

83. "Bo, Don Beat Bears Twice," *Arkansas Democrat*, August 9, 1961, 19; "Belinsky and Bradey Pitch Travs to Sweep Over Bears," *Arkansas Gazette*, August 9, 1961, 14; "Saner Settles 'Short' Game in 13th, Travs Sweep Pair," *Arkansas Gazette*, August 16, 1961, 16; Jack Keady, "Travs' Sweep Comes After 22 Innings," *Arkansas Democrat*, August 16, 1961, 17.

84. "Sports to Tackle Final Road Trip," *Shreveport Journal*, August 21, 1961, 29.

85. "Consecutive Homers Give Travs 9-7 Edge Over Vols," *Arkansas Gazette*, August 27, 1961, 17; "Boozer Earns His Honor, Looks 12-1," *Arkansas Gazette*, August 31, 1961, 18.

86. Allen, 47-50.

87. "Vols' Five-run Surge Sinks Travs," *Arkansas Gazette*, September 3, 1961, 13; Jim Bailey, "A Fortunate Third for the Travelers," *Arkansas Gazette*, September 5, 1961, 15.

88. Allen, 57.

89. *Ibid.*, 61.

90. "Angels Draft Bo Belinsky," *Arkansas Democrat*, November 28, 1961, 21; "Trenton Hurler Belinsky Drafted by Angels; Minoso to Cardinals," *Trenton Evening Times*, November 28, 1961, 23.

Chapter 2

1. "Angels Sign All But Seven," United Press International, *Daily Record* (Banning, CA), January 26, 1962, 7.
2. Myron Cope, "Bo Belinsky's Dilemma, Baseball or Dames?" *True*, October 1962, 48.
3. Braven Dyer, "Belinsky Concedes He's True 'Screwball,'" *Los Angeles Times*, March 2, 1962, B1.
4. Ross Newhan, "Belinsky Threat to Piersall as Baseball's Clown Prince," *The Independent* (Long Beach, CA), March 2, 1962, 29.
5. Bill Rigney, "Rigney Needs Pitching; New Park Will Help," *New York Daily News*, January 30, 1962, 46. The preamble to the article read, "This is another in the series of letters written by major league managers to Joe Trimble and Jim McCulley, baseball writers for THE NEWS. Bill Rigney wears his halo as Chief Angel jauntily as he predicts Los Angeles will improve over last year if his youngsters make fewer mistakes and if he can get a solid pitching rotation lined up."
6. Newhan, "Rigney Needs Pitching; New Park Will Help."
7. "Angel Belinsky Turns in Uniform," Associated Press, *Evening Vanguard* (La Ballona Valley, CA), March 5, 1962, 7.
8. "Belinsky Fails to Win Point, but Signs Pact," *Los Angeles Times*, March 6, 1962, B2.
9. Braven Dyer, "Bo Belinsky in Angels' Dog House," *Los Angeles Times*, March 7, 1962, B1.
10. *Ibid.*
11. Braven Dyer, "Autry Gives Bo Ride, Advice," *Los Angeles Times*, March 11, 1962, J5.
12. Maury Allen, *Bo, Pitching and Wooing ... with the Uncensored Cooperation of Bo Belinsky* (New York: Dial Press, 1973), 67.
13. *Ibid.*, 69.
14. *Ibid.*, 73.
15. "Bo Belinsky Out of Angel Doghouse; Impresses Rigney," *Daily News-Post* (Monrovia, CA), March 8, 1962, 8; Braven Dyer, "M'Bride Sparkles In No-Hit Stint," *Los Angeles Times*, March 8, 1962, B1; "Three Angels Hurl Shutout," Associated Press, *San Bernardino Daily Sun*, March 8, 1962, 15.
16. "Bo Belinsky Boasting Throwing Hard Says Mgr.," *Daily News-Post* (Monrovia, CA), March 20, 1962, 14.
17. Maxwell Styles, "Styles in Sport," *Citizen-News* (Hollywood edition), March 24, 1962, 9.
18. Braven Dyer, "Belinsky Bombed; Colts Blast Angels, 7 to 0," *Los Angeles Times*, March 27, 1962, B1.
19. Braven Dyer, "Colts Bomb Bo Belinsky, Angels, 20–5," *Los Angeles Times*, April 5, 1962, B1.
20. Bud Furillo, "Bo Arm Good as Mouth," *Los Angeles Herald Examiner*, April 19, 1962, D-1.
21. Bud Furillo, "Bud Furillo's Steam Room, Trenton Swings Late, and Bobo Calls His Dad," *Los Angeles Herald Examiner*, April 19, 1962, D-3.
22. Braven Dyer, "Angels Win, Belinsky in Hero's Role," *Los Angeles Times*, April 19, 1962, B1.
23. Bud Furillo, "Bargain Bo Wins Again," *Los Angeles Herald Examiner*, April 26, 1962, C-1.
24. Ross Newhan, "Belinsky Throws No-Hitter," *Independent-Press-Telegram* (Long Beach, CA), May 6, 1962, 50.
25. *Ibid.*
26. Al Wolf, "Champagne Fails to Make Hit with Belinsky," *Los Angeles Times*, May 7, 1962, B1.
27. "Bo Belinsky Dies of Apparent Heart Attack," Associated Press, *Courier-Post* (Cherry Hill, NJ), November 25, 2001, 26C.
28. Newhan, "Belinsky Throws No-Hitter."
29. Wolf, "Champagne Fails to Make Hit With Belinsky."
30. Maury Allen, *Bo, Pitching and Wooing ... with the Uncensored Cooperation of Bo Belinsky* (New York: Dial Press, 1973), 2.
31. Bo Belinsky, "Bo Belinsky's Steam Room," *Los Angeles Herald Examiner*, May 7, 1962, C-2.
32. Braven Dyer, "Belinsky, Ex-Pool Shark, Pockets Wins for Angels," *The Sporting News*, May 9, 1962, 20.
33. Braven Dyer, "Angels Win, Take Third; Bo Fans 11," *Los Angeles Times*, May 12, 1962, A1.
34. Bob Speck, "Bo First to Win Five in Row," *Citizen-News* (Metropolitan Los Angeles edition), May 12, 1962, 16; John

B. Old, "Wouldn't Take Mint for Bobo, Haney Insists," *Los Angeles Herald Examiner*, May 12, 1962, C-1.
35. Bud Furillo, "Belinsky Eyes TV Series," *Los Angeles Herald Examiner*, May 12, 1962, C-1.
36. Old, "Wouldn't Take Mint for Bobo, Haney Insists."
37. Braven Dyer, "Belinsky Belted; Angels Lose, 6–4," *Los Angeles Times*, May 18, 1962, B1.
38. Resolution of Congratulations and Good Wishes for Future Success to Robert (Bo) Belinsky; Proclamation for Robert "Bo" Belinsky Day, May 21, 1962, Bo Belinsky File, Trentoniana Department, Trenton Free Public Library, Trenton, NJ.
39. Braven Dyer, "Bo's Success No Surprise to Scout Who 'Found' Him," *Los Angeles Times*, May 24, 1962, B4.
40. Ibid.
41. Al Wolf, "Belinsky Refuses to Alibi for Bombing by Yankees," *Los Angeles Times*, June 2, 1962, A2.
42. "Rigney Tells Bo to Cut Out 'Activities," *Los Angeles Times*, June 8, 1962, B2.
43. Allen, 95.
44. Ibid., 96.
45. Bud Furillo, "Rigney Irate But Picks Bo to Pitch," *Los Angeles Evening and Sunday Herald Examiner*, June 14, 1962, A-1.
46. Melvin Durslag, "It's All the Fault of Burton," *Los Angeles Herald Examiner*, June 15, 1962, C-2.
47. Walter Winchell, "Bobo, Chance Only Drinking Milk—Winchell," *Los Angeles Herald Examiner*, June 14, 1962, C-1.
48. Bud Furillo, "Bud Furillo's Steam Room," *Los Angeles Herald Examiner*, June 14, 1962, C-2.
49. "Belinsky, Chance Fined After 5 A.M. Ruckus," *Los Angeles Times*, June 14, 1962, B1.
50. Sid Ziff, "Too Much Too Soon," *Los Angeles Times*, June 15, 1962, C3.
51. Myron Cope, "Bo Belinsky's Dilemma, Baseball or Dames," *True*, October 1962, 48.
52. Ibid.
53. Braven Dyer, "Bo Belinsky Censured by Haney," *Los Angeles Times*, July 8, 1962, C2.
54. Maxwell Stiles, "Bo Booed as Angels Beaten," *Citizen-News* (Metropolitan Los Angeles edition), July 7, 1962, 13;
Wells Twombly, "Angels, Dodgers Take Battering, Lee Starts Tonight; Club in Third Place," *Valley Times* (San Fernando Valley, CA), July 7, 1962, 8.
55. Braven Dyer, "Belinsky Beats Twins on 4-Hit Shutout, 3 to 0," *Los Angeles Times*, August 12, 1962, G1.
56. "Woman Sues Bo Belinsky for $150,000," *Los Angeles Times*, August 16, 1962, 32.
57. Allen, 97.
58. Dan Hafner, "Angels Sell Belinsky to A's for Delivery in '63," *Los Angeles Times*, September 5, 1962, B1.
59. "Frick to Probe Bo 'Deal'; A's, L.A. Deny Trade Set," *Los Angeles Times*, September 6, 1962, B1.

Chapter 3

1. "L.A. 4½ Behind; Belinsky Deal Vetoed," *Los Angeles Times*, September 7, 1962, C1.
2. Ross Newhan, "'Rig' Elated; Angels Cinch Third Place," *Independent-Press-Telegram* (Long Beach, CA), September 30, 1962, C-4.
3. Myron Cope, "Bo Belinsky's Dilemma, Baseball or Dames?" *True*, October 1962, 48.
4. Ibid.
5. "Bowsfield Sent to Athletics in Belinsky Deal," United Press International, *Los Angeles Times*, November 27, 1962, B1; Braven Dyer, "Bowsfield Fall Guy in Belinsky Deal," *Los Angeles Times*, November 28, 1962; B2.
6. "No-Hitters Belinsky, Monboquette, Wilson to Be Feted at Times Dinner," *Los Angeles Times*, December 24, 1962, D1. Jack Kralick and Sandy Koufax also threw no-hitters, but the article neither acknowledged them nor indicated they would be honored.
7. Sid Ziff, "Oh Me, O'Malley," *Los Angeles Times*, December 12, 1962, B3.
8. Bob Crane, "It's Bob Crane, the Hip Hogan," *San Diego Union*, September 1, 1966, C-6.
9. *Star Trek*, Opening Credits, Narrated by William Shatner, Aired on NBC, 1966–1969.
10. Tom Nahigian, "Bo and Dean, a Lifetime of Fun and Friendship," *The National Pastime—Endless Seasons,*

Baseball in Southern California, Society for American Baseball Research, 2011.
11. *Ibid.*
12. Brett Chance, email to author, March 24, 2024.
13. Mike DiGiovanna, "Cy Young Winner with the Angels," *Los Angeles Times*, October 12, 2015, B7.
14. "Savarine's .353 Average Best in Appy Hit Parade," *Roanoke Times*, September 12, 1959, 9.
15. Bob Thomas, "Sinatra Planning 'Biggest Show' for Kennedy's Inauguration," *Los Angeles Mirror*, December 9, 1960, 18.
16. Robert Sullivan, "B of A Starts Bookkeeping Brain Here," *Los Angeles Times*, December 8, 1960, 104.
17. Myron Cope, "The Angel Who Doesn't Fear to Tread," *Saturday Evening Post*, April 10, 1965, 95. Chance is awarded 28 retroactive saves according to the original 1969 criteria for the statistic.
18. Braven Dyer, "Debut of Angel Pitcher Chance Has 'Em Talking," *Los Angeles Times*, September 14, 1961, 80.
19. "No Tears for Chance After Nifty One-Hitter Over Twins," Associated Press, *Progress-Bulletin* (Pomona, CA), September 11, 1962, 8.
20. Chuck Such, "Chance Choice Chuck—on Mow or Mound," *The Sporting News*, January 26, 1963, 3.
21. Angel Stadium débuted in Anaheim in 1966. The Van Nuys Chamber of Commerce had proposed the Sepulveda Flood Control Basin in Van Nuys as a stadium site. "Van Nuys Site Urged for Angels Ball Park," *Los Angeles Times*, December 15, 1960, E1. Los Angeles Mayor Sam Yorty suggested the Baldwin Hills Reservoir, which had an "empty shell." Henry Sutherland, "Yorty Suggests Baldwin Hills Reservoir as Home for Angels," *Los Angeles Times*, April 22, 1964, 37.
22. Floyd Schneiderman, "Phils Trip Dodgers; Angles Win—by One, 2-Hitter Pitched by Chance," *The Independent* (San Gabriel Valley, CA), June 3, 1964, 64.
23. Will McDonough, "Lamabe Luckless Loser to Chance's 2-Hit Blazer," *Boston Globe*, June 3, 1964, 47. Chance is referring to the August 10, 1963 game, which the Yankees won 2–1. He pitched eight and one-third innings, allowed four hits and two walks, and struck out five.
24. Russell Schneider, "'We're Proud of Dean,' Mom Beams," *The Sporting News*, November 21, 1964, 3.
25. Joe Donnelly, "The Cockiest Guy in Baseball," *Baseball Yearbook*, 1965, 4.
26. Braven Dyer, "Feuding Over, Chance Signs $41,000 Pact with Angels," *The Sporting News*, February 27, 1965, 27; Cope, 95.
27. *Ibid.*
28. Rube Samuelsen, "Is There a Chance Dean Has Grown Up?" *Evening Vanguard* (Venice, CA), February 12, 1965, 9.
29. Dyer, "Feuding Over, Chance Signs $41,000 Pact with Angels," *The Sporting News*, February 27, 1965, 27.
30. Cope, The Angel Who Doesn't Fear to Tread," *Saturday Evening Post*, April 10, 1965, 95.
31. Ross Newhan, "'Shocked That Angels Traded Me to Contender,'" *Press-Telegram* (Long Beach, CA), December 3, 1966, 10.
32. Max Nichols, "Chance Remains Calm, Jokes on Bench in No-hitter," *Minneapolis Star*, August 26, 1967, 12.
33. Brett Chance, email to author, March 24, 2024.
34. Maury Allen, *Bo, Pitching and Wooing ... with the Uncensored Cooperation of Bo Belinsky* (New York: Dial Press, 1973), 106.
35. *Ibid.*, 102.

Chapter 4

1. Maury Allen, *Bo, Pitching and Wooing ... with the Uncensored Cooperation of Bo Belinsky* (New York: Dial Press, 1973), 17.
2. Walter Winchell, "Walter Winchell of New York," *New York Mirror*, August 26, 1962, 10.
3. Allen, 89.
4. Walter Winchell, "Walter Winchell of New York," *New York Mirror*, June 17, 1962, 10.
5. *Ibid.*
6. Allen, 101.
7. Walter Winchell, "Walter Winchell of New York," *New York Mirror*, July 9, 1962, 10.
8. Walter Winchell, "Walter Winchell of New York," *New York Mirror*, July 11, 1962, 10.

9. Walter Winchell, "Walter Winchell of New York," *New York Mirror*, July 12, 1962, 10; Walter Winchell, "Walter Winchell of New York," *New York Mirror*, July 19, 1962, 10.
10. Walter Winchell, "Walter Winchell of New York," *New York Mirror*, July 19, 1962, 10.
11. Walter Winchell, "Walter Winchell of New York," *New York Mirror*, August 6, 1962, 10.
12. Walter Winchell, "Walter Winchell of New York," *New York Mirror*, August 16, 1962, 10.
13. Walter Winchell, "Walter Winchell of New York," *New York Mirror*, August 22, 1962, 6.
14. Walter Winchell, "Walter Winchell of New York," *New York Mirror*, July 12, 1962, 10.
15. Allen, 91.
16. Walter Winchell, "Walter Winchell of New York," *New York Mirror*, July 18, 1962, 10.
17. Walter Winchell, "Walter Winchell of New York," *New York Mirror*, July 25, 1962, 6.
18. Walter Winchell, "Hurler Actress Tell Romance," *San Diego Union*, August 13, 1962, A13.
19. Vernon Scott, "How Does Tina Keep Gym Dandy Figure?" United Press International, *Evening Press* (Binghamton, NY), August 11, 1962, 11; Jack Gould, "TV, New Play Offered," *New York Times*, January 17, 1956, 67.
20. "Tina Louise Joins 'Li'l Abner,'" *New York Times*, August 3, 1956, 12; Brooks Atkinson, "Theatre, 'Li'l Abner,'" *New York Times*, November 16, 1956, 23.
21. "Bo Belinsky Reveals Playboy's Guide to America After Dark," United Press International, *Los Angeles Times*, August 31, 1962, B3.
22. *Ibid.*
23. Allen, 119.
24. *Ibid.*, 93.
25. *Ibid.*, 94.
26. Jack Murphy, "Belinsky's Angel Halo Askew Despite Rigney's Rules of Order," *San Diego Union*, February 20, 1963, b-5.
27. "Belinsky Says Actress Has 'Calmed Me Down,'" Associated Press, *Fitchburg* [MA] *Sentinel*, March 16, 1963, 8.
28. Mamie Van Doren with Art Aveilhe, *Playing the Field, My Story* (New York: G.P. Putnam's Sons, 1987), 46–50.
29. Harold Heffernan, "Mamie Van Doren's Career Hitting Peak," *Standard-Star* (New Rochelle, NY), May 28, 1957, 11.
30. Van Doren with Aveilhe, 59, 60, 77–81, 99.
31. Abraham Weiler, "'Untamed Youth' Full of Rock 'n' Roll," *New York Times*, May 11, 1957, 24.
32. Mamie Van Doren, X (aka Twitter), February 2, 2024.
33. Geoffrey M. Warren, "'Untamed Youth' Takes Over Theater Screens," *Los Angeles Times*, May 17, 1957, 24.
34. "Double Dose of Glamor Hits Vegas," *Herald Journal* (Cache County, UT), October 8, 1957, 2.
35. Alice Pardoe West, "Behind the Scenes," *Ogden Standard-Examiner*, August 4, 1957, 5B.
36. Gary Wagner, "The Broadway Party Line," *Helper Journal* (Helper, UT), October 17, 1957, 6.
37. Vernon Scott, "Mamie Is Aiming Higher," *Pittsburgh Press*, June 15, 1959, 20.
38. Sheila Graham, "Bad Luck Still Dogs Lex Barker," North American Newspaper Alliance, *Deseret News and Telegram* (Salt Lake City), March 18, 1957, A15.
39. "Mamie Van Doren Divorced," *New York Times*, March 23, 1960, 31.
40. Van Doren with Aveilhe, 176–177.
41. Braven Dyer, "Angel Playboys Bo, Dean Fined Again," *Los Angeles Times*, March 31, 1963, J1.
42. Braven Dyer, "Bo Loses Bank Roll, Game, But Not 'Fan.'" *Los Angeles Times*, April 1, 1963, B1.
43. "Bo, Mamie Engaged; No Wedding Date Set," Associated Press, *Los Angeles Times*, April 2, 1963, B1; "Belinsky Plans to Marry Mamie," Associated Press, *North Adams* [MA] *Transcript*, April 2, 1963, 9.
44. "Blurb on Bo and Bride-to-Be Brings Boycott," United Press International, *Los Angeles Times*, April 3, 1963, B1.
45. Allen, 144.
46. Van Doren with Aveilhe, 180.
47. *Ibid.*, 181.
48. *Ibid.*, 183.
49. Allen, 144.
50. Van Doren with Aveilhe, 184.
51. Allen, 9.

52. Myron Cope, "A Dialogue Between Baseball's Bigmouths," *True—The Men's Magazine*, August 1965, 30.
53. Allen, 142.
54. Ibid., 145.
55. Ibid., 147. Allen says that Van Doren entertained a "young man in the show."
56. "Bo, Mamie Break Off Engagement," *Los Angeles Times*, June 24, 1963, C3; "Jilted Mamie Says Bo Should Be Pitching Baseball—Not Woo," *Los Angeles Times*, June 25, 1963, C2.
57. Allen, 147.
58. Ibid., 148–150.
59. Phil Collier, "Dejected Bo Belinsky Ponders 'Loose Ends,'" *San Diego Union*, May 27, 1963, b-3.
60. Van Doren with Aveilhe, 186.
61. Vernon Scott, "Mamie on Prowl After Losing Bo," United Press International, *Boston Globe*, July 25, 1963, 26.
62. "Mamie Visits Bo in Tacoma, Will Sit in Section Reserved for Wives," Associated Press, *Sunday Tribune-Herald*, July 28, 1963, 8; "Mamie Joins Bo for Look at Life in Minors, United Press International, *Los Angeles Times*, July 28, 1963, G6.
63. "'So What,' Bo Declares," Associated Press, *Baltimore Sun*, July 30, 1963, 19.
64. James Bacon, "Mamie Is 'Through with Men,' But Not Bitter About Bo Romance," Associated Press, *Honolulu Star-Bulletin*, August 12, 1963, 18.
65. Earl Wilson, "It Happened Last Night," *Courier-Post* (Camden, NJ), August 15, 1963, 50.
66. Frank Quinn, subbing for Walter Winchell, "Walter Winchell of New York," *New York Mirror*, August 29, 1963, 10.
67. Sheila Graham, "Bill Looks Younger, But Rumors Wrong," *Edmonton Journal*, September 7, 1963, 20. Graham's first name is misspelled as Shelah in the byline.
68. "Sentinel TV Log," *Santa Cruz Sentinel*, September 4, 1963, 24.
69. Walter Winchell, "Walter Winchell," *New York Mirror*, September 9, 1963, 10.
70. "Monbo Fails Again in Try for 20 Wins," Associated Press, *Greenfield* [MA] *Recorder-Gazette*, September 11, 1963, 18.
71. "Mamie Cancels Her Wedding Date with Bo," *Los Angeles Times*, October 5, 1963, D20.
72. "In Politics—In a Way," Associated Press, *Kansas City* [MO] *Star*, October 26, 1963, 7.
73. "Strip Tease for GOP by Actress Is Off," Associated Press, *Democrat and Chronicle* (Rochester, NY), October 28, 1963, 5A.
74. "Mine Host Bo Shows He Has 'Little Class,'" United Press International, *Sunday News* (New York), November 3, 1963, 146. This is the Sunday edition of the *Daily News*.
75. Ibid.
76. Allen, 133–134.
77. Sid Ziff, "Bo Talks of Future," *Los Angeles Times*, January 26, 1964, H4.
78. Mamie Van Doren, Author's page on X (formerly known as Twitter), April 25, 2024.
79. Allen, 279.
80. "Mamie Van Doren Reveals Her Marriage to Young Minor League Ball Player," United Press International, *Lebanon* [PA] *Daily News and Lebanon Daily Times*, June 23, 1966, 40.
81. "Mamie to Watch Husband Pitch," United Press International, *San Diego Union*, July 16, 1966, A10.
82. "Best Regards—Bo," *Oakland Tribune*, June 24, 1966, E57.
83. "Ex-Spartan Ace Killed in Crash," *Los Angeles Times*, April 29, 1972, A2.
84. Allen, 100.

Chapter 5

1. Sid Ziff, "Price on Angels," *Los Angeles Times*, January 18, 1963, C3.
2. Maury Allen, *Bo, Pitching and Wooing... with the Uncensored Cooperation of Bo Belinsky* (New York: Dial Press, 1973), 122.
3. Braven Dyer, "Reformed Bo Gets Pay Hike for '63," *Los Angeles Times*, January 22, 1963, B1.
4. Braven Dyer, "Belinsky Late As Angels Open Camp," *Los Angeles Times*, February 13, 1963, C1.
5. "Angels' 'New' Belinsky Up to Old Tricks," *Los Angeles Times*, February 18, 1963, B1.
6. Sid Ziff, "Daddy Wags," *Los Angeles Times*, February 22, 1963, B3.
7. Ross Newhan, "Bo Takes New Grip on Baseball," *Independent-Press-Telegram*

(Long Beach, CA), March 3, 1963, C3; Braven Dyer, "Cronin Sees Chance Take Play Away from Belinsky," *Los Angeles Times*, March 3, 1963, I4; "Chance Sparkles on Mound," United Press International, *Santa Barbara News-Press*, March 3, 2024, C1.

8. "Belinsky Picks Business Over Pleasure," Associated Press, *Pensacola News-Journal*, March 3, 1963, 3E.

9. Milton Gross, "Angels Take Risk with Belinsky," North American Newspaper Alliance, *Orlando Sentinel*, March 3, 1963, 2B.

10. Braven Dyer, "Lil Albie Predicts Banner Year for New Roommate—Belinsky," *Los Angeles Times*, March 8, 1963, B2.

11. Braven Dyer, "Bo Wins Raves But Angels Lose Game," *Los Angeles Times*, March 12, 1963, B1.

12. Braven Dyer, "Belinsky Shoots Blanks at S.F.," *Los Angeles Times*, March 16, 1963, A1.

13. Braven Dyer, "Belinsky Hurls Six Scoreless Innings, 2–1," *Los Angeles Times*, March 21, 1963, B1.

14. Braven Dyer, "Angels Playboys Bo, Dean Fined Again," *Los Angeles Times*, March 31, 1963, J1.

15. Braven Dyer, "Bo Loses Bank Roll, Game, But Not 'Fan,'" *Los Angeles Times*, April 1, 1963, B1.

16. Allen, 103.

17. Ibid.

18. "Bo, Dean Run Out of Gas on Freeway," *Los Angeles Times*, April 6, 1963, A1.

19. "Belinsky, Dean in Doghouse Again," *San Pedro News-Pilot*, April 6, 1963, 7.

20. Joe Jares, "Errant Angels Bo and Dean Skip Banquet," *Los Angeles Times*, April 6, 1963, 1; "Belinsky, Dean in Doghouse Again."

21. John Hall, "Wagner Says Giants Will Beat Dodgers," *Los Angeles Times*, April 8, 1963, B1.

22. "Bo's No Hero to Hometown Newspaper," United Press International, *Los Angeles Times*, April 12, 1963, B1.

23. Braven Dyer, "Rube Marquard, Ex-Mound Ace, Sounds Warning to Bo and Dean," *Los Angeles Times*, April 13, 1963, A2.

24. Sid Ziff, "Waddell vs. 'Bo,'" *Los Angeles Times*, April 16, 1963, B3.

25. "Belinsky, Angels Looking for Friendly Face Today," United Press International, *Evening Vanguard* (Venice, CA), May 20, 1963, 7.

26. "Bo Headed for Bullpen," *Los Angeles Times*, May 20, 1963, C1; "'Rig' Denies Bo Going to Minors," United Press International, *Los Angeles Times*, May 21, 1963, B1; Braven Dyer, "Rigney Huddles with Paul; Item, Belinsky," *Los Angeles Times*, May 22, 1963, B1.

27. "Hawaii Ready for Bo, Locker Set in Advance," United Press International, *Los Angeles Times*, May 23, 1963, B2.

28. Fred Borsch, "Islanders Get Bo Belinsky," *Honolulu Star-Bulletin & Advertiser*, May 26, 1963, C1.

29. Bo Belinsky, "'I'll Be Back,' Says Hawaii-Bound Belinsky," Associated Press, *Honolulu Star-Bulletin*, May 27, 1963, 27.

30. "Bo Belinsky Must Report to Islanders or Be Placed on Disqualified List," United Press International, *Honolulu Advertiser*, May 30, 1963, B-8.

31. Braven Dyer, "Bo Gets Ultimatum—Report or No Pay," *Los Angeles Times*, May 30, 1963, B1.

32. Bob Speck, "Angels Win, Bo AWOL," *Citizen-News* (Los Angeles), May 31, 1963, B1.

33. Coy Williams, "From This Angle...." *Citizen-News* (Los Angeles) June 1, 1963, B2.

34. Jim Murray, "Buttons & Bo's Ties," *Los Angeles Times*, June 3, 1963, Part III, 1.

35. Sid Ziff, "Dancing Champion," *Los Angeles Times*, June 4, 1963, Part III, 3.

36. Ross Newhan, "Losses, Injuries Mounting but Angels' Crowds Aren't," *Press-Telegram* (Long Beach, CA), June 4, 1963, C1.

37. Photograph caption, *Citizen-News* (Los Angeles), June 5, 1963, C6.

38. "Belinsky Eyes Career as Actor," *Honolulu Star-Bulletin*, June 7, 1963, 20; "Bo to Quit, Says Friend," *The Independent* (Long Beach, CA), June 7, 1963, C1.

39. "Hollywood Still Loves Belinsky," Associated Press, *Baltimore Sun*, June 14, 1963, 26; Hedda Hopper, "No Riding Into Sunset for Autry," *Los Angeles Times*, June 14, 1963, C10.

40. "Bo Belinsky Decides to Report to Hawaii," Associated Press, *Hilo Tribune-Herald*, June 26, 1963, 1; "Haney Nixes Bo's

Request," *Los Angeles Times*, June 26, 1963, C1.

41. "Bo Hopes Mrs. Du Pont Would Buy Him Ball Club," Associated Press, *Hilo Tribune Herald*, June 27, 1963, 20; "Bo Belinsky Shows Up at Angel Game," *Los Angeles Times*, June 27, 1963, B4.

42. "Bo Decides He Will Report to Islanders," *Hilo Tribune-Herald*, July 16, 1963, 4; "Belinsky Agrees to Go to Hawaii," *Los Angeles Times*, July 17, 1963, C1.

43. "Is Hawaii Ready for Bo Bolinsky [sic]," *Hilo Tribune-Herald*, July 17, 1963, 6.

44. "30,000 Hawaii Girls in Bikinis Lure Belinsky," Associated Press, *Boston Globe*, July 20, 1963, 13.

45. "Belinsky Reaches Hawaii Equipped with Pool Cue," United Press International, *Boston Globe*, July 21, 1963, 61.

46. "Bo Likes Hawaii; Will Be Ready on Next Road Trip," Associated Press, *Hilo Tribune-Herald*, July 25, 1963, 8.

47. Allen, 129.

48. "Tacoma Shells Belinsky in His 'Minor' Debut," United Press International, *Boston Globe*, July 29, 1963, 15; "Bo Smashed in Islander Debut," Associated Press, *Hilo Tribune-Herald*, July 29, 1963, 8.

49. "'So What,' Bo Declares," Associated Press, *Baltimore Sun*, July 30, 1963, 19.

50. *Ibid*.; "Belinsky Says He'll Be Beach Boy in Waikiki If He Doesn't Make Angels," Associated Press, *Hilo Tribune-Herald*, July 31, 1963, 8.

51. "Seattle Whips Islanders, 7–4," Associated Press, *Hilo Tribune-Herald*, August 2, 1963, 8.

52. "Belinsky Chucks Shutout in First Islander Start," Associated Press, *Hilo Tribune-Herald*, August 6, 1963, 5.

53. "Bo Belinsky Determined to Return to Big Leagues," *Honolulu Advertiser*, August 10, 1963, A10.

54. Ferd Borsch, "Islanders Clobber Portland Nine, 10–1," *Honolulu Star-Bulletin & Advertiser*, August 11, 1963, C1.

55. Ferd Borsch, "Knoop's Homer Beats Bevos," *Honolulu Advertiser*, August 15, 1963, B-7.

56. Tom Hopkins, "9th Straight Win Ups Hawaii to 2nd Place," *Honolulu Star-Bulletin*, August 20, 1963, 36.

57. Ferd Borsch, "Islanders' Win Streak Ends," *Honolulu Advertiser*, August 24, 1963, A10; "Hawaii Outstanding Franchise, PCL Chief Says," *Honolulu Advertiser*, August 24, 1964, A10.

58. Ferd Borsch, "16,954 See Islanders Belt Spokane, 6–0," *Honolulu Advertiser*, August 27, 1963, B6.

59. "Angels Recall Five and a Guy Named Bo," *Los Angeles Times*, August 30, 1963, B2; "Oklahoma City Stops Islanders," Associated Press, *Hilo Tribune-Herald*, August 31, 1963, 8.

60. Bo Has Nose for News—He Wins, Too," *Los Angeles Times*, September 1, 1963, H6; "Islanders Win Two Over Oklahoma," United Press International, *Sunday Star-Bulletin & Advertiser*, September 1, 1963, A-11.

61. "Belinsky's Streak Broken," United Press International, *Honolulu Advertiser*, September 6, 1963, B-7.

62. Braven Dyer, "Angels Eke Out 6–5 Win in 10th," *Los Angeles Times*, September 11, 1963, B1.

63. Sid Ziff, "Big Frog in Puddle," *Los Angeles Times*, September 11, 1963, B3.

64. "Angels Use Same Bait, Bo Snaps It Up," *Los Angeles Times*, October 10, 1963, B1.

65. "Belinsky Fearful Surfboard Rap May Ruin Singing Voice," United Press International, *Los Angeles Times*, November 7, 1963, B1.

Chapter 6

1. Maury Allen wrote that Belinsky got a $2,000 salary raise to $15,500. Maury Allen, *Bo, Pitching and Wooing ... with the Uncensored Cooperation of Bo Belinsky* (New York: Dial Press, 1973), 136.

2. Al Wolf, "Odds Shaky on Bo Showing Up," *Los Angeles Times*, January 14, 1964, B2.

3. Sid Ziff, "Bo Talks of Future," *Los Angeles Times*, January 26, 1964, H4.

4. Braven Dyer, "Angels Leave 'Em Laughing as Good-Will Tour Continues," *Los Angeles Times*, January 28, 1964, B5.

5. Ziff.

6. Braven Dyer, "'It's Up to Me,' Says Angelic Bo Belinsky," *Los Angeles Times*, February 21, 1964, B1.

7. "Belinsky Gives Up Homer in 9–7

Loss," *Los Angeles Times*, March 11, 1964, B1.

8. Braven Dyer, "'Bring On Dodgers!'—Bo Sharp," *Los Angeles Times*, April 7, 1964, B1.

9. Frank Finch, "Belinsky on Key, And Angels Sing, 5–0," *Los Angeles Times*, April 13, 1964, C1.

10. John Hall, "Even Belinsky's Impressed by Angels' Defensive Improvement," *Los Angeles Times*, April 13, 1964, C2.

11. Allen, 152, 170. Photos occupy pages 153–169.

12. "Angels Routed from Hotel by Fire at 5 a.m.," *Los Angeles Times*, May 16, 1963, B1; Ross Newhan, "'Don't Know What to Do'—Rigney," *Press-Telegram* (Long Beach, CA), May 21, 1964, C-1.

13. Braven Dyer, "Angels Rally in 9th, Edge Tigers, 3–2," *Los Angeles Times*, April 23, 1964, B1.

14. Braven Dyer, "Last Gasp Rally Robs Angels, 4–3," *Los Angeles Times*, May 20, 1964, B1.

15. Braven Dyer, "Angels, Twins Divide," *Los Angeles Times*, May 28, 1964, B1.

16. "Belinsky Has New Twist, Asks to Be Farmed Out," Associated Press, *Progress-Bulletin* (Pomona, CA), June 19, 1964, 33.

17. Ross Newhan, "Bo Is Fed Up as 'Nice Guy,'" *The Independent* (Long Beach, CA), June 18, 1964, 43.

18. Braven Dyer, "Father's Day Good to Bo—Anyway," *Los Angeles Times*, June 22, 1964, B1.

19. Charles Maher, "Bo Happy with Angels," *Progress-Bulletin* (Pomona, CA), June 22, 1964, 16.

20. Braven Dyer, "Belinsky Blanks Chisox on 2 Hits," *Los Angeles Times*, July 10, 1964, B1.

21. *Ibid.*

22. Sid Ziff, "Bo Wants Fine Back," *Los Angeles Times*, July 12, 1964, G3.

23. Charles Maher, "I'm Quitting, Says Belinsky," Associated Press, *Fort Worth Star-Telegram*, August 14, 1964, Section 3, Page 4.

24. Braven Dyer, "Bo Hedges on Plan to Give Up Baseball," *Los Angeles Times*, August 14, 1964, B5.

25. "Belinsky Asks for Release Plus Pay," Associated Press, *Daily News-Post* (Monrovia, CA), August 15, 1964, 10.

26. Allen, 175.

27. *Ibid.*, 176.

28. "Suspended Belinsky Plans Return Here," United Press International, *Citizen-News* (Los Angeles), August 15, 1964, 4.

29. Allen, 177.

30. "Angels Put Southpaw Hurler on 'Indefinite Suspension,'" Associated Press, *Progress-Bulletin* (Pomona, CA), August 15, 1964, 6

31. "Belinsky Back, Bemoans 'Bad' Side in Press," *Los Angeles Times*, August 16, 1964, C1.

32. Allen, 179.

33. *Ibid.*, 180.

34. Alex Kahn, "Bo Faces Deadline on 'Exile' to Hawaii," *Citizen-News* (Los Angeles), August 19, 1964, 6.

35. "Bo Suspended—Again," *Los Angeles Times*, August 23, 1964, D2.

36. "Belinsky Will Play 'For Any Major Club,'" *Citizen-News* (Los Angeles), August 28, 1964, 1.

37. "Belinsky Desires Trade to Major League Club," *Los Angeles Times*, August 29, 1964, A5.

38. "New Angels' Home," Artist's Rendering of Angel Stadium, *Evening Citizen* (Los Angeles), August 28, 1964, 7.

39. "Bert Lahr to Appear in Baseball Musical," *Los Angeles Times*, October 10, 1964, 19; "Bert Lahr Better," *San Pedro News-Pilot*, October 14, 1964, 8; "Bracken Replaces Bert Lahr," *Los Angeles Times*, October 15, 1964, 78.

Chapter 7

1. Allen Lewis, "Phillies Seek Bo Belinsky, Name Cal McLish as Coach," *Philadelphia Inquirer*, December 2, 1964, 46.

2. Allen Lewis, "Phillies' Chances for Landing 2d Pitcher Grow Slim," *Philadelphia Inquirer*, December 3, 1964, 44.

3. "Nats Get Howard; Belinsky to Phillies," United Press International, *Los Angeles Times*, December 5, 1964, A1.

4. Jack Disney, "This Is Wonderful, Exclaims Belinsky," *Los Angeles Herald Examiner*, December 4, 1964, D-1; Bud Furillo, "Steam Room, Bo's a Man in a Hurry Now," *Los Angeles Herald Examiner*, December 5, 1964, C-1.

5. Frank Dolson, "Phillies Acquire

Belinsky from Angels," *Philadelphia Inquirer*, December 5, 1964, 22.

6. "Chance Likes New 'Image,'" Associated Press, *San Diego Union*, March 10, 1965, B-4.

7. Melvin Durslag, "Philly Is Bo's Kind of Town," *Los Angeles Herald Examiner*, December 6, 1964, E-1.

8. "November 27, 1963, Address to Joint Session of Congress," https,//millercenter.org/the-presidency/presidential-speeches/november-27-1963-address-joint-session-congress (last accessed April 11, 2023).

9. "Liston Heavy Choice to Win," *Reno Evening Gazette*, February 22, 1964, 10.

10. "Walter Winchell," *Philadelphia Inquirer*, January 18, 1965, 17. The *New York Mirror* had ceased operations in 1963, but Winchell continued to syndicate his column to newspapers.

11. Melvin Durslag, "Fred 'Shows' Dean Who's Boss," *Philadelphia Inquirer*, January 18, 1965, 26.

12. Allen Lewis, "Major League Outlook, Team Balance Called Keynote to Phillies," *Philadelphia Inquirer*, February 7, 1965, 6.

13. "Stuart, Belinsky Must Aid Team to Play—Mauch," Associated Press, *Philadelphia Inquirer*, February 9, 1965, 32.

14. "Phillies Pulled Shrewd Deal on Bosox," *Philadelphia Inquirer*, February 11, 1965, 34.

15. "Bennett Calls Stuart Popoff; 'Won't Fit In,' Ex-Phil Says," *Philadelphia Inquirer*, March 2, 1965, 27.

16. Allen Lewis, "Feud with Bennett 'Just a Joke,' Stuart Tells Phils," *Philadelphia Inquirer*, March 3, 1965, 34.

17. Allen Lewis, "Mauch Predicts 40 HRs for Stuart, 12 Wins for Bo," *Philadelphia Inquirer*, February 25, 1965, 31.

18. "Practice Pitch Sends Infielder to Hospital," *Philadelphia Inquirer*, March 2, 1965, 27.

19. "Haney Gathers Shockley to Angel Fold," *Desert Sun* (Palm Springs, CA), March 8, 1965, 7.

20. John Hall, "Angels Are a Mutual Admiration Society as Vets Help the Kids," *Los Angeles Times*, March 29, 1965, 36.

21. Melvin Durslag, "Dodger 'Jets' Look Smooth to Osteen," *Philadelphia Inquirer*, March 6, 1965, 19.

22. "Torn Thumbnail Benches Stuart for Few Games," *Philadelphia Inquirer*, March 12, 1965, 32.

23. Joe Gergen, "'New' Belinsky Pitches Three Scoreless Innings," United Press International, *Daily Times-Advocate* (Escondido, CA), March 16, 1965, 12; Joe Gergen, "'New' Belinsky Calls It Quits as Far as His Nightlife Goes," *Conejo News* (Thousand Oaks, CA), March 16, 1965, 5; Joe Gergen, "The 'New' Belinski Shuts Out Phils 1–0," United Press International, *Press Democrat* (Santa Rosa, CA), March 16, 1965, 18. (The third article misspelled Belinsky's name in the headline.)

24. Allen Lewis, "Belinsky Sharp in NL Debut as Phils Nip Mets," *Philadelphia Inquirer*, March 16, 1965, 31.

25. Allen Lewis, "Mauch Is Ejected as Tigers Nip Phils After Dispute, 5–4," *Philadelphia Inquirer*, March 20, 1965, 22.

26. Allen Lewis, "Phillies Beat Twins for 4th in Row But Belinsky Hurts Back in 6–4 Win," *Philadelphia Inquirer*, March 25, 1965, 38.

27. Allen Lewis, "Phillies Foil Braves, 3–2; Belinsky Fans 8," *Philadelphia Inquirer*, April 3, 1965, 21.

28. Stan Hochman, "Belinsky Shines Under the Lights," *Philadelphia Daily News*, April 3, 1965, 23. This article said that Belinsky threw 87 pitches rather than the 89 reported in the *Inquirer*.

29. "Your Ticket to a Great Season," Advertisement, *Philadelphia Inquirer*, April 9, 1965, 20.

30. "1965 Baseball Guide," *Philadelphia Inquirer*, April 11, 1965, 197.

31. Melvin Durslag, "Dean Tags Sandy's Curve, 100G's," *Philadelphia Inquirer*, April 21, 1965, 42.

32. George C. Langford, "Shockley Cashes In on Adcock's Tutoring," *Daily Times-Advocate* (Escondido, CA), May 5, 1965, 14.

33. Jim Bunning threw a perfect game on June 21, 1964. The franchise's most recent no-hitter before Bunning's took place in 1906, when Johnny Lush blanked the Brooklyn Dodgers.

34. Frank Dolson, "Belinsky Still Can't Win on Any Decision," *Philadelphia Sunday Inquirer*, May 9, 1965, 67.

35. Allen Lewis, "Mauch Says Cards 4th Best," *Philadelphia Inquirer*, May 13, 1965, 37.

36. Allen Lewis, "Who Goofed? Phils 'Fess Up, Admit Bo Injury," *Philadelphia Inquirer*, May 29, 1965, 21.

37. Gimbel's advertisement, *Philadelphia Inquirer*, May 28, 1965, 12.
38. Lewis, "Who Goofed? Phils 'Fess Up, Admit Bo Injury."
39. Allen Lewis, "Phils' 3 Homers Beat Cards, 7-1; Belinsky Victor," *Philadelphia Inquirer*, June 30, 1965, 1.
40. Allen Lewis, "Redlegs Thwart Phils, 4-1, As Nuxhall Hurls 5-Hitter," *Philadelphia Inquirer*, July 5, 1965, 20.
41. Red Foley, "Stengel-less Mets Win, 8-1, Then Boot 2d to Phils, 3-1," *New York Daily News*, July 26, 1965, 46.
42. Stan Hochman, "Belinsky Demoted to Bullpen; Culp Saves Starting Job as Phils Split," *Philadelphia Daily News*, July 26, 1965, 45.
43. Myron Cope, "A Dialogue Between Baseball's Bigmouths," *True—The Men's Magazine*, August 1965, 30.
44. Ibid.
45. Bill Conlin, "The Weekend That Was in 'Frisco," *Philadelphia Daily News*, August 16, 1965, 51.
46. Stan Hochman, "Belinsky Had Great Stuff But...," *Philadelphia Daily News*, August 26, 1965, 59.
47. Maury Allen, *Bo, Pitching and Wooing ... with the Uncensored Cooperation of Bo Belinsky* (New York: Dial Press, 1973), 196.
48. Stan Hochman, "Bo Finds Autry Tough Innkeeper," *Philadelphia Daily News*, September 9, 1965, 56.
49. Frank Dolson, "First Bunnies, and Now Bankruptcy," *Philadelphia Inquirer*, December 21, 1965, 36. Dean Martin had created a persona of being a friendly drinker in his live performances. In September, he premiered in *The Dean Martin Show*, a comedy-variety stalwart for NBC. It ran for nine seasons.
50. Bob Smith, "Playboy Who Won't Play," *Corpus Christi Caller-Times*, December 5, 1965, 12F.
51. Donald Freeman, "'Hopelessly Hammy' Sands Makes a Hit with Critic," Copley News Service, *Press Democrat* (Santa Rosa, CA), December 5, 1965, 8B.
52. "Belinsky Agrees to Phillies Pact," *Philadelphia Inquirer*, February 16, 1966, 39.
53. "11 Unsigned on Phils List," *Philadelphia Inquirer*, February 13, 1966, 69.
54. Allen Lewis, "Belinsky Skips First Practice," *Philadelphia Inquirer*, February 26, 1966, 21; Allen Lewis, "Belinsky Is Still Missing; Culp, Quinn Near Accord," *Philadelphia Inquirer*, February 27, 1966, 65.
55. Allen Lewis, "Bo Arrives Despite Snow, Flu, Movie Role," *Philadelphia Inquirer*, February 28, 1966, 24.
56. Allen Lewis, "Mauch Reveals Lineup for First Exhibition Tilt," *Philadelphia Inquirer*, March 11, 1966, 31.
57. Allen Lewis, "Cardenas's Homer Beats Phillies, 4-2," *Philadelphia Inquirer*, March 12, 1966, 21.
58. Allen Lewis, "Phils, Mets Play 15 Innings to 3-3 Tie; Belinsky Sharp," *Philadelphia Inquirer*, March 18, 1966, 36.
59. Allen Lewis, "Phils Beat Dodgers on Wine's HR in 12th," *Philadelphia Inquirer*, March 23, 1966, 43.
60. Stan Hochman, "Waist Pitch Baffles Culp," *Philadelphia Daily News*, March 24, 1966, 58; Allen Lewis, "Twins Edge Phillies in 9th on Rookie's Home Run Off Green," *Philadelphia Inquirer*, March 24, 1966, 42; Allen Lewis, "Astros Top Phils in 8th on Brand's Hit, 6-4," *Philadelphia Inquirer*, March 25, 1966, 34.
61. Allen Lewis, "Astros Outgun Phillies in 12-9 Slugfest," *Philadelphia Inquirer*, April 1, 1966, 33.
62. Allen Lewis, "Jackson, Herbert Hurl Phils to 2-0 Win," *Philadelphia Inquirer*, April 6, 1966, 38.
63. "Phillies 1966," *Philadelphia Inquirer*, April 3, 1966, 199.
64. Edgar Williams, "Team with a Split Personality," *Philadelphia Inquirer*, April 10, 1966, 186.

Chapter 8

1. John Dell, "Bo Misses Sign on Aaron's 500-Footer," *Philadelphia Inquirer*, April 21, 1966, 40.
2. Allen Lewis, "Belinsky Wants to Pitch Again, Even in Minors," *Philadelphia Inquirer*, June 4, 1966, 23.
3. Frank Dolson, "Bo's 'Wrong Pitch' Made Lanier Right," *Philadelphia Inquirer*, June 6, 1966, 22.
4. "Phils Farm Belinsky; Bike Dents His Car," *Philadelphia Inquirer*, June 14, 1966, 31.
5. Maury Allen, *Bo, Pitching and Wooing ... with the Uncensored Cooperation of Bo Belinsky* (New York: Dial Press, 1973), 205.

6. Bob Ortman, "Belinsky Just Wants to Pitch," Copley News Service, *Sunday Oklahoman* (Oklahoma City), June 19, 1966, 4.
7. "Belinsky, Phils Are Strongest," Associated Press, *Sacramento Bee*, June 19, 1966, F2.
8. "Belinsky Sent to Padres," *San Diego Union*, June 14, 1966, B-7.
9. "Hawaii Scores 4-3 Win Over Padres," *San Diego Union*, June 25, 1966, A-25.
10. Wayne Lockwood, "Belinsky, Pads Nip Bevos, 4-3," *San Diego Union*, June 30, 1966, A-47.
11. Wayne Lockwood, "Pads Viewed as 'Salvation' by Well-Traveled Bo," *San Diego Union*, July 4, 1966, B-5.
12. Allen, 205.
13. Don Page, "Stay-at-Homers Will Have 'Feast,'" *Los Angeles Times*, July 2, 1966, Part III, Page 2.
14. Wayne Lockwood, "Phoenix' 3-Run Rally Shades Padres, 6-5," *San Diego Union*, July 4, 1966, B-5.
15. Wayne Lockwood, "Padres Back Belinsky with 12 Hits, Win, 10-1," *San Diego Union*, July 9, 1966, A-25.
16. Frank Rhoades, Column, *San Diego Union*, July 10, 1966, A-19.
17. Wayne Lockwood, "Seattle Blanks San Diego, 6-0," *San Diego Union*, July 13, 1966, B-3.
18. "Padre Averages," *San Diego Union*, July 18, 1966, B-1; "Tardy Bo Fined $50," *San Diego Union*, July 24, 1966, J-1.
19. "Denver Rally Turns Back Padres, 5-3," *San Diego Union*, July 30, 1966, C-1.
20. Harrington's advertisement, *San Diego Union*, August 2, 1966, A-10.
21. Wayne Lockwood, "Padres See Oiler Jinx by Daylight, Lose, 5-4," *San Diego Union*, August 7, 1966, H-1.
22. Wayne Lockwood, "McNight's Hits Topple Phoenix," *San Diego Union*, August 12, 1966, C-1.
23. Wayne Lockwood, "Padres 22 Hits Rout Tulsa, 15-9," *San Diego Union*, August 17, 1966, C-1.
24. "Phils Call Sutherland, Schaffer, Three Pitchers," *San Diego Union*, August 31, 1966, C-1; "Phils Call Two from San Diego; Wine to Return," *Philadelphia Inquirer*, August 31, 1966, 32; "Padres Receive 4 Phillie Players," *San Diego Union*, October 5, 1966, C-4.
25. "Bo Aims to Keep Dodger Scoreless String Going," *Honolulu Star-Bulletin*, October 13, 1966, D-4.
26. Jim Hackleman, "Dodgers Kick Runless Habit," *Honolulu Star-Bulletin*, October 17, 1966, B-1; Tom Hopkins, "Sportraitures," *Honolulu Star-Bulletin*, October 18, 1966, C-2.
27. "TV Crosswords," *Shreveport Journal*, September 9, 1966, D17.
28. Red McQueen, "Hoomalimali, Could Dodgers Use Belinsky?" *Honolulu Advertiser*, October 18, 1966, B8.
29. Jim Hackleman, "Dodgers Rout Old Enemy," *Honolulu Star-Bulletin*, October 18, 1966, C-2.
30. Phil Collier, "Dodgers Speed Past Mets, 3-2, Pad Lead, Dodger Notes," *San Diego Union*, September 13, 1966, C-1.
31. "Astros Tap Belinsky in Draft's 1st Round," Associated Press, *Austin American-Statesman*, November 29, 1966, 27.
32. "Houston Astros Draft Swinging Bo Belinsky," United Press International, *Valley Morning Star* (Harlingen, TX), November 29, 1966, 6.
33. "Astro's [sic] Belinsky Only Lukewarm Toward Game," Associated Press, *San Angelo Standard-Times*, February 9, 1967, 20.
34. Murray Chass, "Bo Belinsky Has Changed with Astros," Associated Press, *Corpus Christi Caller-Times*, March 12, 1967, 39.
35. "Belinsky Likes His Newest Assignment with Houston," Associated Press, *San Angelo Standard-Times* (San Angelo, TX), March 28, 1967, 13.
36. "Bo Fined $100 for Missing Curfew," Associated Press, *Fort Worth Star-Telegram*, March 30, 1967, 19.
37. "Belinsky & The Terrier," United Press International, *McKinney* [TX] *Courier-Gazette*, March 2, 1967, 5.
38. Allen, 216, 219.
39. "This Couldn't Be the Bo We Know," Associated Press, *Fort Worth Star-Telegram*, April 6, 1967, 24.
40. "Houston Falls Again to Reds; Bo Belinsky Only Bright Spot," Associated Press, *Kilgore* [TX] *News Herald*, April 24, 1967, 2.
41. Neal Russo, "Astros Enjoy Feast in Cardinal Famine," *St. Louis Post-Dispatch*, June 8, 1967, 45.

42. Lou Smith, "Lou Smith's Notes," *Cincinnati Enquirer*, June 12, 1967, 35.
43. George Vecsey, "Houston Has Reformed Belinsky," *Newsday*, August 1, 1967, 24A.
44. Vecsey, "Houston Has Reformed Belinsky."
45. Allen, 221, 226.
46. Dan Hafner, "Wynn's 36th Homer Gives Astros Split with the Dodgers," *Los Angeles Times*, September 11, 1967, 39.
47. "Astros Assign 6 Players to OC," Associated Press, *San Angelo Standard-Times*, November 18, 1967, 4B; "Bo Unhappy Over Move to Okla. City," United Press International, *El Paso Herald-Post*, November 18, 1967, B3.

Chapter 9

1. Lanky Long, "Alfie Here, But No Bo," *Evening Tribune* (Cocoa, FL), February 21, 1968, 15A.
2. "People in Sports," *Fort Worth Star-Telegram*, February 21, 1968, 2-C.
3. "Rain Forces Astros Inside," Associated Press, *Austin American-Statesman*, February 24, 1968, 21.
4. Maury Allen, *Bo, Pitching and Wooing ... with the Uncensored Cooperation of Bo Belinsky* (New York: Dial Press, 1973), 232.
5. Ibid., 233–234.
6. Ibid., 237.
7. Ibid., 230.
8. Ibid., 243.
9. Ibid., 246.
10. John Wilson, "Bo Vanishes—It's Over a Gal," *Houston Chronicle*, March 18, 1968, Section 1, Page 1.
11. Joe Heiling, "Bo Is AWOL from Astros," *Houston Post*, March 18, 1968, Section 4, Page 1.
12. "Belinsky Packs Up and Leaves Astros," United Press International, *Honolulu Advertiser*, March 18, 1968, A-12; "Belinsky Suspended," United Press International, *Honolulu Advertiser*, March 18, 1968, A-12.
13. "Bo Says He Has Found True Love," United Press International, *Valley Evening Monitor* (McAllen, TX), March 21, 1968, 2B.
14. Ibid.
15. Frank Luksa, "Belinsky No Sex Maniac? Say It Ain't So, Bo," *Fort Worth Star-Telegram*, April 5, 1968, 2-C.
16. Ed Levitt, "Will Jo Spoil Bo?" *Oakland Tribune*, March 22, 1968, 55.
17. Luksa, "Belinsky No Sex Maniac? Say It Ain't So, Bo."
18. Levitt.
19. Red McQueen, "Hoomalimali," *Sunday Star-Bulletin & Advertiser* (Honolulu), March 24, 1968, E-4.
20. "Belinsky Offered to Islanders," *Honolulu Star-Bulletin*, March 27, 1968, F-1.
21. "Quinn to Confer with White Sox on Belinsky," *Honolulu Advertiser*, March 28, 1968, E-8.
22. Frank Luksa, "Charlotte Bo's Dish," *Fort Worth Star-Telegram*, April 1, 1968, C1.
23. "Bo Belinsky Feels He's 'Trading Bait,'" *Austin American-Statesman*, March 6, 1968, 30.
24. Allen, 248.
25. "Astrolog," *Houston Post*, April 2, 1968, Section 4, Page 4.
26. "Bo Back with Hawaii," *Honolulu Star-Bulletin*, April 2, 1968, D-5.
27. Bill Kwon, "Islander Report," *Honolulu Star-Bulletin*, April 8, 1968, C-9.
28. Monte Ito, "Looks Like an Exciting Club," *Sunday Star-Bulletin & Advertiser*, April 14, 1968, F-5.
29. Luksa.
30. Hal Wood, Column, *Honolulu Advertiser*, April 16, 1968, C-6.
31. "Vancouver Beats Islanders, 5 to 1," *Sunday Star-Bulletin & Advertiser*, April 21, 1968, D-1; Ferd Borsch, "Bo Baffles Beavers, 5 to 1, *Honolulu Advertiser*, April 26, 1968, E-5.
32. Bill Kwon, "Head's-up Ball Gives Bo 5–1 Win," *Honolulu Star-Bulletin*, April 26, 1968, C-2.
33. Bill Kwon, "The Billboard," *Honolulu Star-Bulletin*, April 26, 1968, C-2.
34. "The Bo Bows in 1–0 Duel," United Press International, *Honolulu Advertiser*, April 30, 1968, 25.
35. "Islander Averages," *Honolulu Star-Bulletin*, May 1, 1968, C-1.
36. "Moeller Shuts Out Hawaii on 6 Hits," United Press International, *Sunday Star-Bulletin & Advertiser*, May 5, 1968, D-1.
37. "Islanders' Win Streak Cut," *Honolulu Star-Bulletin*, May 13, 1968, B-1; Ferd

Borsch, "Belinsky Hurls Tonight," *Honolulu Advertiser*, May 14, 1968, B-5; Ferd Borsch, "Islanders Shut Out, 4–0, on Four Hits," *Honolulu Advertiser*, May 15, 1968, C-3.
38. Bill Kwon, "Spokes Spook the Islanders, 4–0," *Honolulu Star-Bulletin*, May 15, 1968, B-4.
39. Hal Wood, Column, *Honolulu Advertiser*, May 16, 1968, B-11.
40. Ferd Borsch, "Islanders Nip Spokane, 4–3," *Sunday Star-Bulletin & Advertiser*, May 19, 1968, D-1.
41. Hal Wood, Column, *Honolulu Advertiser*, May 21, 1968, B-5.
42. Ferd Borsch, "Bo Fires 2-Hitter as Islanders Win, 5 to 0," *Honolulu Advertiser*, May 23, 1968, C-9; Bill Kwon, "It's All Bo and Third in a Row," *Honolulu Star-Bulletin*, May 23, 1968, D-4.
43. Lois Taylor, "The Girls in the Dugout," *Honolulu Star-Bulletin*, May 24, 1968, B-2.
44. Bill Kwon, "Bo Fires a First for the Islanders," *Honolulu Star-Bulletin*, August 20, 1968, B-4.
45. Ibid.
46. Ibid.
47. Ibid.
48. Allen, 249.
49. Ibid.
50. Ibid., 250.
51. Bill Kwon, "A Sad Aloha for Islanders," *Honolulu Star-Bulletin*, August 23, 1968, B-2; Ferd Borsch, "Tacoma Ruins Aloha with 3–0 Win," *Honolulu Advertiser*, August 23, 1968, C-6.
52. "Belinsky Purchased by Houston Astros," *Honolulu Advertiser*, September 25, 1968, C-5; "Astros Select Gary Geiger In Draft; St. Louis Takes Belinsky," *Sacramento Bee*, December 2, 1968, C-1.
53. "Belinsky Confident New Career to Blossom with Trade to Cards," United Press International, *Sapulpa [OK] Daily Herald*, January 30, 1969, 3.
54. "Bo Belinsky Drafted by St. Louis Cardinals," United Press International, *Honolulu Star-Bulletin*, December 2, 1968, D-4.
55. "Cards' Briles Keeping Busy," Newspaper Enterprise Association, *Long Branch [NJ] Daily Record*, February 22, 1968, 11.
56. "Bo Belinsky Drafted by St. Louis Cardinals."
57. "Indians Acquire Versalles," Associated Press, *St. Louis Post-Dispatch*, December 3, 1968, 28.
58. "Cardinals Sign Bo Belinsky, Mike Torrez," Associated Press, *St. Joseph News-Press*, February 22, 1969, 2B.
59. Bob Broeg, "Belinsky's Broke, Welcomes Chance with Redbirds," *St. Louis Post-Dispatch*, February 23, 1969, 2B.
60. Allen, 255–256.
61. "Irate Bo Given Cut by Cardinals," *Springfield [MO]) Daily News*, April 1, 1969, 14.
62. "$12,500 Price Tag for Bo," *Honolulu Advertiser*, April 4, 1969, C-4.
63. Bill Kwon, "Islanders Buy Bo," *Honolulu Star-Bulletin*, April 3, 1969, D-1.
64. Ferd Borsch, "Hawaii Wins 7th in Row," *Honolulu Advertiser*, May 21, 1969, E-1.
65. "Belinsky, Vinson Bring Islanders Back in Groove," *Honolulu Star-Bulletin*, June 5, 1969, D-3.
66. "Births," *Honolulu Advertiser*, June 28, 1969, C-6.
67. Allen, 257.
68. Bill Kwon, "The Billboard," *Honolulu Star-Bulletin*, July 25, 1969, C-2; "Bo Beats Emeralds for Eighth Win in a Row," *Honolulu Star-Bulletin*, July 25, 1969, C-2.
69. "Islanders Barrel with Belinsky," *Honolulu Star-Bulletin*, July 29, 1969, E-1.
70. Bill Kwon, "Bo Belinsky Purchased by Pittsburgh Pirates," *Honolulu Star-Bulletin*, July 30, 1969, D-1.
71. Roy McHugh, "Belinsky Is Back," *Pittsburgh Press*, July 31, 1969, 28.
72. Charley Feeney, "Roamin' Around," *Pittsburgh Post-Gazette*, July 31, 1969, 21.
73. Ibid.

Chapter 10

1. Phil Musick, "The Sound of Musick, 'Sweet' Belinsky," *Pittsburgh Press*, August 1, 1969, 23.
2. 1 Corinthians 13,11.
3. Maury Allen, *Bo, Pitching and Wooing ... with the Uncensored Cooperation of Bo Belinsky* (New York: Dial Press, 1973), 252–253.
4. Bud Furillo, "The Belinsky Re-Visited," *Los Angeles Herald Examiner*, August 6, 1969, D-2.
5. Al Abrams, "Sidelights on Sports," *Pittsburgh Post-Gazette*, August 1, 1969, 17.

Notes—Chapter 10

6. "Belinsky Says He'll Give Bucs His Best," Associated Press, *Hawaii Tribune-Herald*, August 1, 1969, 9.
7. Bill Christine, "Pirates' Bench Splintering Foes," *Pittsburgh Press*, September 9, 1969, 38.
8. Bill Christine, "Taylor Plays Into Cards' Hands," *Pittsburgh Press*, September 11, 1969, 35.
9. Bill Christine, "Pirates Fire Shepard," *Pittsburgh Press*, September 26, 1969, 1.
10. "Pirates Farm Three Veterans," *Pittsburgh Press*, October 28, 1969, 37; "Pirates Sell Bo, 2 Others to Columbus," *Pittsburgh Post-Gazette*, October 28, 1969, 19; "Bo Belinsky to Columbus," Associated Press, *Hawaii Tribune-Herald*, October 29, 1969, 9.
11. Allen, 253.
12. Bob Hertzel, "Reds Acquire Belinsky from Bucs," *Cincinnati Enquirer*, February 5, 1970, 30.
13. Musick, "The Sound of Musick, 'Sweet' Belinsky."
14. Musick, "The Sound of Musick, 'Sweet' Belinsky"; Bob Hertzel, "Just a Family Man," *Cincinnati Enquirer*, February 5, 1970, 29.
15. Maury Allen, "The Bo Nobody Knows," *New York Post*, February 12, 1970, 93.
16. Ritter Collett, "Maloney Nixes Latest Offer," *Journal Herald* (Dayton, OH), March 2, 1970, 19; Si Burick, "Reds' Rep Believes Compromise is Near," *Dayton Daily News*, March 2, 1970, 17; Bob Hertzel, "Arrigo's Vow Fails As Reds Trim Him, 8–7, Reds Notes," *Cincinnati Enquirer*, March 9, 1970, 44; Jim Selman, "Reds Nose Out White Sox 8–7," *Tampa Tribune*, March 9, 1970 1-C; "Bo Signs, Joins Reds," *Indianapolis News*, March 10, 1970, 27.
17. "Bo Is Back," *Cincinnati Enquirer*, March 11, 1970, 21; Earl Lawson, "Uncle Buddy Gave a Warning," *Tampa Times*, March 12, 1970, 1-C.
18. Frank Klein, "Can Belinsky Bounce Back?" *Tampa Times*, March 15, 1970, 2-E.
19. Max Greenwald, "New Bo Dedicated—With Reds or Tribe," *Indianapolis Star*, March 26, 1970, 51.
20. Earl Lawson, "May Shuns Home Run Talk," *Cincinnati Post & Times Star*, March 30, 1970, 16.
21. Bob Hertzel, Merritt Impressive in Win Over Mets," *Cincinnati Enquirer*, March 30, 1970, 43; Frank Dolson, "Belinsky Near End of Last Chances," *Philadelphia Inquirer*, March 31, 1970, 19.
22. Dolson.
23. Allen, 253.
24. Dolson.
25. "Belinsky Is Likely to Stick Around," *Cincinnati Enquirer*, April 5, 1970, 1-C.
26. Bob Hertzel, "Relaxed Man in the Bullpen," *Cincinnati Enquirer*, April 9, 1970, 51.
27. Bob Hertzel, "Reds Option Belinsky," *Cincinnati Enquirer*, May 20, 1970, 43.
28. Allen, 266.
29. Ibid., 268.
30. "Curfew Halts Tribe After 17," *Indianapolis News*, May 29, 1970, 41.
31. "Curfew Rings Again for Tribe, '89ers," *Indianapolis News*, May 30, 1970, 22; "Tribe Tags O.C. for 3d in Row," *Indianapolis Star*, May 31, 1970, Page 2, Sec. 4.
32. Lester Koelling, "Bo Shows Style, But Victim of Idleness," *Indianapolis News*, June 6, 1970, 12; Max Greenwald, "Grand Slam Homer Wipes Out Tribe," *Indianapolis Star*, June 6, 1970, 25.
33. Lester Koelling, "Bo Credits His Mates," *Indianapolis News*, June 10, 1970, 72.
34. Max Greenwald, "Bo Does Omaha Up 'Royally,'" *Indianapolis Star*, June 14, 1970, 77; "Bo's Slow But He's Hot," *Indianapolis News*, June 14, 1970, 51.
35. "Bo Is Go for Tribe," *Indianapolis News*, June 22, 1970, 28.
36. "Even Bo Fails to Halt Skid," *Indianapolis News*, June 26, 1970, 38.
37. "Tribe Plays the Same Old Tune," *Indianapolis News*, June 30, 1970, 31.
38. Lester Koelling, "Tribe Plays 2; Fireworks," *Indianapolis News*, July 4, 1970, 13.
39. Lester Koelling, "Tribe a Loser in a Victory," *Indianapolis News*, July 8, 1970, 53; Max Greenwald, "Bears Bow in 6–2 Game," *Indianapolis Star*, July 8, 1970, 33.
40. "Aeros Drop Two to Indians," *Wichita Eagle and the Beacon*, July 12, 1970, 1D.
41. Dave Overpeck, "Tribe Loses Two; Rapp, 4 Players Thumbed Out," *Indianapolis Star*, July 14, 1970, 23.
42. Max Greenwald, "Oaks' Power Speeds Bo's Power As Tribe Bows, 3–1," *Indianapolis Star*, July 18, 1970, 19.
43. "Tribe Scores 2 in Sixth for 3–2

Nod," *Indianapolis Star,* July 23 1970, 51; "Vern Rapp Has Gotten Some Relief," *Indianapolis News,* July 23, 1970, 42.

44. Lester Koelling, "Oaks Stand Tall on Tribe's Lot," *Indianapolis News,* July 27, 1970, 24.

45. "Behney Winner in Tribe Debut," *Indianapolis Star,* August 1, 1970, 22.

46. Bob Hertzel, "Reds Sifting Indy for Pitcher," *Cincinnati Enquirer,* August 12, 1970, 27.

47. "Tribe Requests Cincy to Reassign Belinsky," *Indianapolis Star,* August 11, 1970, 21.

48. Lester Koelling, "Bouton's Out, Bo Leaves As Tribe Hosts '89ers," *Indianapolis News,* August 11, 1970, 31; "Indianapolis drops Bo," *Evansville Press,* August 11, 1970, 12.

49. Richard Morris, "Bo Belinsky Is Now a Tourist," *Asheville Times,* August 19, 1970, 32.

50. "Smith Bats A's By Tourists, 6–2," *Asheville Citizen,* August 24, 1970, 13.

51. John F. Pardon, "Belinsky, Tourists Lose, 3–1," *Asheville Citizen,* August 28, 1970, 20.

52. John F. Pardon, "Tourists' Finale Exciting for Fans," *Asheville Times,* September 1, 1970, 12.

53. "'Series' Shares Lower This Year," United Press International, *Troy* [OH] *Daily News,* October 30, 1970, 11.

54. "Bo Belinsky Quitting Baseball," Associated Press, *Reno Evening-Gazette,* January 6, 1971, 29.

55. "Derby Fever Strikes Local Hound Track," *Rapid City* [SD] *Journal,* September 6, 1970, 30.

56. Allen, 11.

57. *Ibid.,* 306–307.

58. *Ibid.,* 280.

59. *Ibid.,* 282.

60. *Ibid.,* 286.

61. "Bo Belinsky Quitting Baseball," 29.

Chapter 11

1. Howie Carr, "Of Bear Markets and Bo Belinsky," *Daily Tar Heel* (Chapel Hill, NC), February 4, 1971, 5.

2. Pat Jordan, "Once He Was an Angel," *Sports Illustrated,* March 6, 1972, 70.

3. *Ibid.,* 70, 72.

4. *Ibid.,* 75.

5. *Ibid.*

6. *Ibid.,* 76.

7. *Ibid.*

8. *Ibid.,* 79.

9. Al Ferrara, telephone interview with author, May 2, 2024.

10. "At 38, Belinsky Doesn't Miss Bright Lights," Associated Press, *Hawaii Tribune-Herald,* May 21, 1975, 8.

11. Steve Oney, "Fallen Angel," *Los Angeles,* July 1, 2005, https,//lamag.com/news/fallen-angel-1 (last accessed March 19, 2024).

12. *Ibid.*

13. *Ibid.*

14. "At 38, Belinsky Doesn't Miss Bright Lights."

15. Jack Whatley, "How Don Henley, a Corvette and a Mound of Cocaine Spawned One of The Eagles' Greatest Hits," *Far Out,* https,//faroutmagazine.co.uk/eagles-don-henley-corvette-cocaine-life-in-the-fast-lane/ (last accessed February 14, 2024).

16. *Saturday Night Live,* "Ask President Carter," NBC, March 12, 1977.

17. Doug Hill and Jeff Weingrad, *Saturday Night: A Backstage History of Saturday Night Live* (New York: Beech Tree Books/William Morrow, 1986), 176.

18. Alice Stone, "'Annie Hall,' Woody Allen's Famous 'Cocaine Sneeze' Was a Complete Accident," *Showbiz Cheat Sheet,* https,//www.cheatsheet.com/entertainment/annie-hall-woody-allens-famous-cocaine-sneeze-was-a-complete-accident.html/, January 26, 2021 (last accessed February 17, 2024).

19. Lee N. Robins, Ph.D., "The Vietnam Drug User Return, Final Report, Special Action Office Monograph, Series A, Number 2," Special Action Office for Drug Abuse Prevention, May 1974.

20. *Eight Is Enough,* "Never Try Eating Nectarines as Juice May Dispense," ABC, March 15, 1977.

21. *Mary Tyler Moore,* "Love Is All Around," CBS, September 19, 1970. The show was also known as *The Mary Tyler Moore Show.*

22. *Maude,* "Walter's Problem, Part 1," CBS, September 11, 1973; *Maude,* "Walter's Problem, Part 2," CBS, September 18, 1973.

23. *The Partridge Family,* "Go Directly to Jail," ABC, November 27, 1970.

24. Oney; Allen, 270–272.

25. Oney; Maury Allen, *Bo, Pitching and Wooing ... with the Uncensored Cooperation of Bo Belinsky* (New York: Dial Press, 1973), 273–275.
26. Allen, 275–276.
27. *Ibid.*, 277.
28. *Ibid.*, 292.
29. Oney.
30. *Ibid.*
31. Allen, 293.
32. *Ibid.*, 295.
33. Oney.
34. Anna Quindlen, "Life in the 30's, Wrong Direction?" *Hawaii Tribune-Herald*, May 20, 1988, 4.
35. Dave Joseph, "Life in the Fast Lane Did It to Bo Belinsky," *Fort Lauderdale News/Sun Sentinel*, December 26, 1982, 1C.
36. *Ibid.*
37. *Ibid.*
38. Dave Anderson, "Where Is Bo Belinsky?" *New York Times*, September 18, 1979, B12.
39. Joseph.
40. Rod Ohira, "Bo's Given Up Life in Fast Lane," *Honolulu Star-Bulletin*, March 28, 1985, D-1.
41. Oney.
42. Ross Newhan, "Belinsky & Chance," *Los Angeles Times*, June 24, 1985, C10.
43. *Ibid.*
44. Oney.
45. *Any Given Sunday*, "Locker Room Speech," Warner Brothers, 1999.

Chapter 12

1. Chris Foster, "Bad Boy Bo Gets Better," *Los Angeles Times*, July 2, 1992, C1.
2. *Ibid.*
3. Rhett Bollinger, "The Halo Who Dated Hollywood Starlets," Major League Baseball, https,//www.mlb.com/news/bo-belinsky-son-remembers-angels-star#,~,text=His%20son%2C%20Don%20Carroll%2C%20who,was%20already%20in%20his%2020s., May 4, 2022 (last accessed May 15, 2024).
4. Foster, "Bad Boy Bo Gets Better."
5. Tyler Corder, responses to author's questions via email, January 30, 2024.
6. *Ibid.*
7. Scott Keene, telephone interview with author, March 21, 2024.
8. "Sports News Briefs," *New York Times*, January 31, 1978, 18; Vic Ziegel, "Matchmaker graduates to Garden," *New York Post*, February 2, 1978, 68.
9. Bruce Trampler, email to author, May 6, 2024.
10. Bob Case, telephone interview with author, March 20, 2024.
11. Ray Dinardi, email to author, April 29, 2024; Ray Dinardi, email to author, September 29, 2023.
12. "Whatever Happened to...," Flamboyant Ex-Islanders and Angels Pitcher Bo Belinsky Now Selling Cars in Las Vegas," *Honolulu Star-Bulletin*, March 21, 2001, A3.
13. Ferd Lewis, "Bo Belinsky Always Felt at Home in the Islands," *Honolulu Advertiser*, November 26, 2001, C1.
14. Linda Dougherty, "Trenton's Belinsky Dead at 64," *The Trentonian*, November 25, 2001, S3.
15. Ross Newhan, "Fame Came Suddenly, and Name Never Left," *Los Angeles Times*, November 25, 2001, D1.
16. "Belinsky Remembered," *Honolulu Star-Bulletin*, November 30, 2001, B8.
17. Foster, "Bad Boy Bo Gets Better."
18. Richard Goldstein, "Bo Belinsky, 64, the Playboy Pitcher, Dies, *New York Times*, November 27, 2001, D6.
19. Pat Jordan, "Once He Was an Angel," *Sports Illustrated*, March 6, 1972, 70.

Bibliography

Books

Allen, Maury. *Bo: Pitching and Wooing ... with the Uncensored Cooperation of Bo Belinsky*. New York: Dial Press, 1973.

Autry, Gene, with Mickey Herskowitz. *Back in the Saddle Again*. New York: Doubleday, 1978.

Donovan, Pete. *Under the Halo: The Official History of Angels Baseball*. San Rafael, CA: Insight Editions, 2012.

Florio, John, and Ouisie Shapiro. *One Nation Under Baseball: How the 1960s Collided with the National Pastime*. Lincoln: University of Nebraska Press, 2017.

George-Warren, Holly. *Public Cowboy No. 1: The Life and Times of Gene Autry*. New York: Oxford University Press, 2009.

Goldman, Robert. *Once They Were Angels*. New York: Sports Publishing, 2006.

McDowell, Sam, with Martin Gitlin. *The Saga of Sudden Sam: The Rise, Fall and Redemption of Sam McDowell*. Lanham, MD: Rowman & Littlefield, 2022.

Newhan, Ross. *The California Angels: The Complete History*. New York: Simon & Schuster, 1982.

Proctor, Mel. *The Little General: Gene Mauch, A Baseball Life*. Indianapolis: Blue River Press, 2015.

Shapiro, Michael. *Bottom of the Ninth: Branch Rickey, Casey Stengel, and the Daring Scheme to Save Baseball from Itself*. New York: Times Books, 2009.

Van Doren, Mamie, with Art Aveilhe. *Playing the Field: My Story*. New York: G.P. Putnam's Sons, 1987.

Newspapers and Magazines

Aberdeen American-News
Amarillo Globe-Times
Arkansas Democrat
Arkansas Gazette
Asheville Citizen
Asheville Times
Atlanta Constitution
Atlanta Journal
Austin American-Statesman
Boston Globe
Cincinnati Enquirer
Cincinnati Post & Times Star
Corpus Christi Caller-Times
Courier-Post
Daily News
Daily News-Post
Daily Tar Heel
Daily Times-Advocate
Democrat and Chronicle
Desert Sun
Dothan Eagle
Edmonton Journal
Evening Press
Evening Tribune
Evening Vanguard
Fitchburg Sentinel
Fort Worth Star-Telegram
Greenfield Recorder-Gazette
Hawaii Tribune-Herald
Helper Journal

Herald Journal
Hilo Tribune-Herald
Hollywood Citizen-News
Honolulu Advertiser
Honolulu Star-Bulletin
Houston Chronicle
Houston Post
The Independent
Independent-Press-Telegram
Indianapolis News
Indianapolis Star
Journal Herald
Kansas City Star
Kilgore News Herald
Knoxville Journal
Knoxville News-Sentinel
Lebanon Daily News and Lebanon Daily Times
Long Branch Daily Record
Los Angeles Herald Examiner
Los Angeles Times
McKinney Courier-Gazette
Minneapolis Star
Nashville Banner
New York Mirror
New York Post
New York Times
North Adams Transcript
Oakland Tribune
Orlando Sentinel
Pensacola News-Journal
Philadelphia Daily News
Philadelphia Inquirer

Pittsburgh Post-Gazette
Pittsburgh Press
Press Democrat
Press-Telegram
Progress-Bulletin
Rapid City Journal
Reno Evening Gazette
Sacramento Bee
St. Joseph News-Press
St. Louis Post-Dispatch
San Angelo Standard-Times
San Diego Union
San Pedro News-Pilot
Santa Barbara News-Press
Saturday Evening Post
Sporting News
Sports Illustrated
Springfield Daily News
Standard-Star
Stockton Daily Evening Record
The Sun
Tampa Times
Trenton Evening Times
The Trentonian
Tribune-Herald
Troy Daily News
True
Valley Evening Monitor
Valley Morning Star
Wichita Eagle and The Beacon
Winnipeg Free Press
Winnipeg Tribune

Index

Aaron, Hank 36, 110, 119–120, 150
Aaron, Tommie 36
Abajian, Rich 178–179, 181, 184–185
ABC 49
Adair, Bill 138, 141
Adam-12 64
Adams, Nick 66
Adcock, Joe 99, 110
Admiral Mason Park 7
Aguirre, Hank 50
Albertson, Jack 66
Allen, Dick 110, 114, 115
Allen, Maury 1, 7, 10, 15, 37, 69, 87, 94, 100, 132, 171, 172–173
Alley, Gene 150
Alou, Felipe 110
Alou, Jesus 150
Alou, Matty 114
Alusik, George 82
Alvis, Max 99
Amaro, Ruben 108, 109, 110, 112
Ambassador Hotel 38
Anderson, Sparky 153, 155
The Andy Griffith Show 49
Annie Hall 167–168
Anthony, Ray 67
Antrim, Harry 66
AP 74, 78, 83, 99
Arkansas Democrat 20
Arkansas Gazette 16, 18, 19
Armored Command 61
Aspromonte, Bob 128, 129, 130
Associated Press 167, 184
Atlanta Constitution 18
Atlanta Journal 18
Atkinson, Brooks 61
Autry, Gene 24, 26, 42, 53, 62, 69, 91, 116, 173
Averill, Earl 30, 31

Bachelor Father 49
Bailey, Charles W. 92

Baldschun, Jack 110, 112, 113, 114, 115
Bales, Lee 132
Ball, Lucille 93
Baltimore & Ohio Railroad 49–50
Banks, Ernie 113, 114, 130
Barber, Steve 28, 30, 31
Barker, Len 164
Baseball Yearbook 53
Basin Street West 84
Bateman, John 128
Bavasi, Buzzie 119
The Beach Boys 50
Beckert, Glenn 113
Belinsky, Anna 5, 69, 160, 171, 173
Belinsky, Bo: and Aberdeen Pheasants 11; and alcohol 1, 57, 156, 165–170, 172–173, 175, 181; 175; and Amarillo Gold Sox 12, 164; and army 14; and arrests 10; and Beverly Hills incident 37–38, 59; and Bill Rigney 36, 38, 69, 94; and Braven Dyer 100–102, 126, 127; and Brunswick Pirates 6–7; and Cadillac 62, 116; and children 145, 166–167, 177; and Cincinnati Reds 152–155, 159; and cocaine 166–167, 171; and Dean Chance 51, 54, 56–57, 59, 75, 76, 79, 80, 81, 107, 109, 111, 172, 173; and death 185–186; and dog 128, 133; and Findlay Automotive 178–179; and fines 37–38, 93–94, 99, 127, 129; and first major league victory 28; and first sexual experience 58; and Gimbel's 110; and guns 156; and Hawaii 72, 74–75, 83–90, 96, 100, 138–143, 144, 155, 173, 183–184; and Houston Astros 126–133, 135, 137–138, 143–144; and humility 154; and Jo Collins 133–139, 141–144, 146, 148–149, 152, 154, 156, 162, 164, 170–172, 187; 156, 170–171; and Knoxville Smokies 10–11; and Las Vegas 3, 65, 67, 74, 90, 92–93, 117, 177–187; and Little Rock Travelers 15–22; and Los Angeles Angels 22; and

211

Index

Mamie Van Doren 63–77, 83, 85, 96, 126, 136, 172, 173, 181, 184, 185, 186; and nickname 33; and no-hitter for Angels 30–33; and Northern League All-Star Game 11; and Oklahoma City 89ers 132; and Pensacola Dons 7–10, 12–13; and Philadelphia Phillies 105–121; and Pittsburgh Pirates 6, 146; and pool 6; 79–80; and reputation 111, 113, 116, 120–121, 126, 143; and rib injury 111; and salary holdout 24–25; and San Diego Padres 121–126; and sister 173; *Sports Illustrated* 162–163, 186; spring training in rookie season 27; and statistics 159–160; and Stockton Ports 12–13; and Trenton 5–6, 7, 34; and Venezuelan League,126, 143; and Walter Winchell 58–60; and WIBF-TV 111; and women 6, 11–12, 13, 14, 15–16, 26, 60–61, 94, 96, 109, 126, 136
Belinsky, Edward 5, 28, 160
Bell, Gary 29
Bell, Gus 36
Ben Casey 93
Bennett, Dennis 107
Benny, Jack 93
Bergen, Polly 92
Berra, Yogi 102, 107
The Best Man 92
Bewitched 46
Bilko, Steve 24, 30
Blattner, Buddy 93
The Bob Cummings Show 66
Boccabella, John 141
Bolling, Frank 36
Bond, James 45
Booker, Buddy 142
Borbón, Pedro 155
Bourbon Street Beat 49
Bouton, Jim 52, 82, 99
Bowden, Earlie 8
Bowen, Rex 6
Bowsfield, Ted 44
Boyer, Clete 131
Bracken, Eddie 102
Brand, Ron 129, 132
Brandt, Jackie 31, 43
Breeding, Marv 31
Brewer, Jim 150
Brewer, Lee 79
Bridges, Rocky 93
Bright, Harry 82
Briles, Nelson 143, 144
Brinkman, Ed 96
Brock, Lou 79, 110, 113
Brown, Gates 97
Brown, Joe 151

Brown, Ollie 120
Bruton, Bill 97
Buford, Don 98
Buhl, Bob 120, 121
Bunning, Jim 24, 118, 127, 149
Burda, Bob 149
Burdette, Lew 28, 29, 113, 115
Burdick, Eugene 92
Burke's Law 61

Callison, Johnny 108, 110, 112, 113, 114, 115
Campbell, Jim 142
Campbell, Judy 69
Capone, Al 58
Capp, Al 61
Cardenas, Leo 115, 118
Carlton, Steve 110, 185
Carroll, Clay 110, 155
Carty, Rico 131
Caruso, Paul 58, 71, 86
Case, Bob 180–183
Cash, Norm 97
CBS 64
Cedeño, César 157
Cepeda, Orlando 129
Chance, Brett 46–48, 50, 57
Chance, Dean 25, 36–38, 44–47, 50–56, 59, 60, 67, 79–80, 81, 105, 107, 109, 111, 130
Chance, Florence 52
Chance, Wilmer 51
Charles, Ed 40, 98, 130
Checkmate 61
Chesapeake & Ohio Railway 49–50
Chicago & Eastern Illinois Railroad 50
Cimino, Pete 55
Cimoli, Gino 40
Cincinnati Enquirer 153, 154–155
Citizen-News 84
Cline, Ty 29
Clinton, Lou 89
Cocoanut Grove 38
Colavito, Rocky 98
Collins, Jo 133–
Collins, Kevin 116
Conigliaro, Tony 95
Conlin, Bill 114
Connors, Chuck 49
Conrad, George 24
Continental League 23
Coogan, Jackie 64
Coogan, Richard 66
Cope, Myron 44, 53, 113
Copley News Service 117
Corder, Tyler 178–179, 187
Corrales, Pat 114, 115
Crane, Bob 45
Critchfield, Hank 54

Cronin, Joe 24, 84
Culp, Ray 112, 114
Cunningham, Joe 39
Curtis, Tony 49, 63
Cy Young Award 48, 51, 52, 55, 57

Daily News (New York) 113
Dal Canton, Bruce 150
Dalton, Harry 13–14, 22
Dalrymple, Clay 108, 119, 121
Damn Yankees 57, 102
Damon Runyon Cancer Fund 60
Dan Raven 49
Davalillo, Vic 55
Davenport, Jim 114, 120, 149
Davis, Ron 128, 130, 151
Davis, Tommy 55, 80, 130
Davis Memorial Park 187–188
Day, Doris 66
Decker, Joe 141, 142
Dehner, John 66
Dees, Charlie 89
The Defenders 92
de la Hoz, Miguel 29
Dempsey, Jack 63
Denehy, Bill 57
Denver, Bob 64
Desilu 58
Devine, Bing 143–144
Diamond, Alan 139
Dierker, Larry 120, 150
Dietz, Dick 149, 150
Dillard, Don 29
Dinardi, Ray 181, 187
Disneyland 56
Dr. Kildare 93
Dr. No 45
Dr. Strangelove (or *How I Learned to Stop Worrying and Love the Bomb*) 92
Dolson, Frank 117, 154
Donohue, Jim 25
Dothan Eagle 13
Douglas, Kirk 92
Dreier, Doug 159
Drysdale, Don 28, 30, 50, 56, 80, 119
Duliba, Bob 89, 98
DuPont, Ricky 70–71, 100
Duren, Ryne 29, 40, 41, 52
Durocher, Leo 150–151
Durslag, Melvin 38, 105, 107, 108
Dyer, Braven 33, 50, 67, 78–79, 83, 93, 96, 98, 100–102, 126, 127

East Side / West Side 92
Eilers, Dave 131, 132
Eisenhower, Dwight 64
Eisenhower, Mamie 63

Elektro 64
Emery, Cal 124
The Enemy Within 92
Engel, Geraldine 188
Essegian, Chuck 29
Estrada, Chuck 43
Eves, Gloria 37–38, 41, 57

Fail-Safe 92
FCC 92
Feeney, Charley 146
Ferrara, Al 132, 165
Firestone, Leonard 80
Fischer, Bill 143
Fischer, Hank 109
Fisher, Eddie (baseball player) 54
Fisher, Eddie (singer) 63
Fitzgerald, Lou 7, 44
Flood, Curt 110
Foley, Red 113
For Those Who Think Young 61
Forbidden 63
Ford, Whitey 24, 30, 50, 90
Fort Worth Star-Telegram 136
Fox, Nellie 34, 39
Fowler, Art 24, 28, 82, 83, 84, 89
Francona, Tito 29, 110
Frawley, William 60
Freeman, Donald 59
Fregosi, Jim 89, 97
Frick, Ford 43, 84
Frings, Ketti 38
Frings, Kurt 38
Fuentes, Tito 121
Furillo, Bud 28, 29, 33, 38, 56, 58, 149

Gable, Clark 66
Gabrielson, Len 114, 121
Gagliano, Phil 110
Gaines, Joe 141
Gallagher, Al 155
Gentile, Jim 30, 31, 120
Gergen, Joe 108
Get Smart 66
Gibson, Bob 110, 143
Gibson, Russ 155
Gilligan's Island 61–62
Gilligan's Planet 62
The Girl in Black Stockings 66
Gleason, Jackie 58, 60
God's Little Acre 61
Golden Globe Award 61
Gonzalez, Tony 112, 116
Goossen, Greg 116, 130, 131
Gosger, Jim 89
Gould, Jack 61
Graham, Sheila 73

Grahame, Gloria 63
Grammas, Alex 151
Grant, Johnny 93
Grant, Lee 71
Grant, Mudcat 30
Grba, Eli 29, 44, 89, 175
Green, Dallas 108
Green, Gene 29
Griggs, Hal 88
Grissom, Marv 27, 28, 33, 35, 39, 76, 84, 94
Groat, Dick 113, 119, 120
Guns, Girls, and Gangsters 67

Hackleman, Jim 126
Hall, Jimmie 55
Haller, Tom 114
Hamende, Joe 158
Hampton, Lionel 84
Haney, Fred 24, 34, 35, 38, 40, 42, 44, 53, 61, 62–63, 69, 76, 79, 80, 84, 85, 89, 91, 98, 99, 100
Hansen, Ron 30, 31, 98
Hardcastle and McCormick 66
Harper, Tommy 111, 115
Harrelson, Bill 158
Harrelson, Bud 130
Hart, Jim Ray 120, 121
Hashem, Tufie 35
Hatton, Grady 126–127, 128, 129, 130, 131, 132
Hawaii 138–139
Hawaii Five-O 66
Hawaiian Eye 38, 49
Haye, Bob 24
Heffernan, Harold 63
Heffner, Bob 95
Hefner, Hugh 117, 133–134, 164
Held, Woodie 29
Helms, Tommy 128
Hemond, Roland 35
Henderson, Ken 149, 155
Hennessy 49
Henry, Bill 114
Herbert, Ray 108, 115, 121
Hershberger, Mike 98
Hershiser, Orel 30
Hertzel, Bob 153
Higgins, Charles 159
High School Confidential 63–64
Hinton, Chuck 55
Hodges, Gil 57
Hogan's Heroes 45, 66
Honolulu Advertiser 126, 140
Honolulu Star-Bulletin 126, 140, 141, 143, 145, 174, 183–184
Hope, Bob 80
Hopper, Hedda 59, 85

Hornsby, Rogers 91
Hornung, Paul 117, 173
Horton, Tony 55
Horton, Willie 109
House, Pat 158
Howard, Frank 94
Houk, Ralph 82
Houston Post 135
Howard, Elston 52, 82, 90
Hunt, Ken 83
Husky, Ferlin 67
Hutton, Tom 150

I Dream of Jeannie 46
I Love Lucy 60
Indianapolis News 159
It's a Bird...It's a Plane...It's Superman 73

The Jackie Gleason Show 49
Jackson, Alvin 103
Jackson, Grant 125
Jackson, Sonny 120
James, Johnny 25
Jenkins, Ferguson 108
Johnson, Alex 112, 114, 129
Johnson, Deron 111
Johnson, Ken 103
Johnson, Lou 115
Johnson, Lyndon B. 106
Johnson, Walter 51
Johnstone, Jay 124
Jones, Clarence 141, 142
Jones, Cleon 130
Jones, Dalton 95
Jones, Gordon 127
Jones, Mack 131
Jordan, Pat 162

Kaline, Al 97
Kasko, Eddie 115
Kaze, Irv 26
Keane, Johnny 102
Keene, Scott 179–180
Kelly, Gene 49
Kelso, Bill 94, 124
Kennedy, John 96
Kennedy, John F. 23, 45, 49, 51, 69, 92, 106
Killebrew, Harmon 39, 96
Kindall, Jerry 29
Kirkland, Willie 82
Kisses for My President 92
Kitt, Eartha 46
Klein, Frank 153
Klimchock, Lou 139
Klurfeld, Herman 58, 60
Knebel, Fletcher 92
Knoop, Bobby 53, 88, 99

Index

Knowles, Darold 120
KOGO-AM 123
Kolb, Gary 150, 151
Koppe, Joe 29, 30, 31, 34, 82, 98
Kostro, Frank 90
Koufax, Sandy 28, 29, 55, 74, 109, 119
Kralick, Jack 97
Kranepool, Ed 116, 131
Kubek, Tony 53, 82, 90
Kuenn, Harvey 79, 120
Kushner, Jerry 122
Kwon, Bill 145

Lamabe, Jack 52
Lancaster, Burt 92
Landis, Jim 39, 129
Landrum, Don 113
Lane, Charles 66
Lanier, Hal 114, 121, 150
La Rose, Vic 141, 142
Larsen, Don 163
Las Vegas Hillbillys 67
Latman, Barry 93, 95, 97
Lau, Charlie 131H
Lee, Don 94, 95, 96, 97
Lefebvre, Jim 115
Levitt, Ed 136
Lewis, Allen 107, 112
Li'l Abner 61
Lillis, Bob 130, 131
Llenas, Winston 145
Lolich, Mickey 54, 97
Lonborg, Jim 130
Los Angeles Angels, created 23-24; Dodger Stadium 24, 38; Gene Autry's ownership 24, 26; Wrigley Field 24
Los Angeles Herald Examiner 28, 33, 36-37, 38, 58, 105, 149
Los Angeles magazine 174
Los Angeles Times 36, 44, 65, 67, 74, 76, 78, 82, 84, 91-92, 93, 100, 123, 177, 184
Louise, Tina 61, 76
Lowenstein, John 157
Lucchesi, Frank 122, 125
Lumpe, Jerry 40
Luplow, Al 29
Luska, Ed 136

Mack, Connie 82
MacMurray, Fred 92
Mahaffey, Art 114-115
Maher, Charles 99, 100
Malzone, Frank 40, 89
Mansfield, Jayne 63
Mantilla, Felix 52, 89, 120
Mantle, Mickey 35, 57
Manuel, Charlie 158

The Many Loves of Dobie Gillis 49, 64
Marichal, Juan 130
Maris, Roger 35, 82, 90
Mark Hopkins Hotel 60
Marquard, Rube 81
Marshall, Dave 149
Martin, Dean 49
Martinez, Marty 150
Mathews, Eddie 6, 36, 130
Mauch, Gene 105, 107, 108, 110, 112, 113, 114, 115, 116, 117, 118, 119, 120, 121, 122, 126, 129, 160
Marvin Hime & Company 69
May, Lee 155
May, Rudy 54, 105
Maye, Lee 55
Mays, Willie 114, 121
McBride, Ken 24, 28
McCall's 75
McCarver, Tim 113, 129
McCormick, Mike 30, 130
McCovey, Willie 114, 121, 149, 155
McFadden, Leon 150
McHugh, Roy 146
McLain, Denny 54
McNertney, Jerry 98
McQueen, Red 126, 137
Méjias, Román 89, 95
Menke, Denis 150
Meriwether, Lee 46
Messersmith, Andy 124
Meyers, Lee 75-76
Michaels, Al 142
Miller, Bob 55
Milner, Martin 64
Mincher, Don 55
Minow, Newton 58
Missouri Pacific Railroad 50
Monboquette, Bill 44, 73-74, 95
The Monitor 81
Monroe, Marilyn 63, 66
Moore, Jackie 109
Moose, Bob 151
Morales, Rich 141
Moran, Billy 30, 31, 33, 39, 43
Morgan, Joe 120, 130
Morgan, Tom 24, 35, 41, 50
Morton, Bubba 124
Moses, Sammy 35
Murphy, Daniel 142
Murphy, Jack 62
Murray, Jim 84
Musick, Phil 148, 153

Naked City 49
NASA 64
Nelson, Lori 65

Ness, Elliot 58
Nettles, Graig 55–56
The New Adventures of Gilligan 61
New York Mirror 58–60
New York Times 61, 65
Newhan, Ross 184
Newman, Fred 54
Newspaper Enterprise Association 143
Nicholson, Dave 30, 31
Nixon, Russ 89
Noren, Irv 86, 88
North American Newspaper Alliance 78
Nottebart, Don 138, 164
Nuxhall, Joe 111, 112
Nye, Louis 64
Nyman, Jerry 143

Oakland Tribune 136
Oliver, Al 150
O'Malley, Walter 23–24
Osinski, Dan 41, 42–43, 44, 52, 89
Osteen, Claude 108
Oswald, Lee Harvey 92
O'Toole, Jim 30
Oyler, Ray 108

Paar, Jack 59
Pagán, José 150
Page, Don 123
Palm Springs Desert Inn 24
Paramount Pictures 63
Parker, Wes 115
Pascual, Camilo 24
Pavletich, Don 115
Pearson, Albie 24, 30, 31, 39, 78–79, 82, 92, 185
Pena, Orlando 43, 82
Pensacola News-Journal 8, 9
Pepitone, Joe 90
Peppermint West 85
Perez, Marty 145
Pérez, Tony 111, 128, 130
Perry, Bob 88
Perry, Gaylord 130, 150
Pesky, Johnny 89, 95
Philadelphia Daily News 114
Philadelphia Inquirer 107, 109, 110, 111, 112, 117, 118, 121, 154
Phillips, Adolfo 114
Phillips, Bubba 29
Phoebus, Tom 164
Piniella, Lou 139
Pinson, Vada 111, 115, 120
Pittsburgh Post-Gazette 146
Pittsburgh Press 146
Pizarro, Juan 24, 34, 126
Playboy 133–134, 154, 164, 170–171

Podres, Johnny 28
Pointer, Aaron 141
popular culture depictions of drugs and alcohol 167–169
Post, Wally 94
Powell, Boog 48
Preston, Lita Leon 61
Price, Lt. John 133–134

Qualls, Jim 141, 142
Quinn, Jack 137, 138, 140, 144, 145–146
Quinn, John 118

Rader, Doug 150
Rapp, Vern 159
Raymond, Claude 129
The Real McCoys 61
Reed, Howie 132
Reynolds, Bob 53, 80
Rhoades, Frank 124
Ribant, Dennis 152
Rice, Del 40
Richardson, Bobby 35, 90
Richardson, Spec 135, 138
Richert, Pete 54
Rickey, Branch 23
Ridzik, Steve 125
The Rifleman 49
Rigney, Bill 25, 28–29, 32, 34, 35, 36, 38, 40, 41, 43–44, 50, 53, 62–63, 67, 75, 76–77, 78, 79, 83, 84, 89, 90, 94, 95, 160
Roarke, Mike 97
Robards, Jason 92
Roberts, Robin 50
Robertson, Jerry 57
Robinson, Brooks 30, 57
Robinson, Floyd 39
Robinson, Frank 111
"Rock Around the Clock" 6
The Rockford Files 66
Rodgers, Buck 29, 30, 97, 149, 185
Roebuck, Ed 125
Rogers, Ginger 85
Rojas, Cookie 112, 120
Rollins, Rich 39
Roman, Bill 108, 109
Romano, John 29, 97
Rose, Pete 111, 115, 120, 156
Roseboro, John 115
Ross, Marion 66
Route 66 49, 61, 64, 92
Roznovsky, Vic 114
Rudi, Joe 140
Rudolph, Don 82

Sadowski, Ed 39
Sakamoto, Gordon 183

Index

San Diego Padres (Pacific Coast League) 121–126
San Diego Union 45, 59, 124, 125
Sands, Tommy 117
Santo, Ron 114
Satriano, Tom 52
Saturday Evening Post 53
Saturday Night Live 167
Saverine, Bob 48
Schaffer, Jim 125
Scheinblum, Richie 157
Schneider, Dan 132
Schoendienst, Red 143–144
Schumacher, Max 159
Seaver, Tom 130, 142
Selma, Dick 130
Sembera, Carroll 128, 131
Seven Days in May 92
77 Sunset Strip 38, 49
Sex Kittens Go to College 64, 65–66
Shannon, Mike 129
Shecter, Leonard 164
Shepard, Larry 149, 150, 151, 153, 156
Sherry, Larry 130, 131
Shockley, Costen 54, 105, 107, 110
Short, Chris 118, 127
Shreveport Journal 126
Siebern, Norm 82
Silk Stockings 71
Silver Slipper 74, 92
Simmons, Curt 110
Sims, Duke 132
Sizemore, Ted 140
Skelton, Red 49, 93
Skowron, Moose 35
Slape, Gregg 159
Slate Brothers night club 38
Smith, Al 34
Smith, Willie 52
Soriano, Dewey 88
Spahn, Warren 30
Spring, Jack 25, 29, 41
The Sporting News 50, 53
Sports Illustrated 6, 162–163
Sprague, Gary 145
Sputnik 64
Stack, Robert 58
Stahl, Larry 130–131
Staller, George 32
Stanley, Mickey 108, 109
Star Trek 45–46
Staub, Rusty 120, 129
Steinhagen, Ruth Ann 39
The Steve Allen Show 64
Stevens, Connie 38, 76
Stevens, Kay 38
Stock, Wes 31
Stottlemyre, Mel 54
Storrowtown Music Fair 71
Strat-O-Matic 91
Stuart, Dick 52, 89, 95, 107, 112, 113
Studio One 61
Sudakis, Bill 150
Sullivan, Haywood 40, 88
Surfside 6 49
Sutherland, Gary 125
Sutton, Don 150
Swoboda, Ron 130

The Tab Hunter Show 49
Tales of Wells Fargo 61
Tamblyn, Russ 63
Tampa Times 153
Tanner, Chuck 144, 146, 161
Taylor, Tony 108, 110, 119, 120
Teacher's Pet 66
Temple, Johnny 30
Terry, Ralph 35, 82
Thomas, Frank 107
Thomas, George 97
Thomas, Lee 29, 39, 43, 89
Thornton, Otis 159
Thorsland, Arne 48
Tiant, Luis 54, 57, 99
Tillman, Bob 89, 95
Time 44
The Tonight Show 6, 59, 73
Torborg, Jeff 94, 149
Torre, Joe 131
Torres, Felix 24, 30, 31, 34, 40, 90, 95, 124
Tovar, Cesar 55
Trampler, Bruce 180
The Trap 61
Trautman, George 84
Trenton Central High School 5–6
Tresh, Tom 82
Triandos, Gus 30, 31
True—The Men's Magazine 113

Uecker, Bob 110, 120
Uhlaender, Ted 55
Universal-International 63
Untamed Youth 65
The Untouchables 58
UPI 62, 75, 100, 108, 110, 143

Van Doren, Mamie 63–76, 83, 84, 96, 126, 136, 184
Vaughn, Robert 117
Venezuela 22, 24
Vice Raid 66–67
Vidal, Gore 92
Vietnam War 133–134
Vinson, Charlie 145

Waddell, George Edward "Rube," 82
Wagner, Gary 113, 114, 125
Wagner, Leon 24, 30, 33, 34, 41, 82, 90
Waitkus, Eddie 39
Warner Brothers 49
Warren, Geoffrey M. 65
Washburn, Ray 155
Waterston, Sam 92
Weiler, Abraham 65
Weld, Tuesday 64
Welsch, Ronald 157
Weltman, Phil 34
Werhas, John 145
Westinghouse 64
Westrum, Wes 130
Weyer, Lee 108–109
Weyerhauser, Jane 166
Wheeler, Harvey 92
Whitaker, Bridget 37–38
White, Bill 120
Wiffle ball 91
Wildcat 73
Will Success Spoil Rock Hunter? 63
William Morris Agency 34
Williams, Billy 113, 114
Williams, Coy 84
Williams, Dick 30
Williams, Esther 84
Williams, Stan 28, 57
Wills, Maury 55, 80, 109
Wilson, Bill 125
Wilson, Don 128
Wilson, Earl 40, 44, 95, 130
Winchell, Walter 38, 58–60, 84, 107
Wine, Bobby 114, 115, 116
Witt, George 25
Wojcik, Stan 140
Wolf, Al 91
Womack, Dooley 158
Wood, Hal 140
Woodling, Gene 51
Wooster, Ohio 48
Wynn, Early 30
Wynn, Jimmy 120, 130, 131, 150
Wynne, Billy 143

Yastrzemski, Carl 89, 95, 130

Ziff, Sid 38, 44, 75, 76, 77, 82, 84, 92, 93, 98

www.ingramcontent.com/pod-product-compliance
Ingram Content Group UK Ltd.
Pitfield, Milton Keynes, MK11 3LW, UK
UKHW021845140426
5217IPUK00022B/1596